THE WINONA LETTERS

BOOK TWO

RICHARD N. WILLIAMSON

THE WINONA LETTERS • BOOK TWO
IN THE *LETTERS FROM THE RECTOR* SERIES

THE COLLECTED WORKS ✦ VOLUME III

ISBN (paper) 9781940306087
ISBN (Kindle) 9781940306094
ISBN (ePub) 9781940306100
ISBN (PDF) 9781940306117

For more information,
or for additional titles, contact:

Marcel Editions
An Imprint of the St. Marcel Initiative
www.stmarcelinitiative.com
c/o BRN Associates, Inc.
9051 Watson Rd., Suite 279
St. Louis, MO 63126
(855) 289-9226

Marcel EDITIONS
A St MARCEL INITIATIVE IMPRINT
Jesu Christo Regi æterno milit
—MARCELLUS CENTURIO, A.D. 298

St. Louis, Missouri ❧ 2019

CONTENTS

NO. 131 | SEPTEMBER 1, 1994   1
A Teenager's Story

NO. 132 | OCTOBER 1, 1994   8
Avoid "Conservative" Catholics

NO. 133 | NOVEMBER 1, 1994   13
Understanding Moral and Natural Liberty

NO. 134 | DECEMBER 1, 1994   24
Pope John Paul II and the Prayer Meeting at Assisi

NO. 135 | JANUARY 1, 1995   29
Words of Encouragement

NO. 136 | FEBRUARY 1, 1995   33
Death of Fr. Urban Snyder

NO. 137 | MARCH 1, 1995   38
Natural Born Killers

NO. 138 | APRIL 5, 1995   43
Democratism in the Catholic Church

NO. 139 | MAY 5, 1995   48
Why is Our Lady Weeping?

NO. 140 | JUNE 6, 1995   55
Sincere Sin

NO. 141 | JULY 1, 1995   60
The Principle of Religious Liberty

NO. 142 | AUGUST 3, 1995   66
    Forebodings & Reassurance from Europe
NO. 143 | SEPTEMBER 1, 1995   73
    Pluralism: Threat to Catholics Today
NO. 144 | OCTOBER 3, 1995   79
    Errors of Liberal Education
NO. 145 | NOVEMBER 9, 1995   84
    25 Years of the SSPX
NO. 146 | DECEMBER 5, 1995   90
    FAQ on the SSPX
NO. 147 | JANUARY 6, 1996   97
    Si Si, No No Congress
NO. 148 | FEBRUARY 1, 1996   104
Nixon's Career: A Liberal View and a Catholic View
NO. 149 | MARCH 1, 1996   109
    Influences of Vatican II
NO. 150 | APRIL 1, 1996   116
    Patrick Buchanan's Campaign
NO. 151 | MAY 7, 1996   122
    Bishop Bruskewitz & the SSPX
NO. 152 | JUNE 6, 1996   128
    The Unabomber Manifesto: Is It Relevant?
NO. 153 | JULY 1, 1996   137
    Has the SSPX Lost Its Charity?
NO. 154 | AUGUST 3, 1996   144
    The Charity of St. Pius X
NO. 155 | SEPTEMBER 1, 1996   150
    The 150th Anniversary of La Salette
NO. 156 | OCTOBER 4, 1996   158
    Asia and England
NO. 157 | NOVEMBER 3, 1996   163
    On Americanism
NO. 158 | DECEMBER 1, 1996   169
    FAQ on the Future of the Church & the SSPX

NO. 159 | JANUARY 1, 1997   186
Pink Floyd's "The Wall"

NO. 160 | FEBRUARY 1, 1997   192
It Always Comes Back To Disregard of God.

NO. 161 | MARCH 1, 1997   199
A New "Concentration Camp"

NO. 162 | APRIL 1, 1997   205
The Resurrection: An Historical Fact

NO. 163 | MAY 1, 1997   210
Woes of Modern Education

NO. 164 | JUNE 5, 1997   215
Is Deep Blue Human?

NO. 165 | JULY 1, 1997   221
Hamlet's Lesson for Modern Man

NO. 166 | AUGUST 5, 1997   227
Devotion to the Immaculate Heart of Mary

NO. 167 | SEPTEMBER 5, 1997   232
The Death of Princess Di

NO. 168 | OCTOBER 8, 1997   237
The Sin of Homosexuality

NO. 169 | NOVEMBER 7, 1997   243
The Film
"The Sound of Music"

NO. 170 | DECEMBER 1, 1997   249
"Perils from False Brethren"

NO. 171 | JANUARY 2, 1998   262
Fugitives to the Woods

NO. 172 | FEBRUARY 4, 1998   267
Neither Sedevacantist nor Liberal

NO. 173 | MARCH 3, 1998   273
The SSPX's Marriage Tribunal

NO. 174 | APRIL 2, 1998   279
"Peter Schlemihl"

NO. 175 | MAY 1, 1998   285
The Film *Titanic*

NO. 176 | JUNE 1, 1998   291
10 Years After the Consecrations

NO. 177 | JULY 1, 1998   296
Unreal Movies & Real Catholicism

NO. 178 | AUGUST 3, 1998   301
"Fiftiesism"

NO. 179 | SEPTEMBER 1, 1998   307
John Paul II's "Personalism"

NO. 180 | OCTOBER 1, 1998   313
Co-education

NO. 181 | NOVEMBER 1, 1998   319
Why We Do Not Cooperate with Rome

NO. 182 | DECEMBER 1, 1998   326
One Year to the Millennium:
Quo Vadimus? –
Where are We Headed?

INDEX   341

A Teenager's Story

IT CANNOT BE repeated too often, the first of the Ten Commandments is also the first in importance: Thou shalt love the Lord thy God with all thy heart, with all thy soul, with all thy strength and with all thy mind, and thou shalt have no other gods before him. If many Catholics lose their children to the Faith, even lose them from home; it can be because despite the appearances, they have not obeyed the First Commandment. They may even have put their child in a Catholic school, but if their own hearts and souls have not put God in the first place, the children follow the example, and under fierce pressure from today's world, slide away from God.

Let us at the beginning of another school year see children, in or out of Catholic schools, with the same problem, calling for the same solution: the parents must live by their Catholic Faith. Firstly the case of a 13 year-old American teenager, as described to me recently by a good friend who had to look after him for a couple of weeks. We will call him Nick. I quote my friend almost word for word:

> These weeks I spent at home looking after Nick were one of the great learning experiences of my life: I en-

tered into the amazing world of a modern teenager. To sum it up in one sentence: for him there is no external reality. Nothing exists outside his head, unless it appears on a screen where he has chosen to watch the dancing images.

When Nick arrived by plane, his luggage happened to have got lost. We had to buy him new clothes, but he would not wear just anything. His self-definition depended on his T-shirt, so to buy him replacements, Nick took me on a visit to the T-shirt industry. I had no idea! Racks upon racks upon racks of T-shirts, and nine out of ten covered in blood, skeletons, corpses, dismembered limbs, all according to the various Heavy Metal rock groups, matching the C.D.'s. There is an extra-ordinary dependency of the youngsters on these groups. As for choice? Non-existent! The shirts, the discs, the groups are all the same: a multi-million dollar industry! As the adults' self-definition is by their personalized license-plates, so the youngsters' is by their T-shirts!

So Nick had to fill out a lost luggage claim form. He did not even know his home address! This I found was part of a pattern: for Nick, anything falling outside of four areas just does not exist: firstly, Heavy Metal – I realized he watches a great deal of MTV (the continuous Rock "music" TV channel). Secondly, hideous movies (but Nick will watch any movie). Thirdly, computer games. In the stores there are hundreds and hundreds of these, each a self-contained world into which the kids vanish, "improving their skills," with accompanying books to explain the fantastical game, all incredibly complex, of the electronic hero diving through labyrinthine halls with a Zoogoo gun to zap the Zogos jumping at him out of every corner, etc., etc. I had no suitable computer at home? Then Nick stood and stared in the stores, spending hours dreaming up absurd new games, hours and hours of meaningless fantasizing. Fourthly, fast food. Nick sincerely believed that the MacDonald's on 3rd street was better than the

MacDonald's on the Plaza! He is a connoisseur of fast food! Pathetic. He could not eat anything else. He is addicted to sugar. I bought him several candy-bars to last a few days. They were gone in a few hours, and he was bouncing off the walls! Fifthly, one must add the TV program, Beavis and Butthead. Nick can quote whole chunks of the dialogue, word for word. This cartoon is sheer nihilism, emptiness and destruction, nothingness. It's Nick's delight. Terrifying!

Has Nick any skills? Reading, I would guess 7th grade, mathematics, 6th grade, while his age is 9th grade. Nick will do nothing that makes any demands, for instance adding numbers in his head is too hard. When we played Scrabble, he would invent words. Yet he gets A's and B's in classwork, and he hopes to go to the Massachusetts Institute of Technology – in order to study and make computer games! But how is this kid ever going to connect with reality? As we were once driving over a famous river, I called out its name – Nick didn't even look out of the window. From one State to another, he had no idea where he was. One evening I told him he had half an hour to get ready to go out – he spent 25 of the 30 minutes watching MTV with no idea of the five minutes to go!

The kid is a SLAVE of MERCHANDISING. As though his entire being exists to give money to the manufacturers and merchants of T-shirts, C.D.'s, Nintendo games, movies and fast food. To them immediately goes every dollar. The kid is a trash junkie. Whatever the screen tells him to do, he will do, this C.D., or that film or MacDonald's, and if he can't do it, he goes mad. His heart and soul have been offered up to merchandising.

In the kid's favor, he has a real sense of humor and there is no pretence about him. Unlike other youngsters I know who have learned how to fool the adults but in private are exactly like Nick, he has no cover-up skills. As least he made no excuses.

I have long known modern philosophy putting reality inside the mind – Descartes said, "I think, therefore I am" – but this kid putting that into practice still took me by surprise – his head is empty except for the content of the screen. I was also surprised by the amount of money he spends to enrich the ruiners of his soul. Some of this money – to his credit – he had worked hard to earn for himself. The rest came from his father who also works hard for his family, and who has tried to help his son, but today's anti-culture has taken over.

Nick's parents are decent folk, I know them, but they have not understood the seriousness of the problem. They allowed Nick to do computer-games and watch TV, but they did not grasp the descent into demonism of what he was watching. Pied pipers of Rock have stolen away their boy while their back was turned. Nick's parents also relied on Nick's being in Catholic school to make him a good kid, but . . . Nick may know the list of the seven sacraments, but his school religion stops there, his heart is not in it, his heart has been sold to the merchants. School cannot replace parents. Nick's dad is mostly at work, his heart is in his business. His mom is a lovely woman, truly feminine, with a touch of New Age, a flower child of the 1960's, no solid basis despite a fairly strict Catholic home. Vatican II has given to them both a loose and sloppy version of Catholicism – no wonder the kid's heart and love are in computer games.

If you ask me what I think can be done for the boy, I would reply that before supernatural seeds of the Faith can be sown, the parched dry field of his soul has first got to be ploughed, watered and nourished with natural nutrients. Until that hard shell is cracked, teaching him is a waste of time. I know supernatural Faith is infinitely higher than natural culture, but so long as a soul is blasted and withered by today's anti-culture, the leap to Faith is too great. There must be a ramp to Rome on the natural level. In school, that should be the glories of Western civilization so-called, meaning, in fact, the natural fruits of Catholic culture. The ground must be prepared, otherwise the seed simply bounces off. Especially with children. We must not fool ourselves – BEWARE OF SHINING FACES, ALL READY TO SNEAK OFF TO THE TRASH MERCHANTS. But for goodness' sake don't think I see no hope for Nick. The first step is to recognize that today's anti-culture is trash, and not to kid oneself that it is alright because it is democratic (it is!), just a matter of taste, or whatever. The second step is to see why it gets hold of the children, because it meets with no resistance, it finds the soul empty. The third step is to start filling the child's soul with good things, not only supernatural, but also natural, otherwise when the anti-natural arrives, it is liable to knock the feet out from under the supernatural. Let little children learn the old nursery rhymes, and after "Couldn't put Humpty together again", there is no need to add "Amen"! The Faith, yes, but common sense also. And the parents must realize that example goes much farther than words. Their children are not toys, but immortal souls for whose formation or deformation God will call them to account. When parents really put God in first place, it will be literally child's play to fill the child's soul with good things. Dad must take time with his boys, Mom must take time with her girls."

Be it said, Nick's parents are now taking action to look after Nick's education, but let us pass to another friend writing to me from France. The problem is transposed into a different key, but it is basically the same problem:

Once I worked with alcoholics, now I am teaching in a Traditional Catholic girls' secondary school which has a good reputation throughout France, but strangely enough, I look back wistfully at the time spent with the alcoholics. Perhaps it's because there was so often buried under layers of misery, and of course sin, a huge desire for God, and once they discovered who He was, for Our Lord. There was no hypocrisy – they had tried to find happiness in every conceivable place and way, and they had no illusions left about finding Paradise on this earth.

Whereas inevitably, for children, the world is full of promise. And the children in our school are often second generation 'Traditionalist'. Unfortunately, in France today, it is a little bit smart to be a 'Traditionalist.' It's quite chic to put on your Gucci scarf and talk about your Royalist sympathies and criticize some modernist bishop. But at the same time, "One mustn't exaggerate," and religion must fit in with one's social life and amusements. That flame and thirst to discover the treasures of Our Lord's Heart are so rare in these nicely brought up Catholic girls. It reminds me a bit of my own boarding-school chapel, which was Protestant: beautiful singing, incense, processions, bells, in fact everything except Our Lord who had no personal relevance in our lives. There are of course amongst our girls exceptions which rejoice our hearts.

But your Excellency, you are damning us if we do not put our children in Catholic schools, and now you are damning us if we do! Dear, dear friends, dear, dear parents, no doubt at all, if it is at all possible, children must be put in Catholic schools, as the Catholic Church has always insisted, and that of course does not mean schools of today's official "Catholic" Church. However, better the alcoholic thirsting for God, or the trash junkie who may learn to hunger for God, than the Traditionalists knowing their way around God, meaning, having learned, as they think, how to get around Him! The poor He fills with good things, those who think they are rich He sends empty away (Lk. 1: 53).

Up hill or down dale, in sickness or in health, in Tradition or out of it, God is all that matters, and the one thing He does not have that is ours to give Him, and that

He wants, is the heart of our hearts, with all our soul, with all our mind, with all our strength. All the rest that matters will follow.

Dear Friends and Benefactors, out of the trashland by miracle and by prayers have stepped forward this year, it seems, ten young men to try a priestly vocation at Winona. Pray that they have "that flame and thirst to discover the treasures of Our Lord's Heart," and be thanked for every prayer you said that helped to bring them here!

Most sincerely yours in the Sacred Heart.

Avoid "Conservative" Catholics

OCTOBER, MONTH OF the Holy Rosary, and today some seminarians are taking part in a "National Rosary March" being organized locally in Winona. However, the Seminary will not be officially taking part. Interesting question – why not?

The problem is not what it might often be, namely some kind or other of naturalism, because the flyer announcing the Rosary March announces also its supernatural motivation: "[T]o save both America and the world, to obtain the conversion of Russia to the Immaculate Heart of Mary, to establish the Reign of Christ the King, to obtain the conversion of all Americans to the Roman Catholic Faith, to restore the Traditional Family; and to perform public reparation for sin." It could be one of our own SSPX Catholics who drew up such a program.

Nor is the problem what again it could easily be, namely one of activism. True, the flyer begins a little disagreeably with the title "Calling all cowards," as though anyone not taking part in the March is faint-hearted or not willing to do something to defend their Faith. Nevertheless, "praying fifteen decades of the Rosary as we walk down the main streets of our towns" is primarily prayer, with little action as such, and with little indication of that spirit of revolt or anger which can, from a Catholic point of view, mar many otherwise apparently well-intentioned marches or parades.

Nor is the problem one of more pressing duties of state. Indeed seminarians have an absolute duty to study and pray in isolation from the world for, normally, six years to prepare themselves to go back into the world as priests of Our Lord Jesus Christ, but midday Saturday they can easily take an early lunch, with minimal interruption of studies, and with fifteen decades of the Rosary said into the bargain.

Nor is the problem one of collaboration or involvement with the Novus Ordo, insofar as the March is being organized, says the flyer, by a group of lay people and surely any such layfolk who believe in public rosaries have the Catholic Faith. And if any Novus Ordo clergy are present and are – naturally enough – invited to take a lead, surely seminarians present can be diplomatic enough to let no action on their part deter any official clergy from taking part in a public Rosary March!

Then where is there a problem? Answer: seminarians being taught and learning to believe the fullness of Catholic doctrine are coming into possession of a treasure beyond price, that Faith without which it is impossible to please God and so to get to heaven. Now it is true that anybody taking part in a public Rosary March must have some Catholic Faith at least, and that all such people should benefit from contact with seminarians being armed with the fullness of Faith. However, the risk is that few such people may grasp the importance of the fullness of integral Catholic doctrine, and so the seminarians could be exposed to a kind of temptation of "TRADECUMENISM": let all of us who believe in the

Rosary just get together, and all will be well; let all of us who love the Mother of God concentrate on the things that unite us and not dwell on the things that divide us, after all we are all Catholics, are we not?

That is how seminarians might be tempted to begin devaluing what makes the specific mission and value of the SSPX, namely its guarding the integrity of Catholic doctrine.

This importance of doctrine, on which follows the need for so-called Traditional Catholics to shun religious fellowship even with so-called conservative Catholics (except to make them see the error of their ways), is difficult for many people today, even Catholics, to understand.

Let us think for a moment. A Catholic is a Catholic (i.e., much better placed to get to Heaven than if he were not a Catholic) not by his sex, age, intelligence, or any such thing, but by what he believes, meaning not what he makes up in his own mind, but by what he knows to be true in matters of God.

Thus a Catholic knows firstly that one God exists, and that to associate with atheists on the supposed common ground of benevolence to mankind, while excluding God, is to live a lie and a blasphemy – because anything good at all in man comes only from God. Secondly he knows that God once (only once) took flesh and became man, the God-man Jesus Christ, and that to associate with other religions on the basis of a supposed common belief in God, excluding Jesus Christ, is to live a lie and a blasphemy against the goodness of God who took infinite pain to come down to earth for us men and for our salvation. Thirdly the Catholic knows that Our Lord Jesus Christ, true God and true man, came down amongst us not only once in the Incarnation but also every time Mass is validly celebrated, in the mystery of the Real Presence, and that to associate with other "Christians" on the grounds of a supposed common belief in Christ, is to associate in a lie if these "Christians" insult God (at least objectively) by their refusal of the doctrine of the Real Presence.

These are three classic examples, what one might call the first three classic stages, of the principle whereby to refuse Catholic doctrine is to insult God. Thus he who denies the Real Presence, for instance, gravely underestimates the true love of God. Alas, many Catholics today do not understand this primacy of doctrine, which is a primacy of divine reality, because they put man and his fellowship in front of the interests of God.

However, let us suppose the principle is understood, at least in theory. Then since Vatican II we may say the principle has been carried at least two stages further forward in practice:

Fourthly, a Catholics knows (but not by authority – there is the problem!) that the Second Vatican Council departed from Tradition, and that to associate indiscriminately with Novus Ordo "Catholics" on the basis of a supposed common "Catholicism" is to associate in a lie and a blasphemy if these "Catholics" insult God (at least objectively) by trampling on Catholic Tradition.

Fifthly, a Catholic knows (this is even more controversial, but, day by day, events prove Archbishop Lefebvre to have been right) that the "conservatives" who put themselves back under Rome around or after the fateful Consecrations of June 1988, also thereby departed from Tradition, and that to associate in friendship or solidarity with them is implicitly to betray the Catholic Faith by saying in actions if not in words that the Faith is something that today's Roman Protestants are capable of guarding – for who protects a child by throwing him amongst thieves? So whoever does throw a child amongst thieves, what value does he put on the child? And if he thinks thieves are not thieves, what is his judgment worth? And if he pretends they are not thieves, what is his honesty worth? In any case the child is ruined.

Dear friends, this letter has often (and recently) taken us "Traditionalists" to task for our laziness, complacency, vanity, hypocrisy, all the sins in the book! For, subjectively, we are all of us poor sinners, and we are liars if we deny it (I Jn. 1: 8). Objectively however, we are carriers of glorious Tradition, the fullness of Catholic Truth. Our own misery as carriers makes no less glorious the Truth we carry, indeed the more lowly we may (must) think of ourselves, the more highly by contrast we should uphold the Truth.

In that case the seminarians may go down the hill to join with all other devotees of the Rosary and of the Mother of God, and they may mix with there to do them all the good they can, but the greatest good they can do them – always with all due prudence – is to give them to understand that, fourthly the Novus Ordo, and fifthly its "conservative" branch, are: not adequate ways to honor the Mother of God or to serve her Divine Son.

"With the Rosary and the Scapular one day I will save the world," said the Mother of God to St. Dominic.

Understanding Moral and Natural Liberty

B ACK IN MAY when this letter disentangled the dignity of man with God from the very different dignity of man without God, you were promised a letter to disentangle the two even more confused liberties, corresponding to the two dignities. As the arrival of winter gives us longer evenings by the electronic fireside, let us attempt the second disentangling.

Liberty, like its Germanic synonym, freedom, is one of those words which in modern times is so charged with emotion that the moment it is mentioned, most people stop thinking because their brains are awash in cosy feelings. However, anybody with a grain of common sense, looking at the world around him, appreciates that the world produced by these feelings is not cosy at all, and so it is not only Catholics who need to do some thinking.

Let us start by defining liberty, or freedom, in the way most people use the word, as an absence of constraint. Now constraint may be external or internal. For instance if a bird is in a cage or has a thread tied to its foot, it is constrained externally, because the cage or thread are not part of the bird but are external to it. But if the bird is externally free or free from any external constraint, that does not mean it is internally free, because all its actions, for instance wherever it flies or whenever it eats, are governed, or constrained, by its instincts. Watch a dog caught in a conflict between two of its instincts. The dog is not freely choosing, or deciding. Eventually one instinct prevails, and the dog acts accordingly. On the contrary men have a superior faculty of reason or intelligence with which they can override their instincts, so men are not normally constrained by their instincts, so they can use their reason to choose which instinct to follow or not to follow, and so men have both external liberty (if they are not for instance in prison) and internal liberty.

Thus a man in prison has internal but not external liberty, a bird in the sky has external but not internal liberty a man in the open air has both, a bird in a cage has neither. What interests us here is not the external liberty, called physical liberty because it means an absence of physical or material constraint. What interests us here is the internal liberty, called "natural liberty" because it is part of man's rational nature, or sometimes "psychological liberty" because it is part of man's psychological makeup.

This natural liberty as we shall call it, following on man's reason, is nothing other than his free will, as it is called in English, meaning man's faculty to choose without constraint of instinct between alternatives presented to his reason. This faculty of free will, or natural liberty, is at the heart of the confusion over "liberty" and it is one of the two liberties continually confused, so let us look at it well to observe its true nature. Let us establish four points: it is a (1) inalienable (2), faculty, a (3) unlimited (4) capacity, which for purposes of illustration we shall compare to a motor car.

Firstly, in its roots, natural liberty is an inalienable feature of rational nature. Wherever there is the faculty of reason, wherever there is a man not deprived of the use of his reason, there is natural liberty or free will. If a man loses, for instance by drink, the use of his reason, then he is no longer free, but otherwise his natural liberty is inalienable from his being a man. So long as a car is mechanically in working order, it has or is, until the car "dies," an inalienable ability to drive.

Secondly, in the man, natural liberty or free will is a faculty and not an act. It is a faculty or ability to act, built into his nature, but it is prior to any of a man's rational acts, presupposed by all of them and so identical with none of them. The car, purely as car, is an ability to drive, it is not yet, purely as a car, driving anywhere. It can be sitting in a garage.

Thirdly, in action, natural liberty is unlimited from within, that is to say the faculty is not limited to this act or that act, to this kind of act or that kind of act, but it is a faculty wide open to any and all acts physically available to a man in his circumstances. The faculty is only limited from without, for instance, a man has no natural liberty to fly (without a machine) because that alternative is not physically available to him. But from within, free will is not limited. Similarly the car, again purely as a motor car, is not limited to driving north, or south, or east, or west, but it can drive in any of these directions wherever a car can drive, only not for instance across water, because that is not a possibility physically available to it.

However, fourthly, in morals, natural liberty is a capacity or ability, and not a right, to act without limitation. For just as certain acts like flying by himself are physically unavailable to man, so too certain acts are morally unavailable to him, for instance murder, adultery or theft. Natural liberty has the capacity to commit these wrong acts, but it has no right to commit them. Similarly the motor car has the physical capacity to drive down the wrong side of the road, but it has no right to do so because it will suffer and cause accidents. The car's natural ability to drive wherever it can drive comes from within it as a car, but its right to drive wherever it may drive comes not from within but from without, for instance from the highway code. Thus natural liberty gives me the ability from within to do whatever I can do, but the right to do what I may do comes not from within but from without. The ability or capacity alone does not constitute a right.

Of course if there was no highway code, then the motor car would have the right to drive on the road wherever it had the ability, then ability and right would be the same thing. But when it comes to morals, there is a highway code. Man constantly dreams of having the right to do as he likes, but as Catholics know, and as all the truly great pagans and non-Catholics have taught, this universe has a moral framework whereby, from outside of us, certain acts are objectively and unchangingly right whilst others are objectively and unchangingly wrong. From which it follows that natural liberty is an ability but not a right.

So all experience teaches that of all the acts available to be chosen by natural liberty, some are right, or morally good, and some are wrong, or morally evil, and here we come to the second of the two liberties continually confused.

If the faculty of free will is misused to choose evil acts, then we have the misuse of natural liberty which is commonly (and reasonably) called license, each act of which is sinful, or a sin. On the other hand – always assuming that human acts divide into those that are morally good and those that are morally evil – if the faculty of free will is rightly used, to choose good acts, then we have the right use of natural liberty which we call moral liberty. Let us again look well, to establish, the true nature of this moral liberty, in four points: it is the (1) alienable (2) use of a faculty, a (3) limited (4) right.

Firstly, in its roots, moral liberty is alienable in the sense that every time I misuse my natural liberty by choosing sin, then I may have sinful liberty, or license, but I certainly have no moral liberty to do good, in fact Our Lord says that he who sins is the slave of sin (Jn. 8: 34). Similarly if a car is misdriven so that it is wrecked, it can no longer be driven anywhere until its natural ability to drive is repaired. The car's being misdriven excludes or alienates for the duration its being driven. Of course a man's liberty cannot be wrecked beyond repair so long as he is living. He retains until death his inalienable faculty of natural liberty but misuse of the faculty excludes or alienates its right use for as long as the misuse lasts. Therefore moral liberty is alienable.

Secondly, in the man, moral liberty or the right use of free will is the use of a faculty as distinct from the faculty used, like the safe driving of the car as opposed to the car driven. There must be the faculty prior to the use, as to the misuse, and so every use, like every misuse, presupposes the faculty, as all driving or mis-driving presupposes a car, but the faculty is different, from its use or misuse because it is always in itself open to both and so it is identical with neither. Natural liberty is by itself only potential, moral liberty and license are always at least partly actual. It is because there will never be moral liberty without natural liberty, that the Catholic Church values and defends natural liberty against all heretics who deny that man has free will; nevertheless it is moral liberty that adds the actual goodness to the mere potential of the faculty of free will. As driving presupposes a car, so all drivers look after their cars; nevertheless no car in the garage, can ensure it will be well driven on the road; the good driving is distinct from the car.

Thirdly in action, moral liberty is limited from within, that is to say moral liberty is limited to all good acts, it excludes and is excluded by the evil acts of license. Thus in terms of the variety of acts open to it, moral liberty is more limited than natural liberty which is open to all acts good or evil. Therefore moral liberty is comparatively limited. As good driving excludes bad driving, so good driving limits the variety of ways in which a car can be driven.

However, fourthly, because moral liberty's limitation is to acts that are good, then moral liberty can be called a right, because if I have no right to do wrong, or commit sin, I do have a right to do what is right. One can say then that moral liberty is a right which is confined to right acts. So moral liberty is by definition confined to right acts, whilst natural liberty is open to right or to wrong acts. Therefore moral liberty is a right to act whereas natural liberty is only a capacity or a potency to act. It is obeying the highway code and all laws concerned which gives me the right to drive my car out of the garage and on the road.

Thus we arrive at the following clear distinction in four points between natural and moral liberties, the two liberties which it is necessary above all to distinguish: whereas natural liberty is an inalienable faculty, a (from within) unlimited capacity, moral liberty is an alienable use of that faculty, a (from within) limited right. Natural liberty and moral liberty are thus as distinct as the motor car sitting in the garage and its being well driven along the road; as distinct as the bottle empty and the bottle filled with wine.

Well, if the two liberties are so clearly distinct, how can they ever be confused with one another? A swift answer is that while I live I cannot lose my natural liberty which is open to all acts, good or evil. Now moral liberty is a right. If then I blur the two, my natural liberty becomes a right, and I have the right to do whatever I like, right or wrong! In fact claiming natural liberty as a right is a convenient way of abolishing right and wrong. Everything becomes legitimate, an old dream of naughty man. We are then all "liberated" and "emancipated," we can all "let it all hang out," we can do as we like, in theory as long as it does not hurt someone else, but in practice (and in logic) even if it does hurt someone else – drive-by shootings, natural-born killers, etc, etc. Teach youngsters that their natural liberty is a right, and, in logic and justice, they will punish their teachers by destroying them.

However, many liberals will admit the difference between right and wrong, and still claim that they have a natural right to do wrong. So the real reason for the confusion must go deeper.

The real reason is the self-glorification of man. The wine bottle is seen to be so valuable that it is of no importance whether it is filled with wine or dishwater. The car is seen to be such a superb model that it does not matter whether it drives or crashes – look, what a superb wreck it makes, wrapped around that tree! Man is seen to be by nature of such dignity, his natural faculties have such intrinsic value, that howsoever he uses or misuses them they show forth that transcendental dignity, and so their use or misuse becomes of secondary importance. Man's natural liberty thus becomes a right, because whatever he does with it, it shows forth his dignity. Look, what superb wrecks Lucifer and Judas Iscariot are, in the eternal fires of Hell! What a dignity of defiance!

This glorifying of man's nature in itself forgets (or denies) that man is not a value in himself. As the bottle exists only to contain wine, as the car exists only to be driven without crashing, so a man exists only to fill his life with merits so that when he dies he can go to Heaven. No human soul is on earth for any other reason. But the liberals and secular humanists deny that man is relative in this way to any value above him. He is the supreme value in himself, therefore he is a value above right and wrong. Now in truth God alone is above right and wrong (in the sense, that He alone can by nature do no wrong). Therefore the liberals in fact make man into God.

Moreover the liberals have gained such influence over the last several hundred years that they have molded the whole world around us. Their glorification, in fact deification, of man seeps into our being through their music, arts, media, schools, universities, politics, economics, "patriotism," and so on and so on. As a result, when a man-glorifying error like the right to do wrong is put before us, it finds through the cast of our minds and the tilt of our emotions, molded by the liberal world around us, such a sympathetic reception that the error and the confusion are liable to drop into us as easily as a letter drops into a letter box.

That is why, if we are asked such a question as whether moral liberty or natural liberty is the true liberty, our instinctive reaction is to say that it is natural liberty, because moral liberty is limited, and limits take away liberty. Now that answer would be correct if man was an end in himself, because then he would be the measure of right and wrong, which means he could do no wrong, which would give him the right to choose whatever he liked, which would make moral liberty meaningless. But whoever recalls that man is even more for Heaven than the wine bottle is for wine or the car is for safe driving, realizes that true liberty is liberty for the bottle from dishwater, liberty for the car from crashing, liberty for man from sin (whoever sins is the slave of sin, says Our Lord), so that the true liberty is in fact moral liberty. Thus natural liberty rejects any limitation or law, but moral liberty greets any limitation or law helping it to attain its end. If natural liberty, which is open to sin, were the true liberty, then neither God nor the angels in Heaven who can no longer sin, would have true liberty!

Alas, these arguments have difficulty biting when a man's emotions from his background, friends, education and even "patriotism" all run in the opposite direction. However, if the whole world were steeped in the error of deifying man and glorifying natural liberty, it would still not be so grave as long as the Catholic churchmen resisted and condemned the error. But now listen to a few examples of Vatican II's teaching on religious liberty:

- "The human person has a right to religious freedom" (Dignitatis Humanae #2) – he has a natural faculty to choose any religion, yes; he has a moral right to choose any religion other than Catholicism, no.

- "The right to religious freedom is founded in the dignity of the human person" (D.H.#2) – man is so dignified that he has a right by moral liberty to go to heaven, yes; a right by misuse of natural liberty to go to hell, no (unless "right" simply means ability).

- "Men retain the right to religious liberty even when they misuse it by not seeking the truth" (D.H.#2) – men have the natural faculty to turn away from the truth, yes; they have the moral liberty or right to do so, no.

- "Religious bodies have the right to be allowed to spread whatever is their faith" (D.H.#4) – religious bodies have their members' natural faculty to spread truth or error, and the civic liberty if their society chooses to allow them to do so indiscriminately, but they have the moral right or liberty to spread the Catholic truth alone.

These are just four examples of the almost hopeless confusion pervading this Vatican II document, confusion between the natural faculty of freedom and the moral right of freedom. It is a confusion that easily fits into modern minds feeling the self-value and glory of man, but it will not fit into Catholic minds knowing man's entire relatedness to, and dependence on, God. Yet the mass of Catholic churchmen today are going along with this – in effect – declaration of independence from God!

"It is not, nor it cannot come to, good." To Vatican II making man's natural liberty into a right corresponds the man-centered New Mass; to the New Mass corresponds "Beavis and Butthead," that horrific MTV program whose charming and well-spoken young creator apparently declared on a recent TV talk-show (David Letterman) that the idea for his nihilistic cartoon about two valueless boys came to him all in a flash when, in attendance at the Novus Ordo Mass, he heard a Beavis-style laugh from a youngster two pews behind him; and "Beavis and Butthead," mirror of valueless youth, is the death-knell tolling for a futureless society! Of course, give man the right to do as he likes, and in no time at all human society will become worse than a jungle!

Any reader of today's newspapers cannot fail to observe how fast that is happening around us. Man has put himself in the place of God, he claims natural liberty as a right, that right he has to grant – or he is proud of granting! – to youngsters who have none of the oldsters' residual common sense to restrain them from behaving worse than wild animals. As a result, everywhere the red lights are flashing dissolution and chaos, and the alarm bells are ringing off the wall, but will man put his liberty back underneath God? Never! Anything but that! Catholic adults! Activate your supernatural faith and charity, recognize the absolute supremacy of God and His Divine Son, Jesus Christ, and the primacy of His one Catholic Church; recall that man by his nature alone is not only open to good or evil, but by the original sin in his nature more or less strongly inclines naturally to evil; so resolutely wash out of your own minds the last trace of confusion between the natural faculty of freedom and the moral right, and then, according to your circumstances, do all in your power to censor, curtail, limit and check the youngsters' misuse of their natural faculty, so that it will choose only that to which they have the moral right. They may not understand, and you may not be popular, but at least you will not have been a traitor to them, and by defying your country in its error, if it rests on religious liberty, you will have done all you can to save it from its ruin!

May God have mercy upon us all, and make us slaves of that justice and servants of that truth which alone can set us truly free (Jn.8: 32).

Pope John Paul II and the Prayer Meeting at Assisi

A DIFFICULT BUT valuable book on JP2 has just been published in English translation by the Angelus Press out of Kansas City, Missouri: Volume I of *Pope John Paul II's Theological Journey to the Prayer Meeting of Religions in Assisi* by the German professor and priest, Fr. Johannes Dörmann.

Difficult, because Fr. Dörmann is a Catholic scholar of many years' standing, not a SSPX priest, but a learned writer and teacher within the official Church, with many university level articles and books to his name.

Valuable, because with no concern other than to get at the truth, Fr. Dörmann has applied all his experience and talents as a Catholic scholar to discovering and analyzing what this Pope actually thinks. His analysis and conclusions are to us all the more valuable for having been undertaken and published in Germany quite independently of the Society, indeed upon information and belief Prof. Dörmann does not even celebrate the Tridentine Mass. In no way can he be accused of being a "Lefebvrist." If then he and his book testify that the Church's present crisis is not just a problem of liturgical rites or of Church language or of any superficial feature of Church life, but an upheaval of the very foundations of the Catholic Faith, then his independent testimony is a striking confirmation of the wisdom of the apparently extreme stand taken by Archbishop Lefebvre and the SSPX since the early 1970's. What happened was that Prof. Dörmann was profoundly shocked by the Interreligious World Prayer Meeting held in Assisi in 1986 at JP2's instigation and under his leadership. The Professor asked himself, how could the Catholic Pope have come to give such public recognition and official credit to all of the world's principal false religions? Over some such question Catholics have agonized for years, and it has driven many to resort to more or less far-fetched explanations such as a drugged Pope, a dummy Pope, a KGB Pope, a Freemason Pope, an invalid Pope, or whatever. Instead of wild surmise the Professor assumed – reasonably – that JP2 meant what he was doing and was doing what he meant. In that case, what did he mean? Again reasonably, the Professor set himself to find out what JP2 meant, by studying what he has said in his speeches and writings.

Now it is not as though over the last 20 years, whether as Cardinal or Pope, Karol Wojtyla has been hiding what he thinks, on the contrary there has come from him a constant flow of words, spoken or written. The problem is that his style is difficult. Many a page of his one can read half a dozen times and still not grasp what he is meaning to say. Outwardly it seems pious, but inwardly it seems unclear. At this point the pious majority of the Pope's readers or listeners let themselves be contented with the outward piety of his words, whilst a disconcerted minority are repulsed by their inward lack of clarity. Either way, they give up the attempt to understand what the Pope is meaning, and pass on, contented or disconcerted as the case may be.

In this situation, the immense virtue of Prof. Dör-mann, and the immense usefulness of his book, is that he let himself be neither contented nor disconcerted, but he pursued the Pope's meaning until he found it. What the Professor found is so shocking that many of the pious Catholics mentioned above will be tempted to go into denial, or at least to give his book the silent treatment, but let two indications be given that the Professor really has found the Pope's meaning. First and foremost, it is normal that how a man thinks should correspond to how he acts, and what the Professor discovered of the Pope's thinking corresponds exactly to the event of Assisi and to much else besides. Secondly, it is normal that a man as trained as this Pope is in philosophy and theology, should think coherently, and what the Professor discovered is an entirely coherent system of thought, "with every word calculated and in its right place," the Professor has said.

What system did the Professor – repeat, quite independently of the SSPX – discover? The enclosed red flyer gives an overview of his book, which is only the first of three Volumes to have appeared in German, with another two, maybe three, waiting to be written, if the Professor's health holds up, for which we must pray, for the sake of the truth, which is sacred.

The Pope's thinking starts out from man. Every man alive has deep inside himself, if only he will look within, access to a union of himself with God which exists thanks to Christ's Incarnation whereby Christ united himself to every man. This union of every man with God is inside every man alive whether he knows it or not, whether he wants it or not, and so it has been since the beginning of the human race, but it is only in recent times, thanks to the outpouring of the Holy Ghost upon the Second Vatican Council, that men have become aware of this automatic union of every man with God. The Passion and

Resurrection of Jesus Christ merely made manifest the love of God the Father present already inside every man by God's union with every man. Thus far Fr. Dörmann, who in his successful pursuit of the Pope's meaning has abstained from all emotion, abuse or rhetoric. He has merely laid out the Pope's thinking and then, by contrast, alongside, the thinking of the true Church (see, for example, the "Criticism" sections of the Overview).

But let us spell out a few of the logical consequences of this thinking: all men are saved from birth, so Hell (the old fashioned eternal fire) either does not exist or is empty. Conversion, faith, baptism, the sacraments are no longer necessary for salvation, they merely enhance the human person's awareness of his saved state. Likewise amongst all the religions in which subsists the Super-Church of the God of all men, the Catholic Church's only superiority is that, through its connection to Christ, it has a better grasp of man's full inner dignity, which it is its function to encourage men to live up to.

Hence on the one hand a certain preaching of moral standards, e.g., Cairo, to maintain human dignity, but on the other hand a steady pressure upon the narrow old Catholicism to open up and to allow itself to be absorbed into the brave new Super-Church of all mankind, so much less exclusive, so much more caring for all men! Hence JP2's recent promise that the new Super-Church will apologize for all the sins of the narrow old Church, for instance its warmongering Crusades, its intolerance of other religions, etc.

Not that the Pope disbelieves in the doctrine of the old Church, on the contrary he is convinced that Tradition is true and that amongst all religions, Catholicism alone is the fullness of the truth. However, all other religions contain seeds of truth sufficient for salvation outside the Catholic Church!

Nor does the Pope want to exclude Traditional Catholics from his Super-Church, on the contrary he is convinced that the evolution from Church to Super-Church is the true, "living Tradition." So he would love all Catholics to follow him, so he will formulate the Super-Church doctrine as harmoniously as possible with the old Church doctrine – surely his contriving to express the new thought in the old language causes the above-mentioned obscurity of his style, which it takes the patience and skill of a Prof. Dörmann to penetrate. However, if obstinate "Traditionalists" nevertheless refuse to share his broader vision, then to his sorrow and without his fault they excommunicate or at least marginalize themselves . . .etc, etc.

Dear friends and benefactors, I hope your hair is now quietly standing on end! The depth and objective perversity of this neo-modernist heresy are unprecedented. As remedies, surely there soon remain only the shedding of our blood in martyrdom and/or a divine chastisement. But to understand helps us to endure, and here we owe a great debt to Prof. Dörmann: his book makes sense of an otherwise senseless scene. Read the book if you have a chance of understanding it. Give a copy to any priest with a chance of reading it. The truth must out. How else can souls be saved?

We pray for the Pope. We pray for yourselves, and we sincerely thank each one of you benefactors for all your support through another calendar year. Blessed Advent, Happy Christmas, Happy New Year!

Words of Encouragement

FOR THE NEW Year and for January two magnificent quotes from two great churchmen of the last century, who saw then into the heart of our troubles now. Firstly, from Msgr. Gaume, some words of encouragement for what might seem another daunting New Year:

> See what is happening around you; understand both the signs of the times and things you have been told of, and the terrible dangers threatening you. Seduction surrounds you on all sides: in the laws, in morals, in books, in speeches, in the public and private behavior of the people. The number and authority of Catholic truths is shrinking day by day amongst the children of men. Understand all that well: be firmly convinced that your position was never more critical. Draw the conclusion not that you must withdraw from the world, but that you must keep yourself from evil; and, at all costs, keep what is dear to you from evil. More than in any other time, every Catholic must be a soldier to his last breath. If you have a clear understanding of the formidable trial awaiting you and which you are already undergoing, it will fill you with great courage and holy joy. It is the unshakeable proof of your faith

and the rock-solid foundation of your hopes because it is the tangible fulfillment of the prophecies of your Divine Master.

Did he not say, 1800 years ago, that toward the end of times, the nations would universally apostatize; that the faith would grow so weak that it would give out only a glimmer of light; that iniquity would overflow like an impetuous torrent across the face of the entire earth and that the charity of the great number would grow cold? Did he not say that there would arise a multitude of false prophets, precursors of the Man of Sin; that God would count for nothing; and that at the same time the Gospel would reach all the way around the world? Did he not say that he was foretelling these things to prevent your being scandalized by the passing triumph of wicked men; to prevent your saying in your heart: Christ is asleep; he has given up on us? All these things foretold by God, do you not have the impression of seeing them, at least in part, fulfilled beneath your very eyes? Then have a clear understanding of your position, and lift your head bowed beneath the weight of grief, humiliations and fear. The great struggle against Christ is both the proof of your faith and the dawning of the day of justice, when right order in everything will be re-established, never again to be disturbed.

Do not content yourselves with seeing all this, but also watch; what I say to you, I say to all: Watch. Many men in Noah's time did not recognize the warning signs of the Flood, nor in the century of Our Lord's death the warning signs of the destruction of Jerusalem: so it will be at the end of the times" ("Where Are We Headed?", pages 198–200).

To read such words of a French bishop written one hundred and fifty years ago is no sentimental comfort to us today, because superficially, they are not words of good cheer. However, to read them in the United States at the end of the 20th century is a virile consolation, because their remoteness in time and space highlights their abiding truth.

Woe to the sentimentalists! As the chickens of men's unprecedented wickedness come home to roost in this close of our accursed century, such self-comforters will have to step up their willful blindness to keep pace, until nothing but a miracle can open their eyes, and miracles are owed to none of us. On the contrary, blessed the virile in spirit who prefer to see reality as it is, and who through each New Year they are appointed to live, will know how to "possess their souls in patience," by concentrating on their duty as it comes to them day by day, with few expectations (from men) and with even fewer illusions.

The second quote treats of spiritual virility, and is suited to January, month of the Holy Family, insofar as, without even mentioning the family, it puts its finger on the essential problem today undermining the family, the lack of men. Here is how Cardinal Pie said it, again, an ocean away and a century ago:

> What a disappointment for mothers to realize that the male they gave birth to is not a man, and will never deserve to be called a man! . . . Is not ours an age of mis-lived lives, of unmanned men? Why? . . . Because Jesus Christ has disappeared. Wherever the people are true Christians, there are men to be found in large numbers, but everywhere and always, if Christianity droops, men droop – look closely, they are no longer men but shadows of men. Thus what do you hear on all sides today? The world is dwindling away, for lack of men; the nations are perishing for scarcity of men, for the rareness of men . . .
>
> I do believe: there are no men, where there are no characters; there are no characters, where there are no principles, doctrines, stands taken; there are no stands taken, doctrines, principles, where there is no religious

faith and consequently no religion of society. Do what
you will: only from God will you get men.

And if you had the misfortune to go seek for the remedy to the country's intellectual and moral impover-
ishment in a system of education which the children
would have to attend without having to be Christians;
if, to re-build a generation of men, you were to invent
schools where nobody was to be absent except God;
then such an outrage to human liberty, reason and religion alike would be the final blow, and the country's
death warrant.

Notice, dear friends, that the Cardinal concludes on the
pernicious effects of a godless public school system, but
the real problem he named earlier: the lack of a religion
of society. In fact the real religion of modern societies,
i.e., the foundation stone on which they are built, is religious liberty, or the principle that society has no right to
interfere with individuals choosing what religion (or lack
of it) they like. It is this religious liberty which not only
leads directly to a godless public school system, but also,
by implicitly equating religious truth with religious lies,
discredits all religion and all truth, undermines convictions, and so unmans men – see the Cardinal above.

If Catholics will not condemn a society built on religious liberty, that society will condemn them. By a just
punishment it will dissolve the men, their wives, their
children and their families. Dear friends, the New Year
is in the middle of the 1990's, not the 1950's. Take much
courage. The God of Cardinal Pie and of Msgr. Gaume
is for real.

Death of Fr. Urban Snyder

ANOTHER OLD AND faithful American priest, known to many of you, and an ally of the SSPX in its earliest days, died last month in the United States: Fr. Urban Snyder. He died at 9:30 p.m. on January 25 in the infirmary of the Cistercian Monastery of Genesee, in upstate New York, in his 82nd year. "He had been for a month in the infirmary," said those who were with him, "and for the last two weeks he was unable to talk, but he was serene, and appreciated with a smile anything done for him. It was a very edifying death."

As the faithful veterans of the Catholic priesthood disappear one by one who handed down their Faith to the youngsters of the SSPX, enabling or helping the Society to start and to take up where they left off, it is fitting to pay tribute to their generation:

> Their shoulders held the sky suspended,
> They stood, and earth's foundations stay . . .

Fr. Snyder was actually a late vocation to the priesthood. Born in Louisville, Kentucky, in 1912, in a pious Catholic family, graduating in 1934 with a Master's degree in history from Xavier University in Cincinnati, he may have thought his career lay in the law because through his middle twenties he studied at Jefferson School of Law, being admitted to the Kentucky bar in 1940. However, he never practiced as a lawyer but worked instead as a lay secretary of the Louisville Catholic School board under Msgr. Pitt for a few years.

So the first thirty years of his life were spent in the world, giving him a knowledge of life and an experience of men which those same years spent in the Church would not have given him in the same way. Not that he ever strayed far from the Church. It was the Jesuits who had formed his mind, and in early manhood an annual retreat at the Cistercian Monastery in Gethsemane, KY, had maintained this spiritual life.

Later in life the contrast was striking between the slightness and apparent frailty of the outer man, and the firmness of faith and solidity of reasoning of the inner man, so it is easy to imagine the unassuming exterior of these early years behind which God was preparing his future servant. The hour of God struck in the spring of 1942 when John Francis Snyder met the famous Apostle of the Sacred Heart, Fr. Mateo Crowley, at a retreat at Gethsemane. It was the priest who first mentioned a religious vocation. The young man did not hesitate. He entered the Monastery as a postulant in the autumn.

He took naturally to the Cistercian monk's life, which is proof of his providential preparation. Ordained priest on December 20, 1947, in his 36th year, he was immediately appointed Retreat Master for visitors coming to the Monastery from outside, and then Novice Master for a horde of novices flocking to the Monastery in the wake of the World War. He would in fact over the next few years hold every office in the Monastery except that of Abbot.

But in the 1950's storm clouds were gathering over the Church, and it might be said the Devil began with the monasteries. For example, Gethsemane's most famous monk of that time, Fr. Thomas Merton, had undergone a conversion in the 1940's to the quality of which his early books, and their fruits of many vocations, seem to testify, but in the swing to modernism of the 1950's the self-seeking emotionalism of his Protestant origins regained the upper hand, and worse, he continued to draw a large part of the monastery after him. What was a true monk to do?

Here began for Fr. Snyder tens of years of wandering, again, not outwardly impressive to relate, but revealing to the inner eye a steady fidelity and coherence: "For my thoughts are not your thoughts: nor your ways my ways, saith the Lord" (Is. 55: 8). The monk might be driven out of the unfaithful monastery, but the monastery could not be taken out of the faithful monk. He remained the monk, say friends, to the end of his days.

Firstly, he requested and obtained a transfer to the Cistercian monastery in Genesee, NY, and then, probably harried by the monks' modernism burgeoning there too, obtained a sabbatical year to study in Rome. Here he remained for a good part of the time of the Second Vatican Council, but instead of letting himself be confused or swept away by that collective madness possessing numberless priests from the heart of the Church, he returned to the USA, to work as a chaplain for the Sisters of Charity in Nazareth, Kentucky. This time one would guess the modernism of the nuns drove him to ask for and obtain leave to work in the Diocese of Covington, KY, under Bishop Ackerman, which is where he met in 1970 Archbishop Lefebvre who was just at that time looking for priests to help him found the SSPX, in particular for an English-speaking priest to help look after the several American seminarians then entering the new seminary at Ecône.

Fr. Snyder obviously found in the Archbishop a defender of his own faith, so he agreed to help in forming
faithful priests with him, and he followed the Archbishop back to Europe, this time settling in Switzerland. Fr.
Snyder's official incardination or entry into the new Society in 1971 is a part of Society history, because it was
(and remains) a proof of Rome's recognition at that time
of the Society's canonical standing within the Church,
denied by many. For a few years, crucial years for the
Society, Fr. Snyder helped form the English-speaking
seminarians at Ecône. Few priests saw at that time the
need to stand by the Archbishop, and still fewer had the
courage to do so, but Fr. Snyder was one of them. His
mild and quiet exterior belied his strong faith and clear
mind.

However, about 1975 he left Ecône, at least in part
over a practical disagreement with the Archbishop. The
Archbishop had his reasons, needing men to found his
Society in the USA, but Fr. Snyder was not incorrect in
his assessment of some of those men, who, at least objectively speaking, would betray the Archbishop a few
years later. On the contrary, if Fr. Snyder did not stay at
the Archbishop's side, he nevertheless remained faithful
to his cause and sympathetic to the Society.

For several years more he stayed in Europe, serving
as private chaplain amongst Catholics of the rising Traditional movement, this time in Germany. From now
on, souls from numerous countries in several languages were contacting him to obtain spiritual counsel and
solid advice in a more and more confusing situation of
Church and world. Surely his spiritual wisdom and balance never failed them.

In 1982 he returned permanently to the United States,
based on his beloved home state of Kentucky. From here
he continued to travel, to lecture, to administer sacraments to the scattered remnant flock, to study, to pray,

always the monk, but his main apostolate was perhaps by mail: "His mail was unreal," says a friend who knew him well during this time, "his secret was his spirituality. He drew people. He always had the right words to say. He answered any question spiritually. People wrote to him from everywhere."

He visited the seminary here in Winona a few times in his late 70's, and he was always a welcome and interesting visitor, with useful tales to tell to whoever could stop and listen. But as he reached 80 his strength was giving out, so he finally returned to the monastery in Genesee which was where he could be looked after and where he died and was buried. In fairness, the monastery had always been kind to him. May his soul rest in peace.

His had not been a great public career, but only God knows how many souls are grateful to him for his priceless help in private, at a time when true priests were becoming harder and harder to find. Amongst men, no doubt he could easily be overlooked or passed over, but before God it was surely a faithful servant who hung back from the polluted public arena and quietly did the Good Shepherd's work amongst the scattered sheep. We shall not however assume that he is already in heaven, we shall pray for him and beg prayers for him, because we are grateful for his counsel and his example on our darkening scene. Fidelity is possible, his example proves.

Dear Friends and Benefactors, thank you always for your support. There are many claims on your generosity, but do not forget the seminary. We ourselves always need some of you, and one or another of our good causes needs all of you!

Natural Born Killers

OR THE BEGINNING of Lent this year we enclose a flyer appealing for help for the Dominican Sisters in Idaho. These Sisters belong entirely within Catholic Tradition and work closely with the SSPX here in the United States. As the flyer explains, they have already received a great deal of help – to all concerned, well done! – but they must finish the building. Occupancy permits are liable not to be granted until a new building is completely finished.

But why should the Seminary be intervening on the Sisters' behalf? Unselfishly, because we are all part of the Mystical Body of Christ, His Catholic Church, and one part must help another in need. Selfishly, because without good Catholic families we will hardly have steady vocations to the priesthood, and without good Catholic mothers we will hardly have good families.

Nor are the Dominican Sisters raising only future mothers. Mother Church also has an absolute need of good nuns, or Sisters, to nurse, teach and pray, in the way that only women can do, because of the maternal instinct rooted deep within their nature, upon which grace builds. Wherever the true Church flourishes, these feminine vocations also flourish, as an integral part of the Mystical Body of Christ. Woe to the Catholic who would think he only needs priests!

Thus when it comes to prayer, women who as mothers would be ready to die for their children, have a capacity for self-sacrifice beyond that of men, and so for instance the Carmels in which girls give away their whole lives for prayer, are power houses of grace for the benefit of the whole Church. But the demands of the enclosed life inside the Carmel call for a spiritual health and a mental balance not often found in today's girls, despite all their good will, which is why the Traditional Carmel in the Northwest of the USA already sets high hopes on vocations coming from the girls to be formed by the Dominican Sisters in Idaho.

As for nursing, it so obviously fits the nature of women that Mother Church has always had numerous Hospital Orders of Sisters. Vocations failing (or wanting to be priestesses!) in recent years, the State has had to take over from the Church a large number of her hospitals all over the world, but how many patients in their illness can honestly say they prefer as nurses paid laywomen – or laymen!? – to devoted Sisters? In today's Church crisis the nursing orders seem to be the slowest in reappearing within Tradition, but if the crisis goes on for long enough, reappear they will, with ex-pupils of the Dominican Sisters likely amongst the leading candidates.

As for teaching, women again by their motherly gifts are irreplaceable in schooling the little ones, and as the children grow older, it becomes as desirable and necessary that girls from age eight or nine be taught by women, as that boys from that age – if at all possible – be taught by men. For as men alone should show the virility that must be reared in boys, so women alone should have the (true) femininity that must be both put into and brought out in girls, especially in our feminist age.

Richard N. Williamson

Now one may hope most Catholics are immune to the madness of feminism at work in education today, whereby an adolescent girl's family recently threatened in Wisconsin to sue her public school for refusing to let her take part in the boys' wrestling! But Traditional Catholics might be tempted by an objection from the opposite side, namely, the girl's place being in the home, she needs at least no secondary education.

To this objection a great Catholic educatress of girls, founder of the Sacred Heart Nuns teaching Order, St. Madeleine-Sophie Barat, nearly 200 years ago replied (I would love to find the exact quotation): if the men were men, maybe we would not have to teach the girls, but since the men have turned liberal, we must build our schools to teach the girls how to make up – as best they can – for the lack of men. Now middle-class liberalism is no less a problem in the late 20th century United States than it was in early 19th century France, on the contrary. So good Catholic girls' schools to form loyal wives to save the Faith and souls in their families by skilfully compensating for their husbands' lack of leadership, are more necessary than ever. Until the men pull themselves together, it is a choice, so to speak, between St. Madeleine-Sophie and feminism, because nature abhors that vacuum which will be filled not by the men playing macho sports, but only by their submitting to God. From my recent mail-bag:

> You blame bad churchmen for the condition the world is in. I blame husbands. They are not the priests in their home that God intends them to be. They are unbelievably self-centered, not God-centered. A wife cannot follow where a husband will not lead. He does not value his wife in the home, so to earn his love she is out in the world trying to be a man. These husbands sire many a child with no intention of fathering them.

The wife tries to compensate for the big gap that he is leaving void, and she throws the whole family off balance. Without God, the husband's capacity to love goes no further than what benefits himself . . .

We need the Dominicans to raise true mothers and true teaching and praying sisters in Idaho, and we need them urgently – the alarm-bells are ringing off the wall! Let me tell you briefly about a horrible protest film coming recently from Hollywood, not because of the horror but because of the protest: Oliver Stone's Natural Born Killers. Films are only films, but they do hold up the mirror to their society.

A girl in her late teens in an oppressive suburban home falls in love with the young man delivering meat at the door. Deciding to hit the road together, they begin their joint liberation by murdering her molesting father and her spineless mother, with, as parting words to her younger brother, "Now you are free!" Themselves they proceed to cut loose with a caricatural series of senseless, cold-blooded murders of anybody who gets in their way, and she is just as murderous as he is. Finally they are caught and put in jail, where the jailors vie for vileness and incompetence with the police, and where the distraction caused by a mediaman interviewing them for national TV – "I guess, we are just natural-born killers," they tell the nation – enables them, in yet another shootout, with satirical dozens of corpses, to escape with the mediaman, who is their final victim out in the wilds. Law and order have not prevailed. All that is left is the two orphans of suburbanism, clinging to one another.

Obviously the film is satirical, but it is not enough to dismiss it as satire and/or as brilliant film-making, and/or as a product of that left-winger, Oliver Stone. Like his film JFK, this film is a howl of pain and a shriek of protest at a society which stands by after its elected President is publicly assassinated, and which wallows in its vile media while youth is defiled and law and order are broken down. Oliver Stone does not have St. Madeleine-Sophie's answer, and the lack of answer is driving him mad, but at least he does square up to her problem, and not pretend that the hills are alive with the sound of music!

Today's hills are alive with the drive-by shootings of natural-born killers, because too many Catholics are still arranging God to suit themselves, somewhat in the style of the 1950's or 1960's, instead of arranging themselves to suit God, and that is why St. Madeleine-Sophie's answer is not getting out in the 1990's. But the Dominican Sisters in Idaho are doing their best. Let us get behind them, to show God that we are grateful for His gifts and that we want His graces, that we want to do things His way and not ours. He will not let Himself be surpassed in generosity. He can save our youth. He can save everything. All He needs is our serious good will.

Democratism in the Catholic Church

W HAT WAS THE real story behind the appalling massacre in Rwanda, Central Africa, last year, of some half a million people? A fascinating and well-argued answer is circulating amongst friends of ours in France, and that answer is: modernism, or democratism, in the Catholic Church. Theology is not just theory – from errors in theology flow torrents of blood!

The answer just mentioned does need to be backed with arguments because it violates principles cherished by many people today, which includes devout Catholics, as to how society should be run. This letter is too brief to do more than just outline those arguments, but let Catholics see here that outline, because if they can then take the fullness of the arguments on trust, they will the better grasp the nature firstly of modernism, which concerns us all, and secondly of the problem in Rwanda, which may flare up again.

In brief, God makes different men with widely differing natures, for instance some natural leaders, many natural followers, so that by men's different gifts completing and complementing one another, all men may together make up a harmonious society on earth and the communion of saints in Heaven.

This is the crucial principle of common sense as of Catholicism which was violated in Rwanda by egalitarian and democratist modernism, with catastrophic consequences. However, since the principle so offends against the notion of equality between men widely held today, let us immediately turn to St. Pius X for an authoritative statement made at the outset of his papacy in a Motu Proprio of December 18, 1903:

> I. Human society, as established by God, is made up of unequal elements; to make them equal is impossible and would be the very ruination of society.
> II. The equality between various members of society consists solely and exclusively in the fact that all men originate from God, have been redeemed by Christ, and must, according to the exact measure of their merits and demerits, be judged, and rewarded or punished, by God.
> III. Consequently, it is in conformity with the order established by God that there should be in society rulers and subjects, employers and workers, men educated and uneducated, an upper class and a lower class, all of whom united in the bonds of love are to help one another to achieve their final destiny in Heaven, and their material and moral well-being on earth."

Such a landmark statement of principle, behind which Pius X put his full "apostolic authority," would no doubt today be widely dismissed as "elitism" or "racism," or, more subtly, as "mixing religion and politics," because it crashes into modern ideas of human equality. For instance, does not the venerated Constitution of the leading republic of our age exclude all "Titles of Nobility" (I, 9, 10) from the republic being constituted? Yet does that republic not now have, sure enough, its ruling upper class, better known as the East Coast Liberal Establishment? And is not the problem with this ruling class not its existence but its liberalism?

Likewise in the little "country of a thousand hills" of Rwanda, lost in the center of Africa until the first white man arrived in 1894: for some eight centuries prior to his arrival the minority pastoral Tutsis had peacefully ruled the majority agricultural Hutus because as a tribe the Tutsis had the natural gifts to do so, and they had been wise enough on the whole not to misuse those gifts.

Nor was this natural order disturbed when Catholicism arrived soon after with Belgian missionaries teaching the true religion in the wake of the first World War, in fact Tutsis and Hutus who speak the same language mingled happily in the weeks-long celebrations to commemorate in 1933 the consecration of their joint land to Christ the King by the Tutsi King Mutara III.

The troubles only came when modernism on a large scale began to contaminate Catholics in Europe between the wars: man is God; so man, not Christ, is king; so all men are king, so one man must have one vote. As this democratism spread to Rwanda, so the Hutus were progressively indoctrinated by their clergy and leaders with the insufferability of their undemocratic status as one tribe ruled by another over which they enjoyed numerically a three-to-one majority. Moreover, from 1939 to 1945 did not the whites give a spectacle to the whole world of shedding torrents of blood in the name of "Crusade for Democracy"? Democracy is obviously sacred! Bloodshed between the blacks became inevitable.

The first wholesale slaughter of Tutsis took place in 1963; from 1973 on has followed a series of mutual blood baths between Hutu and Tutsi culminating, not necessarily terminating, in the horror of the half million dead last year.

Well, let us assume this analysis is correct. Let us assume that egalitarian democratism, whereby all men are sovereign and therefore equal, is a deadly virus in human society. How did that virus manage to get inside the Catholic Church in Europe between the wars, especially when Pius X (1903–1914) had been so recently condemning it, as above? Fascinating question. Answer, Pius XI who was Pope for most of those interwar years, 1922–1939, was no Pius X. Thus in 1925 Pius XI issued an encyclical magnificent in theory on the social kingship of Christ the King (Quas Primas), but then in practice, the very next year, in an action speaking (as usual) louder than his words, he went on to proclaim, surely unwittingly, the social kingship of man by condemning the vanguard anti-democratists of "Action Française."

At that time clear Catholic minds (e.g., Cardinal Billot) saw and said that the Pope's left hand was knocking down what his right words were building up, that his course of action despite its appearance of spirituality was heading the Church for disaster, but such warnings were drowned beneath the chorus of "devout" Catholics protesting that the Pope can do no wrong, that democracy is not such a bad thing, that "Action Française" was fascist, etc., etc., in which protestations these "devout" Catholics found to their surprise and delight that the world and the media were for once on their side! Just as at Vatican II! No doubt the world was at last being converted!

Alas, alas.

One of Pius XII's first actions as successor of Pius XI in 1939 was to lift the condemnation of "Action Française" – could he also do no wrong?? – but it was too late. Democratist thinking was by then well established inside the Church in France and Europe, from where it spread to Rwanda with the results we have seen.

At this point some of you readers may again be suspicious that the SSPX (or at least one of its bishops) has a hidden political agenda, fascist and anti-American into the bargain. Let us once more assure any such readers that we have no interest in politics except as manifesting religious problems; that we put no trust in fascism, at its best mere anti-communism, to solve those problems, and that we have nothing against America as America, on the contrary, the problem is liberalism, disguised as politics but in fact an anti-religion, in fact the anti-religion.

Dear friends, this anti-religion is on the point of bringing the house down, both Church and world, around our ears. The time is past for tinkering, or for "going my way" with the 1930's, 1940's, 1950's. It may just be that more souls could be saved at that time by disowning the principles of "Action Française", but no longer! 1995 demands the whole truth about the past. A man cannot be blamed if his foresight is not 20/20, but he is an ostrich if he wants less than 20/20 hindsight. The time is over for "devout" Catholicism!

Pray. Pray the Rosary. Pray the Rosary every day. The Mother of God can still obtain our salvation from her divine Son, and she will obtain it if we pray her Holy Rosary. And remember Winona's Doctrinal Session for men from July 25 to 29, where the thinking of the SSPX is proved to be not fascist but papal!

Why is Our Lady Weeping?

WHAT DOES OUR Lady wish to say to us in her month of May 1995? Answer, she is weeping tears of blood in several places. Here are extracts from a recent newswire report from Rome, which some of you may have seen:

> Two reddish trickles run down a saint's ceramic portrait in Salerno. Red rivulets form on the face of a plaster Madonna near Rome. The cases are among at least nine similar reports by the faithful in the past two months, an unusual proliferation in Roman Catholic Italy.
>
> Tuesday, a forensic pathologist said more blood was found on a Madonna statue in Civitavecchia, a small port city about an hour north of Rome, after it had been taken for safekeeping to the bishop's residence.
>
> The incidents have drawn thousands of the curious and faithful. Newspapers and state television detail each twist and turn of the cases. Prosecutors are investigating possible fraud.
>
> The Church is slow to judge such events as miracles. Some lay activists are condemning the phenomena. Cardinal Joseph Ratzinger, the Church's guardian of orthodoxy, has agreed to study the Civitavecchia Madonna, the Vatican said in a statement.

Prominent experts asked in by the Church said the liquid was human blood. An X-ray and CAT scan found no cavities that could be used to house a device to squirt liquid.

Indeed the Church is slow to judge such events as miracles, but such events have happened all down the history of the Church. A famous Church-approved case in modern times was the weeping Madonna of Syracuse, Sicily, in 1954. The more technology advances with its X-rays, CAT scans, etc., surely the more discoverable a human fraud must be.

Now invisible devils or fallen angels might fake a flow of blood from a dry statue in order to confuse the faithful, something that would have to be judged from the fruits, but there would be no confusion unless the devils had a genuine product to imitate. It is reasonable then to assume that several of these "at least nine similar reports" correspond to real interventions of the Madonna – why is she so weeping?

If she is choosing to obtain from Heaven miracles of blood being wept from dry statues, surely that may be firstly because such occurrences are – are they not? – difficult to fake and easy to authenticate. It may be comparatively easy to argue or to believe that little girls are hallucinating if they claim to be receiving messages from the Mother of God. It is comparatively difficult after photographs and X-rays and CAT scans to explain away blood being wept from a dry statue.

Secondly, such occurrences are surely difficult also to misinterpret. Once the official Church had authenticated the weeping Madonna of Syracuse in 1954, the message was unmistakable: the Sorrowful Heart of Mary was being given as much cause for sorrow as ever. Men were misbehaving. Men were offending her Son with their sins. And if forty years later there seems to be an outbreak of weeping statues, then men would seem to be offending her Son more than ever. Is that likely?

Surely it is. Horror a few weeks ago struck in the United States with the car bombing supposedly by two militia men of a Federal Government building in Oklahoma City. Clips of the newsreels were hardly distinguishable from clips of the horrible film Natural Born Killers, I was told by somebody who saw them both, and a picture became famous around the nation of a fireman holding in his arms from among the one hundred and fifty casualties a crumpled and bloody child.

One cartoonist reproduced the picture and for caption put underneath the one word, "Why?" Did it cross his mind that four thousand American children are crumpled and bloodied every day in their mothers' wombs? That maybe the United States needed an explosive audio-visual to grasp the crumpling and bloodying of children's bodies? Probably not. Probably his "Why?" was pointed at God rather than men! Enough to make many statues of the Madonna weep.

However, she must also be weeping at the diabolical confusion in millions of minds which, if it is not cleared up, risks producing a social explosion that will make the Oklahoma bombing look like no more than the advance tremors of an earthquake. This confusion is the tension between government and citizens.

Governments have rights and citizens have rights, but post-Protestant liberalism so mixes true and false in presenting both sets of rights that unless the Catholic Church comes to the aid of common sense, that social explosion seems inevitable. Thus militia-men and the Federal Government, honored by George Washington and Abraham Lincoln respectively, are two honorable American traditions, but when Protestantism so undermines true religion that liberalism gilds with the glamor of a substitute religion both resistance to tyranny and governmental law and order, then it is simply a matter of time before citizens and government are on a crusade, only they are on two different crusades which are on a collision course! Right now we are certain that the Oklahoma bombers chose for the day of their attack the second anniversary of the Federal Government's burning alive of dozens of its relatively harmless citizens in Waco, Texas. On the other hand the media are now preparing us for the Federal Government to respond by an increased clamp-down on all "home-grown terrorists" who resist it. Whereupon, either the people submit for the sake of peace to losing their liberties, or the resistance merely stiffens. Either the Antichrist, or civil war. As the Mother of God weeps, so the Devil laughs.

Certainly if the Catholic Church was listened to, she could clear up the confusion. She would teach, like Leo XIII in *Diuturnum Illud*, that the people on the one hand are not sovereign, that authority to govern does not come from the people, that all power to govern, or rightful authority, comes from God, and so there is no such thing as a right of the people to revolt or to change their government when they like. On the other hand the Catholic Church would also teach the members of any government that since all authority does come from God, they have no right to use theirs how they like, that God judges rulers with a special severity on how they have used their authority (Wisd. 6: 6,7), and they have no right to be obeyed by the people if they gravely misuse it, by working for instance for the arrival of the Antichrist. Surely Waco was the detonator of the Oklahoma explosion.

This Catholic doctrine, harmonizing rulers and ruled whose interests clash irreconcilably if God and His Catholic Church are pushed aside, could clear up the confusion and defuse the bombs if rulers and ruled would heed it. Alas, not only does modern man pay no heed to the doctrine that would heal his wounds, but, worse cause for the Madonna's tears, the Catholic churchmen, since the true doctrine went unheeded, have given up teaching it! Instead, they have joined in teaching the very doctrines that are the cause of the trouble; religious liberty (discrediting all religion), then separation of Church and State, freeing rulers to pursue the godless New World Order, and then sovereignty of the people, freeing those who are ruled to blow up the government.

Now if it were only the Protestants and liberals who were teaching revolution to governments and peoples, as was the case for 400 years, the damage would be limited; but as soon as the Catholic Church which is the pillar of truth (I Tim. 3: 15) joined in preaching Revolution, as since Vatican II, then confusion reigned unchecked.

Worst of all as one might think, and leaving the Mother of God with no alternative to multiplying her tears, is the perversity of these churchmen pretending that they have not changed Catholic doctrine nor altered the Church. They say, we have renovated the Mass, but it is no different, but you must accept the renovations; we have updated the doctrine, but it is just the same doctrine, but you must not remain stuck in the old doctrine; we have adapted the Church to modern times, but it is still exactly the same Church, but you must go along with all the adaptations.

George Orwell called it "doublethink." Take a moment to ponder this marvelous analysis of intellectual perversity taken from his novel *1984* (inspired, dear friends, by his experiences neither in Russia nor in the USA but in the British Broadcasting Corporation!), then apply the analysis of doublethink to the present-day official churchmen, and ask yourself how the Mother of God could be doing anything other than multiplying her statues that weep:

Winston's mind slid away into the labyrinthine world of doublethink. To know and not to know, to be conscious of complete truthfulness while telling carefully-constructed lies, to hold simultaneously two opinions which cancelled out, knowing them to be contradictory and believing in both of them; to use logic against logic, to repudiate morality while laying claim to it, to believe that democracy was impossible and that the Party was the guardian of democracy; to forget whatever it was necessary to forget, then draw it back into memory again at the moment when it is needed, and then promptly to forget it again: and above all, to apply the same process to the process itself. That was the ultimate subtlety: consciously to induce unconsciousness, and then, once again, to become unconscious of the act of hypnosis you had just performed. Even to understand the world "doublethink" involved the use of doublethink.

In medicine, politics, finance, whatever, today's world is awash in doublethink: "Abortion is good for us," "Our financial system is healthy," "Democracy is thriving," "There is more education than ever," "Never have women and children been so respected," "Communism has collapsed," etc., etc. When one stops to consider that what is common to these examples is men straining to exclude God from what is still His world, it stands to reason that the worst doublethink is that practiced by the guardians of the interests of God. Pray for the militiamen and for the Government agents, but pray especially for the priests and bishops. They are the especial cause of the Madonna's tears.

To help restore Catholic balance to minds, this summer's Doctrinal Session for men, July 25 to 29, will be entitled "Antidote to Oklahoma," and it will concentrate on four famous encyclicals of Pope Leo XIII, presenting God's design for government and society: *Libertas, Diu-*

turnum Illud, Immortale Dei and *Rerum Novarum*. We
will be for both government, and people. We will be for
Catholic government and for Catholic people.

We hope that the four deacons and seven subdeacons
due to be ordained to the priesthood and diaconate respectively here in Winona on Saturday, June 24, will be
imbued with this Catholic doctrine, which alone can
save the world. On their behalf we thank you for your
unfailing support which has sustained their seminary,
and we recommend them to your prayers as you are always in theirs.

Sincere Sin

T HERE IS SO much chaos in men's minds today that good old-fashioned analyses of how men think and behave can need to be carefully reapplied if they are not to come out false. For instance, normally any man who utters heresy all the time is a formal heretic and is to be judged as such, but today, not necessarily. Similarly any man who is plunged in sin and pretends to be doing good, is a hypocrite and there is no sincerity in him, but today, not necessarily, in fact today, sincere sinners are as common as dandelions! If we are not to lose our heads, or lose our footing, in the rising tide of chaos around us, we need to take a look . . .

One such "sincere sinner," and the perplexity of a Catholic priest trying to analyze his case, is well portrayed in the article enclosed, "Pray for the Guy Across the Street, Too." This article consists of a prolonged quotation from a plea for contributions by the Franciscan priest, Fr. Bruce Ritter, who was, at the time he wrote it, running his famous "Covenant House" ministry to abandoned and degraded children in the notorious red-light district of 42nd Street, New York City.

In it he tells how one day the man operating one of the most immoral brothels on 42nd Street – let us name him El Dorado, from his car – took up a collection from his young employees (!) and customers (!!) on behalf of Fr. Ritter's work, and when Fr. Ritter sent the tainted money back to him, he returned to Covenant House the following day to express his righteous indignation – he had meant well in making the gift and Fr. Ritter had had no right to refuse it. See El Dorado's own words at the top of the second column.

Now at this point, following the rule book, Fr. Ritter could simply have ruled out of court El Dorado's second appearance like his first, but, more true to life, Fr. Ritter goes on to describe how, instead, El Dorado's apparent sincerity and good intentions sent his mind "reeling." Fr. Ritter concludes with a paragraph on his own unworthiness and kinship with the sinner and finally appeals for prayers for him, with the wish that he himself understood how such a sinner could seem so sincere.

Now by the rule book it is not difficult to judge El Dorado's actions: by running the brothel, etc., by organizing, promoting and exploiting the wholesale violation by numerous souls of God's 6th and 9th Commandments, he is gravely sinning. When he says he hurts nobody, he lies at least objectively and maybe also subjectively because for one moment he admits he is "in a bad business." It is no excuse that he has four kids, that he has to make a living, that he cleaned up his place and made the girls stop stealing, etc., because it is forbidden to do evil to bring about good, the end cannot justify the means. And that he goes to church, tithes, does not like children getting hurt and says "God bless you," is all irrelevant so long as he intends to go on committing the major sin of running the brothel. Until he seriously repents of that sin and takes serious action to stop committing it, his money is tainted at source, and the priest has the right to refuse it and even the duty to do so, to prevent scandal and confusion.

Yet who with knowledge of real souls in real life today will dismiss as a mere sham the sincerity and good intentions of El Dorado appearing through his words and deeds as related by Fr. Ritter? Yet if El Dorado's sincerity and good intentions are not a mere sham, how are they to be reconciled with his life of sin?

Of course men have always been contradictory in their behavior, a mixture of good and evil, and the contradiction is, strictly speaking, resolved, when one observes that what is good is not evil and what is evil is not good. For instance what is sincere in El Dorado is not hypocritical, and what is hypocritical (he says he hurts nobody, but at the same time he admits he is "in a bad business") is not sincere.

Nevertheless, have "sincere sinners" ever before been the norm as one might say they are today? Nothing Fr. Ritter experienced in those 1980's was beyond the reach of the moral theology he had learned in his manuals at the seminary, yet had any of those manuals prepared him for the scale and degree of what he experienced with the El Dorados of 42nd Street?

The moral chaos of "sincere sin" is rising all the time, it made Fr. Ritter giddy and it threatens to engulf us all, unless we can keep our heads by seeing where it comes from and where it is going.

Essentially, "Sincere sin" on the modern scale comes from religious liberty. In the old days when all men knew that there is a God and that He lays down Ten Commandments, and when they built their nations and ran their social life on that basis, then whenever a man did evil, he and everyone else knew it to be evil, and if he wanted to pretend he was doing good, then he was a hypocrite and again everybody knew it. Good was good and evil was evil. Men may have been naughty but the principles were not confused.

Nowadays on the contrary, when men base their nations and social life not on God and His Ten Commandments but on religious liberty, so that logically God and His Commandments become a matter of choice and all moral principles become in society's view optional and confused, then whenever a man does evil – what is evil any longer? – he and everyone else no more so clearly know it to be evil, so he can that much more easily delude himself and everyone else that he is doing good when he sins, so he can be to all appearances a sincere sinner.

Of course God is not deluded, and no man or society however perverse can escape from His eye or deceive His judgment. Nor can any man not be receiving from God sufficient grace to save his soul and sufficient natural light in his conscience to see what he really is doing – notice how El Dorado knows that looking after four kids is good and 42nd Street business is bad – so that even today "sincere sin" has its limits. Notwithstanding, religious liberty is where almost endless moral chaos comes from.

Where is it heading to? For a long time among the nations only the Unites States of America was founded on religious liberty, the idea of which had been imported from Europe, but with Vatican II, the full-blown practice of religious liberty was re-exported by Cardinal Spellman and the American bishops to Rome, into the heart of the Catholic Church, from where recent Popes are exporting it all over the world, which is why sin is being abolished worldwide and sinners everywhere are becoming more and more sincere! The more widely religious liberty expands, the more it unhooks men's minds from objective truth and morality, the more men's minds are cut adrift, the more El Dorados sincerely sin and the more moral chaos swirls around the feet of a Fr. Ritter, so that many a good priest has lost his footing.

The priest must pray much, to obtain from God indispensable grace, light and strength. He must love truth and have a horror for religious liberty, in all its forms. He must avoid overexposure to chaos, and so must realistically measure his capacities and limit his activities. And he always needs to pray for, and to be prayed for by, his people. And may the one true God who allows no right to religious liberty bless you all abundantly.

The Principle of
Religious Liberty

SINCE LAST MONTH's letter attempted to dispel confusion, let us attempt to clear up a little confusion that it seems to have caused.

The letter enclosed a long quotation from a plea for contributions by a certain priest working in New York City in the 1980's. The letter interpreted this plea as showing the priest's spiritual and mental balance being threatened by the moral chaos in the big city all around him, and the letter argued that if the confusion of "sincere sinners" was enough to make the mind reel even of a Catholic priest conducting a high profile and apparently successful ministry, then the confusion must be a threat to all of us, and should be analyzed. The letter concluded by tracing the sincerity of "sincere sinners" back to religious liberty, on the grounds that that principle undermines every other principle in a man's mind.

Now for purposes of the letter's argument, the quotation could have come from any priest at all. And if he had a high profile ministry, and if in fact – as the letter hinted but refrained from saying – it is reported

that the mentally "reeling" priest did afterwards morally fall, then in principle the letter's argument was only
strengthened.

In practice, however, the choice of this particular
priest to illustrate the argument confused some readers,
especially in or around New York City where his story
is best known. Such readers asked, did the SSPX know
what this priest was accused of? (Yes, it did). Did it know
the evidence for these grave accusations being true? (Yes,
it did). Then how could such a priest be held up for admiration? (Neither his downfall nor his confusion was
held up for admiration, but only the good done by his
ministry and his attempt to handle his confusion. Similarly Our Lord commended the unjust steward not for
his injustice but for his prudence – Lk. 16: 1–9). Is the
Society then promoting the vices of priests? (In no way.
If a man has any vice, does he then have no virtues?). But
is the Society now appealing for funds for such priests?
(In no way). Then why does the Society photocopy and
circulate an appeal from such a priest? (Merely because
it illustrates well the mental confusion leading to moral
chaos which the Society wishes to combat).

If some readers were confused by the letter's illustration, others may have been confused by its argument.
For who can believe that the principle of religious liberty, on which modern nations are founded, is responsible
for moral chaos? Yet it is. Moreover religious liberty is
a substitute religion imperiling the eternal salvation of
more souls than any other error today, especially since
Vatican II enshrined religious liberty within the Catholic Church, so at the risk of making ourselves unpopular,
let us once more explain.

The principle of religious liberty is the principle
whereby all religions which contradict one another (for
instance, Jesus Christ is, is not, true God; God really is, is
not, present beneath the appearances of duly consecrat-

ed bread and wine), are welcomed to co-exist alongside one another. This means not just the practice of tolerating false religions as a necessary evil, something Catholics have always done whenever they could not change the world overnight, which was often, but it means the principle of leaving to one side the truth or falsity of all religions in order to found a new nation, a New World, a Newchurch, a better world, on a permanent and superior foundation of all religions accepting one another's not just existence, but right to exist. For instance yesterday Americans in the United States were (and still are) proud of having got over the religious wars tearing apart the Old World of Europe, by their new American way, and today – infinitely worse – Catholic Church leaders are proud of seeking to overcome religious strife and dissension throughout the world by their new ecumenical way.

Now religious liberty way well have enabled the inhabitants of the New World to harmonize all immigrants of mutually contradictory religions and to blend them into one nation, indeed many Americans will say the United States could not have been founded as a nation on any other cornerstone than religious liberty. Similarly today's Rome is counting on ecumenism to blend all the world's inhabitants into the Newchurch, and John JP2 is insisting that there is no other way to world peace.

So might it be. But there is a terrible price to pay. Be it the New World or the Newchurch, if in order to found the new nation or the New World Order I put peace and unity first, then, necessarily, I put truth and religion second. For if two people run in one race, both cannot win the gold medal; whoever comes in second must take the silver medal. If then I extinguish religious dissension by putting unity first, necessarily truth and religion must come in second or third.

But no religion worth the name can content itself with the silver medal. "I am a jealous God," says the

Lord God of hosts, "and I will have no other gods before me." Therefore in a new Republic founded on religious liberty two things happen: firstly, what are called "religions" become a silver-medal side-show for Sunday mornings, even with Catholics, even with a number of "Traditional" Catholics! Secondly, what has been given the gold medal, namely national unity or the nation, becomes inevitably the real religion in men's lives, without the name of religion, but with all its substance: with President for Pope, with Capitol for Vatican, with Flag for cross, with Constitution for sacred text, etc, etc. As Abraham Lincoln saw and said in his Springfield Lyceum speech of 1838, to fortify the young nation and to attach its people to their government, "Let reverence for the laws be breathed by every American mother, to the lisping babe, that prattles on her lap; let it be taught in schools, in seminaries, and in colleges; let it be written in Primers, spelling books, and in Almanacs; let it be preached from the pulpit, proclaimed in legislative halls, and enforced in courts of justice. And, in short, let it become the political religion (Lincoln's underlining) of the nation; and let the old and the young, the rich and the poor, the grave and the cheerful, of all sexes and tongues, and colors and conditions, sacrifice unceasingly upon its altars."

Now of course Lincoln would have vigorously denied he was promoting here a religious religion, but he was promoting the unity of the nation that he later waged a war to save, and how could that unity be saved if his "political religion" did not take pride of place, or the gold medal? (Otherwise, back to Europe). So his religious language – "reverence," "sacrifice," "preached," "pulpit," "altars" – was no accident. He was promoting the secular religion of the new nation, just as JP2 is promoting the secular Catholicism (!) of the Newchurch, with the United Nations building for Vatican, with Declaration of

Richard N. Williamson

Human Rights for sacred text, with United Nations flag for cross, etc, etc. And that is how Lincoln's and JP2's religious liberty becomes the substitute religion binding on all men.

But a religious religion must have the gold medal, or it is nothing. The true God takes first place, or he is a sham. In the same way truth cannot accept the silver or bronze medal. If I once put a lie in front of a single truth, all truth crumbles. One error in a multiplication table makes it worthless. One virus in a computer program paralyzes the program. Truth is as jealous as the Lord God Himself, because God is the Truth (Jn. 14: 6). Therefore in a new Republic or Newchurch putting unity before truth, similarly two things happen. Firstly, all truth, all thinking, everything of the mind or spirit is discredited, even with Catholics, even with many Traditional Catholics, so that in matters spiritual they refuse to think! Secondly, whatever has been preferred to the truth, either "patriotism" or charismatic globalism or whatever other feeling may be involved, takes the place of thinking. Men cease to be rational, and they become unmanly sentimentalists or animal clusters of emotion. Religious liberty makes wimps. Religious liberty causes feminism.

Thus religious liberty has terrible consequences, destroying religion, destroying truth, destroying reason, destroying men, and it explains countless features of the New World, of the Newchurch and of the coming New World Order. Religious liberty is, quite simply, man rising up in revolt against his Maker. Presently it is triumphing everywhere, thanks to the example of the United States, as the whole world is americanized, but thanks first and foremost to the Primate of all Catholics, presently blackening Mother Church's history in scandalous fashion, in order to please non-Catholics. As the Freemasons boasted, towards the beginning of the last century, by gaining the Pope to their ideas they would spread Revolution to the four corners of the earth. But that triumph is hastening to its necessary self-destruction and collapse.

Helping in the collapse will be, we hope, the four young priests just ordained at Winona, all four from the United States and loving their country, but not one believing in the principle of religious liberty. However, we hasten to add, none of them have plans to persecute non-Catholics! In practice, as is well known from the colonial history of Maryland, Catholics are more tolerant of non-Catholics than the reverse. Our Lord has in practice more respect than His enemies have for the freedom that they talk about.

Also dedicated to the true service of the United States by the putting of absolute truth in first place are the Dominican Sisters of Idaho. The motto of the Dominican Order is "Veritas," or "Truth." The Sisters are rescuing in depth girls from moral chaos by filling their minds and hearts with Truth. They are creating what is most likely already the best girls' school in the United States. Enclosed is a second envelope and flyer to help them, in case you missed the first. They are still needing by the autumn $100,000. For these Sisters we are appealing for funds! St. Dominic's day is August 4th.

Dear Friends and Benefactors, may God bless you all with the fullness of truth in your minds and hearts, and with the love of truth, and may He repay you all for having sustained the seminary through another successful school year!

Forebodings & Reassurance from Europe

FROM FOUR WEEKS in Europe I returned to the United States ten days ago with impressions of foreboding and reassurance curiously entangled. It may be interesting to disentangle them.

Firstly, the foreboding. Europe is under sentence of death. One need not be Catholic to see that. For instance, two brave and serious young Americans saw it and said it back in the 1920's, neither of them Catholic: T.S. Eliot and Whittaker Chambers. Catholics saw it and said it much further back, from the time Freemasonry took root in the 18th century to replace Christian civilization with a dream of life free from nature and free from God. The Catholics warned of darkness descending. On schedule, it has descended.

For example, I was for a few days in Spain in the little village in the north, San Sebastian de Garabandal, where one may think that the rugged virtue of the peasants and their simple way of life in the mountains thirty years ago helped draw down the Mother of God in their midst at the time of the Second Vatican Council for an extraordinary series of apparitions to warn the world and the Church in which direction they were heading. Howsoever that be, certainly in the 30 intervening years television and the paycheck have put paid to that old way of life. As people living in the village told me, the villagers are – interestingly – loath to give up any of the objects "kissed by the Mother of God" those years ago, but otherwise they do not talk about those events long past, and they have given themselves over to the modern ways. If the village streets were once criss-crossed by the Mother of God, now at any rate they resound to the joyful strains of life, liberty and the pursuit of happiness. If the village was the scene of apocalyptic apparitions from 1961 to 1965, now at any rate these have slipped into unreality, their message has been gutted, and except for a few oldsters the true Faith is in the village a thing of the past. Apostasy, even in the Spanish mountains, even where the Mother of God appeared maybe 2,000 times! But of course she had said there, "Many cardinals, bishops and priests are on the road to perdition, and are taking many souls with them," and the Church authorities repaid her by suppressing her! But God is not mocked. One must fear a frightful chastisement.

Secondly however, reassurance. Besides Spain, I was in Switzerland for the ordaining of 15 new priests at Ecône in bright sunshine before a crowd of thousands. Young, courageous, well-trained, these young priests take off in mid-August for the four corners of the earth, with Missal and Ritual for sling-shot and with the five priest-administered sacraments for pebbles – a handful of Davids to take on a Goliath of modernity! What a gift of God! What an achievement of Archbishop Lefebvre, for it to be continuing smoothly after him!

Also I was in England, launching-pad of Freemasonry and motherland of liberalism, whose capital city is still corrupting the world with its Babylonian money and materialism, yet in this London there is still enough

Faith for a medium-sized Society church to be filled twice each Sunday for Mass with Catholics who put God far enough in front of country not to mind, even to enjoy, England being lashed by a visiting preacher for her blindness from 400 years of nationalized heresy. Such Catholics could remake Merrie Englande!

Then I was also in Belgium to visit the Traditional Carmel in Quiévrain where a few older Carmelites (including a natural sister of Archbishop Lefebvre, Mother Marie-Christiane) have been joined by a dozen generous young women who turned their backs on everything the modern world had to offer them, and have now for several years given themselves over to the rigor and renunciation of the strict Carmelite life. For modern girls that passage from world to Carmel must be especially difficult, but there they are, and some 50 more in several other locations (including Spokane, WA) offer their lives and prayers to God for all of us. Those in Belgium listened patiently to a retreat which was not all sweetness and sunshine. Let us pray for them in return. They deserve well of us.

Finally I was in the south of France to lend the solemnity of a Pontifical Mass to the celebration by the teaching Dominican Sisters in Fanjeaux of the 20th anniversary of their young Congregation. Those 20 years are another epic story of Providence leading and youthful generosity following. The Sisters now number 119, their schools are forming nearly a thousand girls to become truly Catholic women, including some 140 in Idaho here in the USA, and they are still as radiant as sunflowers! Many thanks, dear friends and benefactors, for all your recent help to them. Their school goes ahead.

But thirdly, the foreboding returns, despite such encouraging signs of vitality of Tradition in these several countries. Why? Because the world is naughty, and I cannot help wondering if these dear young priests and nuns know just how naughty it is; if, in brief, they know what they are doing. For indeed even the servants of Our Lord are, whether they like it or not, part of the society that surrounds them. "I have sent them into the world . . . I pray not that thou shouldst take them out of the world," says Our Lord to his Father (Jn.17: 18,15), and today's society is insidiously undermining people's sense of reality.

Of course the young shock troops of Tradition, priests or nuns, do not accept the great lie of man's independence from God, or man's being God, which is the foundation stone of the great fantasy of modern life, whereby man is the measure of all things and may do as he likes, there being no objective reality nor objective truth nor moral law, but only the present day to eat, drink and enjoy, for tomorrow we are all saved. However, when the minds of nearly all men around me are slipping their anchor in reality, when even what would normally be the minds of good and serious men are launching out on the dreamy waters of everything being allowed with no unpleasant consequences, when there seems to be no longer anything or anybody to administer a reality check or rebuke or warning, is it not difficult to remain untainted by the folly?

Take for instance the present enormous bubble on Wall Street. The American stock exchange has been going up and up, especially in the last few years, with no foundation in reality: the US government owes a huge and unpayable debt of soon five trillion dollars, US heavy industry is being dismantled, the dollar is sinking, the people have no savings and their mentality – "me, the people" – renders their government incapable of taking any serious action. The system is not working. There must be a huge crash, but it is being delayed and delayed, perhaps because, as a friend in France surmises, the criminals leading the dance are now even themselves afraid of losing control, so everybody is conspiring to keep the party going on and on. In any case, reality is kept at bay, and the facts of life are hidden from the best of men.

Another example: a Californian radio newscaster matter-of-factly announces news of research to discover hormonal treatments for men to enable them to produce breastmilk! The horror here is not only the declaration of independence from the biological structure of men and women, but the taking for granted of the assault upon that structure (Might the friends of women's trousers at last see the wisdom of taking a stand on dresses?).

Now the Wall Street bubble and male milk may seem fantasies too gross to deceive or even to interest the young servants of Our Lord, but beware! Did not these fantasies follow on, were they not made possible by, the most senior and respectable Catholic churchmen, "cardinals, bishops, and priests," being tricked onto "the road of perdition," almost to a man, in the 1960's? Are not now numberless Catholics (from the Pope downwards) buying into a brand-new religion (whereby all men are saved – fantastic!), while remaining convinced they are Catholics? Are not the churchmen and churchwomen in fact prime targets for the devil to draw into fantasy land, and has not his "operation of error" intensified since the 1960's, with fewer and fewer people to recognize it or call it by its name? The world is going completely mad, and the madness is more and more normal.

That is why I am afraid for the brave young shock troops of Tradition, priests or nuns. Of course their youth is an ailment they get over day by day – each Dominican Sister was one year older, wiser and stronger than last year, and the SSPX now has a phalanx of priests in their 30's or 40's with 10 to 20 years of priestly experience. Nevertheless, never having known the relative normalcy of even the 1950's, how can these comparative youngsters have the measure of what they are up against? May they not be tempted to ignore how naughty a world they live in, and be deceived accordingly?

But then, fourthly and lastly, several considerations arise to give reassurance. Above all, the young priests and nuns may be blissfully unaware of the depth and breadth of iniquity around them, but so long as they guard the ancient and unchanged Catholic Faith, they have the means of rising above any storm of wickedness let loose beneath them. Their Faith is their victory over the world. Contrast how the mass of poor materialists will react when their material goods, the only goods they know, are stripped away! Already the frustration and despair are coiled up inside! The young priests and nuns will need to be angels of mercy!

Then there is a God, He is in control, the devil cannot lift a finger to tempt anyone without His permission, He will not abandon anyone who has not first abandoned Him (St. Augustine), and He will not allow anyone to be tempted above his strength (St. Paul). Let the young servants of Our Lord be faithful and continue fervent in His service, and He will lead them safely through fields of landmines, to the perplexity and fury of their enemies!

Then again God can use the very ignorance of His own servants. Outside of Our Lord Himself, which of them ever had a total vision of his own situation? How many might have given up out of discouragement if they had seen what they were up against? The architect of the Second Spring of Catholicism in 19th century England for one, St. Dominic Barberi. Archbishop Lefebvre always sought for older priests to help him with building the SSPX, but with a few noble exceptions only the ignorant youngsters would take the heat!

Richard N. Williamson

Dear readers, take heart, you are in good hands. As the preacher at Ecône said on June 29, the SSPX offers Our Lord a handsome collection of nobodies, but that is what he can work with! "Watch and pray." "Have confidence, I have overcome the world." "Pray without ceasing." "He that perseveres to the end will be saved."

Pluralism: Threat to Catholics Today

A SUPERB CONFERENCE was given recently by an American university professor on what these letters have often denounced as the major threat to the Faith and salvation of Catholics today: Pluralism, which is the practice of which religious liberty is the principle.

Dr. John C. Rao, Associate Professor of History at St. John's University in Queens, New York, gave this conference at the celebration of the first anniversary of the Dietrich von Hildebrand Institute, indeed the conference explains how the Institute was founded to help solve the problem set by Pluralism. Whatever we may think of his solution, his analysis of the problem is brilliant.

Pluralism, says the Doctor, paralyses Catholics, because as Catholics they know that truth is single, unique and exclusive of all error, and in their Faith they possess the fullness of that truth. Pluralism on the contrary is that which persuades Catholics that for the sake of getting along amidst the diversity and divisions of modern life, they need to be "open to freedom for all faiths and cultures to coexist peacefully, subject to the dictates of a 'basic common sense'." In other words, says Pluralism, by all means believe what you believe as Catholics, and even do go on believing it, because it makes you good citizens for everybody else's sake, but just do not behave as though your "truth" is absolute or exclusive, because that would be divisive and elitist. Just behave as though you have a truth while everybody else has a truth as well, even if all these "truths" contradict one another. It does not matter how exclusive you believe your Catholic truth is, just so long as you do not behave as though it is exclusively true.

Do readers see the subtlety of the temptation? Pluralism, as Dr. Rao suggests, does not directly require Catholics to abjure their Faith, on the contrary it may positively invite them to keep it, only they must act as though other faiths may also be true. Thus Pluralism tempts Catholics to have it both ways – they may go on believing their absolute beliefs, but at the same time they can mush in with everybody else in the dear modern world without having to constantly fight them, fight them, fight them! Oh, what a relief! Friends with God and friends with the world, friends with everybody, the hills are alive with the sound of music!

But in fact if my Catholic beliefs really are absolutely true, then I cannot mush in with sentimental error and idiotic heresy; whereas if my beliefs do allow me to mush in with sentimental idiots, then my beliefs are not absolutely true, but they are sentimental idiocy! That is why Catholics, if they buy into Pluralism, can no longer defend themselves as Catholics, but are reduced to those little pools of kissy-kissy huggy-huggy mush with which the mainstream Church is awash.

That is why Dr. Rao denounces "this seemingly benign, open, peace-and-freedom-loving pragmatic Pluralism, this mere common-sensical 'methodology'" as being "a subtly monstrous lie that destroys everything that it touches. Rather than being a practical tool, it is a dogma: in fact the One and Only Dogma . . . a heretical dogma into the bargain . . . a Super Dogma."

This is very important to understand. Go-along-to-get-along Pluralism pretends not to contradict Catholic belief, or any other belief, it pretends not to get into the whole question of beliefs, and if it is accused of interfering with beliefs it vigorously denies having anything to do with them. At the same time, to achieve its mushing together of all people with contradictory beliefs, it requires of all of them to act as though their particular beliefs are not what is most important, in other words to subordinate to itself their particular dogmas, in other words to treat itself in action as their Super dogma.

That is why Dr. Rao calls Pluralism a lie – it pretends not to be a dogma, but it imposes itself in fact (or in action) as a Super dogma. "Oh, no, I am not a dogma," says Pluralism, "but all your dogmas must submit to me!" Thus Pluralism is the one dogma that no (other) dogmas are really important; the one belief that all (other) beliefs do not matter; the one absolute truth that all (other) truths are only relative. Which means that all non-pluralist dogma, belief and truth are reduced to mush. Which is why, since a Catholic is a Catholic by the absoluteness of his dogma, belief, and truth, then Catholics, if they accept Pluralism, are reduced to mush and rendered incapable of defending themselves.

For, as Dr. Rao explains (#25, 26), Pluralism "tells a Catholic that he can think but not act, since acting in line with one's thought could be divisive in our world of inevitable and growing diversity." Now this disjunction of thought from action deforms personality, turns a man in on himself, makes introspective sterility normal, creates psychological disorders and drives individuals and societies insane. Hence the modern obsession with sterile contraception. Hence so many people acting willfully, because action from reason is ruled out. The Doctor logically concludes that this emasculation of human thought, reason, action, especially harms the masculine sex which is natured to think, to reason and to command. Pluralism is the deep down reason for the unmanliness of today's men, and for the consequent rise of feminism!

Dr. Rao next (#27) uses his analysis to explain the otherwise completely puzzling behavior of so many bishops and priests in today's Church: how can they be so orthodox in their doctrine yet so destructive of the Church in their behavior? Answer, because by submitting to Pluralism, they have not ceased to believe in or to preach whatever the Catholic Magisterium teaches, but in their action that Catholic Magisterium is always subordinate to the Pluralist Magisterium. This means that the beautiful Catholic truths may be spoken in words, indeed they must be spoken, but they may only be spoken, because if they were to be taken seriously in action they would become dangerous and divisive.

The Doctor goes on to quote an example he knows (#28) of a Catholic bishop of impeccable personal orthodoxy who gives excellent public talks on Catholic doctrine, yet in whose diocese insane modernism is running rampant. Why? Because the "good" bishop fears that any action taken by him against the modernists would, as the Pluralist Magisterium pronounces, render him naive, unpractical, undemocratic and divisive. Then if one criticizes this split between his right thinking and wrong acting, he replies with an appeal, which he considers unanswerable, to the "spirit of the Council," pluralist again. Thanks to this Pluralism, his mind is closed to anything but the effective destruction of his diocese and of the Church! Pluralism has reduced him, like countless other Catholics, to a cheerleader for those who will destroy him! Truly, as the old proverb had it,

"Those whom the gods wish to destroy, they first make mad."

When it comes to a solution for all this madness (#37–43), Dr. Rao proposes the Dietrich von Hildebrand Institute as a means of teaching Catholics the fullness of their Church's culture and history so that their minds can escape from the glamorous trap of the modern world, so that they will no longer be afraid of being divisive with regard to its manifold nonsense. A good idea as far as it goes, but many a cultivated and learned Catholic historian has still let himself be corrupted by Pluralism.

Of course there is a mystery of grace involved, the mystery of the election of a remnant by grace (Rom. 11: 5), and not one of us can prescribe to the Lord God how he will give out His grace, or to whom, so that none of us has a fail safe answer to this appalling crisis of the Catholic Church. However one thing is certain, and that is that the key to the Church's future lies always with its priests, and another thing we have on the authority of St. Vincent de Paul with regard to priests is that it is easier to make a new priest than to convert an old one.

That is why Archbishop Lefebvre's solution to the problem so brilliantly analyzed by Dr. Rao was to make a new generation of priests who would have nothing to do with Pluralism or with pluralists, with all their pomp or with all their works. Plenty even of friends and admirers of the Society he founded have since then urged it to come to some kind of understanding with those pluralists, but it has with the grace of God so far refused to adopt the least bit of plurality, deadly for the singleness of God's truth. And as time passes, more and more of these friends and admirers are forced by the devastation of Pluralism to admit that the single-minded Archbishop was right.

Dear friends and benefactors, a trickle of such priests continues to flow off the hilltop here in Winona. Fourteen young men are due to enter the Seminary to try their vocation in a few weeks' time, seven of them having come through St. Mary's, Kansas! "Fr. Angles, as principal of St. Mary's boys' school, what advice do you give to a Society school principal wishing for vocations?" "Do your duty," he growls in reply, "and do not curry favor with the boys!" But then, dear friends, you have also been praying for vocations!

Thank you for your prayers. Thank you for your necessary support. If all goes well this school year, eight young Americans should be ordained priests on Winona hilltop on Saturday, June 22, 1996.

Errors of Liberal Education

IN THE LAST few years the SSPX has opened up numbers of new schools here in the United States, especially primary schools in the basements of its chapels and church buildings. This reaction to the degeneracy of the public and church schools all around us is normal on the part of Catholic parents and priests. However, starting schools from scratch is still a brave venture in today's circumstances, so, Mother Church having centuries of experience in education, let us recall a little of her ancient wisdom.

The mess into which the world has got itself today flows from heresy; and nearly all modern heresies come back, said Donoso Cortés (1809–1853), to the denial either of the supernatural or of original sin. Now as to the supernatural, Society schools for the (blessed) time being offer little or no worldly advantage to children, e.g., accreditation, so that if parents had no faith in the supernatural, they would hardly resort to Society schools. But as for original sin, while all Catholic parents pay lip service to the dogma, it is in reality so smothered by liberalism that perhaps few of them realize fully how it spells out in practice, especially in education. So let us begin our help to the schools with the reminder of original sin.

Every one of us, nine months before issuing from his or her mother's womb, was conceived by Adam's fault in a state of disorder and enmity with God – "We were by nature children of wrath" (Eph. 2: 3). Now one may for lack of the Catholic Faith disbelieve in such a mystery as sin not committed by a man personally but belonging to him naturally, yet all centuries and all climates are littered with the evidence of a flaw deep in all men's nature, largely wrecking their noble aspirations. In any case, original sin is a fact, the denial of which constitutes the essential error of liberal education, the fight against which is the presupposition of all Catholic education.

Thus Little Johnny may look as though butter would not melt in his mouth, so that his parents think he is a little angel, but Mother Church and good sisters and priests know that because of original sin, he is not only a little angel but also a little monkey, to the point that Scripture – Word of God – says of him (Proverbs 23: 13,14), "Withhold not correction from a child: for if thou strike him with the rod, he shall not die. Thou shalt beat him with the rod, and deliver his soul from hell." Again – (Proverbs 22: 15) – "Folly is bound up in the heart of a child, and the rod of correction shall drive it away." And then to think that liberals are proud of looking on corporal punishment for school children as a barbaric relic that they in their superior wisdom have left behind! Blind idiots!

Dear parents, support those priests, sisters and teachers who are ready to correct your children. Do not believe Little Johnny when with those melting blue eyes he tells you tales of how cruel and unjust his teachers are! Give him a kiss, put him to bed, then ring up the teacher to hear no doubt a very different story! And then (as long as it is not forbidden by "law") spank Little Johnny for fibbing when he gets up in the morning! In the old days, if Johnny told at home how Sister Battle-Axe had paddled him at school, far from being sympathized with, he was paddled again at home! He soon learned to stop complaining of his teachers!

Thus Catholic education then was, as it always ought to be, a conspiracy between priests, teachers and parents for what they are all agreed on is the good of the child, and Catholic parents used to have the good sense to trust the priests and teachers. That trust was destroyed by Vatican II, but it must be rebuilt. Catholic education cannot work if the parents pull against the teachers. Alas, in many Society schools the complaint is heard that the children are educable; it is the parents who are uneducable! Of course not always, but all too often they are unaware how the false liberal ideals they take for granted paralyze the teaching of true Catholic ideals to their children. Given what efforts such parents have often made, this unconscious self-paralysis is sad.

A second major error of liberalism in education is the glorification of the individual over the common good. As homeschoolers know, boys especially miss being taught amidst a group of boys. Peer pressure does great good or ill, because man is a social animal, designed by God to live and learn in society. Therefore a good school forms boys – and girls – in groups, in classes, in a whole society. Therefore if one rotten apple is spoiling the whole barrel, as often happens until a school is well up and running, and even after, then that rotten apple must go, for the common good of all the other children. Of course if a child is naughty, one will be patient for a while, especially if the naughtiness comes from high spirits rather than malice. But if an apple proves to be rotten, it must be mercilessly thrown out! A Catholic school is not a remand home for misfits, it is NOT a Delinquents' Tender Loving Day Care Center! It has to teach, not just babysit, and individuals who render themselves unfit to be taught in the group because of their bad influence on it have no business to be wasting the time of those who are fit and ready to be taught. Delinquents must go! The common good exists, especially in a school, and it is much more important than any one individual on his own. Oh, how liberals lose all sense of this common good!

A third grave error of liberals is their denial of any difference between boys and girls, error crucial at all times, but especially in education from, say, the age of 8 or 9 upwards. From then girls, it is well known, mature earlier than boys biologically, and immediately begin distracting the boys, who are liable to grow into being quite happy to be distracted. Nor is the mixed company from puberty onwards a danger only for chastity, grave though that danger is (unless one denies original sin!). The mixed company is also a tremendous waste of educational time, because as any teacher worth his salt will tell you, even in a subject like literature, suitable to be taught to both sexes, if you teach the boys, the girls switch off, whereas if you teach the girls, the boys tune out. This is because God has built boys and girls for entirely different functions (how often must one today say it?) in society, so that He has given them quite different receivers to pick up the quite different things they need, so different that it is impossible even for a genius of a teacher to teach on the wavelength of both of them at the same time. Hence in a mixed class of adolescents, half of the time is being constantly wasted. But do you think liberals will believe that? Deaf and dumb idiots!

And then do you think any self-respecting boys will let themselves get into a competition with girls? Elementary error, to have them compete! Separate their tests! Let the girls excel at what girls should excel in, whatever will form them to be good wives, mothers or sisters (a mother does not have to be dumb!), but let the boys excel at what boys should excel in, and let no girl near the sacred process of making boys into men. The girls around the boys will only block the formation of the men they so need. But teach the boys to respect and to protect the difference of girls, so that the girls no longer feel the obligation imposed on them by our sick society to make themselves second-rate men in order to have any respect!

But above all, dear parents, go right ahead! Take the bull by the horns (take the cow by her eyelashes!), and get that school up and running! St. John Bosco said God has special graces for adults who look after abandoned youth. Catholic youth are universally abandoned by an anti-Christian society and a modernist Church. You will have trials, because the devil hates true Catholic schools, because he knows how much good they do for the salvation of souls. In fact the early years of any of our little schools are liable to be more or less of a roller-coaster (switch-back railway ride, for English readers!). But the rewards are immense, as the Gospel says, even in this world, let alone in the next.

And dear parishioners, if you cannot contribute as a teacher, then contribute to your parish school from your pocket. Schools are always costly, especially today when there are few unsalaried priests, brothers or sisters to teach. And those who have the children often do not have the funds, whereas vice versa. God will most certainly reward those also who support the unabandoning of youth.

25 Years of the SSPX

O NE QUARTER OF a century of the SSPX – an astonishing Silver Jubilee!

As most of you readers of this letter know by now, nine days ago marked the 25th Anniversary of the Society's being set up as an official Catholic congregation within the official Catholic Church, by the approval of the then diocesan Bishop of Geneva, Lausanne and Fribourg, Bishop Charrière, of the Society's constituting Statues. Since that first day of November in the year of Our Lord 1970, what a dramatic 25 years!

They began quietly, humanly, without heroics. The Archbishop spent most of his time looking after his handful of young seminarians in a seminary built around the Tridentine Mass, because from the beginning he said that if he were to take the Novus Ordo Mass, it would cause such tensions and divisions in a seminary striving to be Catholic, that he might just as well put the key in the door and send everyone home.

Now the New Mass had only just been imposed on the Church at the end of 1969, so it was not immediately clear just what an anti-Revolution the Archbishop was launching. Apparently, he was continuing the true Church and priesthood dating from before the Council at a time when many bishops and priests seemed to be abandoning them, and so a number of devout young men and a few faithful priests followed in the Archbishop's sweet Catholic footsteps, enough to maintain through the early 70's a steady expansion of the young Society with its seminary in Ecône, Switzerland.

However, now began the heroics. As Pope Paul VI clamped down on conservatism whenever it reared its "out-of-date" head throughout the Catholic Church, so the expanding seminary, built on the heart of the old order, the Tridentine Mass, could not escape Rome's attention. Two official Visitors were sent to Ecône towards the end of 1974 to check out the Archbishop's operation. There was little they could find fault with, for the good reason that the Archbishop's seminary was actually fulfilling the letter of the Council's directives as to the running of priestly seminaries!

But when the Visitors in the course of interviewing seminarians uttered heresy, the Archbishop could no longer lie low. In his immortal Declaration of Nov. 21, 1974, he proclaimed to city and to world that in order to keep faith with Eternal Rome, he and his seminary and his Society would have to refuse to follow the neo-Protestant, liberal Rome, which had just been showing itself in, for instance, the Roman Visitors' heretical utterances. The heroic Declaration began a heroic struggle.

In 1975 the Archbishop was summoned to Paul VI's Rome, which resorted to one trick after another in order to incapacitate the author of the Declaration, and his Society. With an appearance of legality, Rome acted to dissolve the Society in May-June of 1975. Sweet souls in Ecône had to choose between Rome and the – still sweet? – Archbishop. A number left at the end of the school year, including several of the seminary's professors. "I will not abandon you," said the Archbishop to his seminarians, most of whom stayed with him.

Through the school year 1975–1976, the tussle was fierce between the sweet Frenchman and Paul VI's Rome. It culminated in the "hot summer" of 1976, when, Archbishop Lefebvre proceeded at the end of June to ordain 12 Society priests despite the Pope's order not to do so. Rome immediately punished the Archbishop and his new priests by suspension, forbidding them to exercise their sacred functions as bishop or priests. Such a punishment coming from the hierarchy within the hierarchical Catholic Church should normally have alienated all Catholics from the suspended Archbishop, but to Rome's horror, there was a spontaneous upsurge of support all over the world and especially in France, from Catholics alienated rather by the modernist antics of suspending Rome. The so-called "Traditionalist" movement was born.

Serenely, the Archbishop began another school year at Ecône, while Rome more prudently sought again to negotiate him out of existence. The Archbishop continually hoped for support from a handful of bishops who might have the courage to stand with him in resisting Rome's destruction of the Faith, but, year after year, those bishops never came forward. After all, Rome did still appear to be Rome.

And Rome's appearing to be Rome caused ongoing tension within Ecône. At the beginning of the next school year in 1977, a palace revolt within the seminary pulled away several more professors and threatened to empty the seminary. Finally, most seminarians stayed and the Archbishop managed to patch together a staff to keep teaching them, but the heroics of resisting Rome were clearly not to everyone's taste! Had the Archbishop not personally been sweet as well as heroic, one may wonder if Society and seminary could have survived.

However, the honey in the lion's jaws could be in a certain way deceptive. He himself did not enjoy resisting

Rome. He asked no better than to cease having to do so. He did not, contrary to what some people think, surround himself with hardliners supposedly responsible for his recalcitrant decisions, on the contrary he seemed to enjoy rather having around him gentle and orderly clerics natural to the Catholicism prior to Vatican II. Hence whenever there was no need for heroics, a sweet normality – how welcome in an ever crazier Church and world! – would tend to re-establish itself. Then that Church and world would close in again, threatening extinction, and it would take his heroism to make the saving decisions, while it would take his sweetness to keep with him on the heroic heights a good part of his following.

Notwithstanding, the worsening chaos of Church and world through the 1980's made the balance of his wisdom more and more clear, so that more and more followers came to understand what he was doing, and the Society grew stronger and steadier. So much so that when the moment came in the summer of 1988 to take the most daring step of all, the consecration of bishops disapproved by Rome, only some 15 of the Society's over 300 priests flinched, all the rest followed the Archbishop and were more strongly united than ever. Similarly, to his own surprise, the overwhelming majority of so-called "Traditionalists" stood firmly behind him, rejoicing not in the defiance of Rome but in the assurance that "Tradition" now had the means of surviving until God would bring Rome to its senses. Their Faith would be protected.

Thus the Archbishop had brought off the extraordinary feat of founding and consolidating a Catholic congregation in the teeth of sustained disapproval from two Vicars of Christ. The only possible explanation was this unprecedented split between Catholic authority and truth following on Vatican II, whereby he could have authority against him but truth with him. From that truth came and comes the Society's unity, strength and authority.

So after an especially stiff final climb to the Consecrations of June 30, 1988, the Society found itself to its delight emerging on a sunny upland where Catholics could again lead normal Catholic lives. Behind, the heroics. Ahead, a vista of sweetness – pre-conciliar Catholicism now had the ultimate protection, its own bishops. Ah, we human beings, how we enjoy being comfortable and normal!

A grand occasion of that normalcy was the principal celebration at Ecône nine days ago of the Society's Silver Jubilee. The Society's Superior General, Bishop Bernard Fellay, celebrated a Pontifical Mass of thanksgiving in a tent specially erected beneath the seminary. Some 2,000 people attending enjoyed the temperature and weather, delightfully mild for late autumn, making of the Rhone valley, splashed in autumnal colors, if not a sunny upland, at least a sunny lowland!

At the following luncheon for 1,000 guests, there spoke in succession Bishop Bernard Tissier de Mallerais, one of two survivors from the Society's very earliest days, who gave fascinating details of the beginning of the epic; Fr. Pierre Epinay, parish priest of the parish in which Ecône is situated also from the seminary's earliest days, and who has been one of the Society's staunchest friends ever since; Fr. Marie-Dominique, Prior of the Traditional Dominicans owing much to the Archbishop and to Ecône for their separate foundation; Mr. Gratien Rausis, one of two survivors from the five Swiss laymen whose purchase of the ancient house of the Great St. Bernard Canons at Ecône made possible the installation there of the Seminary; Mr. Joseph Lefebvre, natural brother of the Archbishop who much resembles him; and finally Bishop Fellay who drew attention to the family spirit of the friends of Ecône present, a spirit which he said could be met with in the Society's houses anywhere in the world – a truly universal or Catholic spirit.

Luncheon was followed by the ceremony of the laying of the foundation stone of the seminary's new church; fast rising in complex slabs of concrete out of a huge hole in the ground dug out of a vineyard to the west of the seminary's old buildings. The Archbishop had for many years wanted to build for his seminary a worthy church, but the local authorities for as many years refused building permission. In God's good time that opposition came to an end, so the building goes ahead. Now two electric cranes and dozens of Swiss workmen buzz with one of Mother Church's favorite activities – building. What institution was ever remotely as constructive as the Catholic Church?

Solemn Pontifical Vespers, i.e. Vespers with a bishop, concluded the memorable day, of which the Seminary Rector, Fr. Michel Simoulin, and his 40 seminarians could be proud: It had been well organized and must have given a handsome impulse to the building program. Americans will no doubt be solicited for a contribution to the heavy building costs. Think at that time of helping to provide a worthy final resting-place for the mortal remains of the hero of the Faith. Where would we all be without him? As the new religion installed in Rome is progressively shown-up for the sand-based sham that it is, and as more and more people come to understand how great a churchman Archbishop Lefebvre was, building on rock, so more and more Catholics will be making the pilgrimage one day to Ecône. But we must work and pray for the Archbishop not to be then turning in his handsome new grave, as has been known to happen with prophets! (Mt. 23: 29)

FAQ on the SSPX

SOME READERS OF this letter send in questions to which others would no doubt like to have answers. Here are a few, Q for questions and A for answers:

Q: Where is the true Church today? Is it with the official Catholic Church, as usual, or with the Protestants, as the Pope seems to say, or with the so-called Traditionalists, as they say?

A: The true Church founded by Our Lord Jesus Christ is One, Holy, Catholic, Apostolic. Wherever you find those four marks, you find the true Church. Now Protestantism destroys oneness; produces little holiness; is not catholic, i.e., universal, in time or in space; and refuses apostolicity, i.e., submission to the Pope. As for the official Catholic Church, it becomes more Protestant in belief and practice day by day. But the so-called Traditionalists are remarkably united (one), producing good fruits (holy), in the faith of all time throughout the world (catholic), with complete respect for the Pope's authority (apostolic). Therefore it is in the direction of the so-called Traditionalists that you must today look for the true Church of Christ.

Q: Are you saying that the SSPX is the Catholic Church, and that outside of the Society there is no salvation?

A: By no means. Wherever you find the four marks, there you find the Catholic Church. Please God, the four marks are to be found in the SSPX, but they are certainly not to be found only in it.

Q: But does the SSPX recognize John Paul II as Pope?

A: Yes. Following Archbishop Lefebvre, the Society has always refused to say that the See of Rome is vacant, because that position is liable to raise more problems than it solves. The recent Popes may not be good Popes, but they are Popes.

Q: But if the SSPX recognizes John Paul II as Pope, how can it disobey him?

A: Because Jesus Christ did not make His Popes as infallible as many Catholics wrongly think, and so to obey the Catholic Faith one must sometimes "disobey" the Pope, as Paul "disobeyed" Peter himself (Gal 2: 11–14), as the great St. Athanasius had to "disobey" Pope Liberius. But such apparent "disobedience" is not real disobedience, because it is putting obedience to God first.

Q: But the heretic Luther also pretended he had to disobey the Pope.

A: Look at what Luther taught. It is not Catholic teaching. Look at what Archbishop Lefebvre taught. It is Catholic teaching. Look at what the Archbishop's adversaries in Rome teach against him. It is not Catholic teaching.

Q: That is what the SSPX claims, but many theologians say the opposite.

A: Then, as Our Lord told us to do, look at the fruits. Which teaching fills confessionals and seminaries, and which empties them?

Q: *Then is John Paul II the head of two different Churches?*

A: There is only one Catholic Church, recognizable by the four marks recalled earlier. But to members of that Church until the day they die, Our Lord leaves their free will so that churchmen especially can – consciously or unconsciously – betray that Church and tear masses of souls out of it. Such a process, often seen in history, is usually gradual, like in Reformation England, because souls need to be deceived little by little. That is what we are seeing in Rome today. On the one hand (as the SSPX believes) JP2 is head of the one true Church, and whenever he talks or acts as such by, for instance, condemning priestesses or by condemning divorce laws in Ireland, then the SSPX heeds him and the liberals in the Church disregard him. But – men can be walking contradictions – whenever he talks or acts as a liberal by, for instance, promoting false ecumenism or religious liberty, then the liberals look up to him as their head, but since the very Catholic Faith is endangered, Catholics cannot follow him. So JP2 is head of the Catholic Church, but whenever he misuses – consciously or unconsciously – his papal office to promote liberalism, his misuse of it makes him head of the liberals.

Q: *So when Archbishop Lefebvre said he never belonged to the Church from which he was excommunicated for consecrating four bishops on June 30, 1988, what he meant was not really the Church but the community of liberals?*

A: Exactly. To speak of the "Church" of the liberals is a way of speaking. Their "Church" should be called the

"Newchurch", to show that it is not the real Church but is deceitfully designed to resemble it.

Q: But then how could Archbishop Lefebvre go on calling John Paul II Pope of the real Church?

A: Because men are contradictory creatures, and one and the same man is capable at different times of acting in contradictory ways. Talking and acting in a gravely liberal way need not disqualify a pope from being pope. Catholics must not exaggerate papal infallibility beyond what the Church teaches about it.

Q: But what entitled the Archbishop to say that his apparent excommunication of June '88 was not a real excommunication?

A: A Catholic excommunication must take place either positively by a solemn ceremony, or automatically by Church Law. Now Rome never performed any ceremony to excommunicate the Archbishop. It merely declared he had automatically excommunicated himself by Church Law. This declaration was false.

Q: How can that be? Is not Church Law what Rome says it is?

A: If Rome changes the law, then the law is (within limits) what Rome changes it to be. But until then, the law is what it is, and in the summer of '88 Church Law said, and it still says, like common sense, that if a man is driven by an emergency to break the Law, he does not incur the penalty for breaking the Law. Now the Archbishop consecrated four bishops only because of the massive emergency created in the Church by the liberals. Therefore he did not incur any Catholic or real excommunication.

Q: Is there any evidence that the Pope did not have all the facts prior to the excommunication?

Richard N. Williamson

A: No. It was liberal thinking that naturally made him expel from the communion of liberals the arch-anti-liberal.

Q: *Has any excommunication in Church history been later recognized as invalid?*

A: Several. St. Athanasius and St. Joan of Arc were both "excommunicated," obviously invalidly. Above the Pope there is a God.

Q: *What is the SSPX doing to get this "excommunication" lifted?*

A: It is persevering in its witness to the Truth so that Rome will continue to have at least that means of recognizing its liberal error.

Q: *But is the SSPX in dialogue with Rome?*

A. Rumors are flying around to that effect, originated perhaps by enemies or false friends of the Society who would like to see its annoying witness brought to an end – the Society rains on the liberal parade – but the Society Superior General, Bishop Fellay, quashed all such rumors at the end of November this year when he said there were no contacts presently with Rome, and if there were he would disapprove of them.

Q: *But did not Archbishop Lefebvre once say that five years after the Consecrations he expected contacts to re-open? How can Bishop Fellay be so haughty?*

A: The Archbishop hoped and trusted that five more years might bring Rome to its Catholic senses. But neither by wishful thinking nor by imprudent contacts can Bishop Fellay or anybody else change the fact that Rome is persevering in its belief that liberalism will save the Church.

Q: But isn't this lack of contacts with Rome dangerous for a Catholic Society wanting to remain Catholic?

A: So long as Rome perseveres in its liberalism, distortion by distance is less of a danger for the Society than is contamination by contact, especially when so many of the liberals are "sincere" and "well-meaning." We must want Rome to recover, and we must be looking for Rome to recover, but in the meantime, "Facts are stronger than the Lord Mayor." Neo-modernism is a deadly disease.

Q: But is it not pride and insolence to take the position that unless Rome comes to us, we will have nothing to do with them?

A: To submit to the Truth is not pride, and to expect Rome to submit to the Truth is not insolence. The Truth is above us all.

Q: Well, if consecrating bishops without Rome's approval was such a wise action of Archbishop Lefebvre, why did he not approve of Archbishop Ngo-dinh-Thuc doing the same thing?

A: Within the SSPX properly founded inside the Catholic Church in 1970, Archbishop Lefebvre knew that candidates for the bishopric were assured of a proper priestly formation in the past, experience in the present, and a measure of protection in the future. One or more of these things he could not be sure of for priestly candidates outside of the Society.

Q: If liberalism is the problem, why attack Protestants who are often decent men and might be our allies in the fight against liberalism?

A: Unfortunately modern liberalism is rooted in Protestantism. All credit to decent Protestants as being decent, but as being Protestant they carry within them the seeds of all indecency. Protestantism is heresy, and heresy matters.

Q: *In any case, let the Society concentrate on the Faith, and leave politics alone!*

A: If politics and politicians would leave the Catholic Faith alone, then men of God could happily leave politics alone. But in the modern world, politics crash into God's law on questions like abortion, and blow it sky-high with principles like religious liberty. Such politics become in fact a graven image, an idol, a substitute religion. If the SSPX left such politics alone, it would be practicing liberalism, and it would be breaking the First Commandment.

Q: *But one cannot help wondering if the Society has a hidden political agenda: anti-semitism, neo-nazism, anti-americanism, revisionism?*

A: The Society's only agenda is that of Christ the King; but Christ the King in a real sense, not just as one more Sunday devotion at the end of October or November. If then a Jew or a neo-Nazi or an Americanist or a Revisionist is for the real kingship of Christ, he should have every Catholic and the SSPX for his friend. But if Jews want the Jewish race to be king, if neo-nazis want the State to be king, if Americanists want religious liberty to be king, then it is not a hidden political agenda to oppose them, but it is the agenda of Christ the King, which should be the agenda of every Catholic. Christ must reign!

We thank you seriously for all your support through another calendar year, especially for greetings in the image of Benjamin Franklin and Ulysses Grant – little did the bishop dream these would become his favorite American statesmen, until he became American Seminary Rector!

Si Si, No No Congress

A RICH DIET of Catholic doctrine, analysis and information concerning the Second Vatican Council was provided here at a SSPX house in Italy to the ninety-odd participants in the second Theological Congress of *Si Si, No No,* from January 2 to 5.

Sixteen speakers in turn addressed 55 seminarians and priests, including three bishops, and a few dozen laity in Albano Laziale, about half an hour by train or car southeast of Rome, on the theme "The problems posed for the Catholic conscience by the last Council." Seminary letters are a somewhat cramped medium in which to present the breadth and depth of the case for the prosecution against Vatican II, such as it was laid out by the sixteen high-level conferences. However, the main ideas will not fail to interest and benefit readers.

The tone was set for the Congress by the first conference, entitled "Tradition against the Council", and given by Msgr. Spadafora, a venerable Italian scripture scholar who has been in the front line of the battle for truth in the Church since the 1950's. Enjoying free access to the floor of the Council when it took place from 1962 to 1965, he had firsthand knowledge of what happened there. He said that the "inert mass" of 2,350 bishops were dominated by "a dynamic minority" who turned the Council into a "complete disappointment." They were cunning neo-modernists worse than Luther. Outwardly pious, inwardly heretics, they succeeded in getting the heresy which they had launched in Scripture studies taken over by the teaching authority of the Church, from where it was transmitted to the Church as a whole. Pope Paul VI had no real understanding of Catholic theology, and the Pontifical Biblical Commission, as it now operates, is a fraud. Msgr. Spadafora's testimony was as eloquent as it was humble and direct.

Another general view of the Council was taken by the following speaker, Fr. Alain Lorans, Rector of the Society's university faculty in Paris, who undertook with not a little French irony to analyze the famous "Spirit of the Council," summed up by Pope John XXIII himself as "Aggiornamento," an Italian word meaning "updating." Essentially, said Fr. Lorans, this meant a shift from objective doctrine of the faith to subjective living or existential living of the faith, in other words a shift from Church teaching to man – the question is no longer what I must believe to be true, but what it suits me in my own life to accept as true. But, concluded Fr. Lorans, supernatural truth is too true to suit man's fallen nature. God's love makes demands upon us which we may not find at all suitable.

Another famous word frequently used to characterize Vatican II, that of being the "pastoral" Council, was studied by the third speaker, Bishop Licinio Rangel, successor of Bishop de Castro Mayer as the head of the Traditional Catholics in the Diocese of Campos, Brazil. Bishop Rangel began by pointing out that very few of the previous 20 ecumenical Church councils were purely disciplinary, most were preoccupied with doctrine, but as such they were all pastoral in the true sense because what the true Catholic pastor feeds his flock with is doctrine. Therefore the word "pastoral" is falsely opposed to doctrinal, and what it in fact meant, when applied to Vatican II, was a turning or conversion to the modern world. Yet suddenly this non-doctrinal or non-dogmatic Council was made into the super-dogmatic Council which Catholics must obey absolutely above all other Councils! The bishop concluded that Vatican II was in many respects a failure, which a Cardinal Ratzinger tries in vain to disguise.

The next two conferences dealt with the run-up to the Council. Fr. Michel Simoulin, Rector of the Society's main seminary in Ecône, Switzerland, gave an overview of the replies made just before the Council by the world's 2,812 bishops and prelates to the official request by Rome that they make known their desires and wishes for the coming Council. Extraordinary! These replies showed few revolutionary desires, and no desire for such a Church revolution as would actually take place at the Council. Thus one critic dismissed the replies as too orthodox, wishing merely "to prepare another Council of Trent!"

Similarly Fr. Philippe Lovey, Superior of the Society's Swiss District, showed how the documents or schemata prepared beforehand for the Council to discuss and approve were all thrown out because of their orthodoxy, except for the schema on the liturgy, retained because of its relatively revolutionary character. The "inert mass" of orthodox bishops allowed the "dynamic minority" of neo-modernists to wrench the Council off its orthodox course within two days of its opening!

The next two conferences tackled the actual thinking of the Council. First of four high quality conferences by Italian lay university professors was Professor Pasqualacci's presentation of an analysis by Fr. Johannes Dörmann of the thinking of Cardinal Wojtyla, future Pope John Paul II and a leading figure at the Council. Readers of this letter already have a familiarity with the Cardinal's system of errors as elucidated from his writings by Fr. Dörmann: Vatican II was a new Pentecost, "enriching" the Catholic Faith with insights "complementing" Tradition, such as the union of God with every human nature; the natural possession by every man of sanctifying grace, whether he knows it or not; the automatic salvation of all men whether they want it or not, independently of repentance, faith, baptism or charity; and so, naturally, the extension of the Newchurch to include all mankind.

It may be objected that such wildly anti-Catholic ideas belong to Cardinal Wojtyla and not to the Council, but the fact remains that that is what he as one leading participant and fervent believer in the Council took it to be saying. It may also be objected that if that is what Karol Wojtyla continues to think, then he cannot be Pope, but the fact surely is that especially in our super-confused times, one man can hold in his head quite opposite notions. Were the Dörmann-Pasqualucci system of errors all that this Pope believed, his being pope might present a more serious problem, but surely he believes besides still much that is Catholic, and is convinced that the contradictory mixture, or Newfaith, is the true Catholic Faith for today! Such are at least the fruits of Vatican II. Heaven help us!

By comparison, the following conference of Fr. Franz Schmidberger, former Superior General of the Society and now its First Assistant, was plain sailing. His subject was "Protestants and the Council." He gave a clear account of the Protestant system of errors flowing from an exaggeration of the ruination of human nature by original sin. He showed the presence and influence at the Council not only of Protestants officially invited to observe, but also of leading Catholics infected by Protestant ideas. Of particular interest was his presentation of Cardinal Bea, deeply Catholic in his personal piety, at any rate as shown by his retreat notes recently published, and yet a vigorous liberal in his campaigning for everything revolutionary at the Council!

Men are contradictory! For the Church to swing from pre-Conciliar Catholicism to post-Conciliar apostasy, there had to be a transition, and surely that transition was incarnated in certain men. Between day and night there is dusk, when one cannot say there is no light. Between an apple ripe and an apple rotten, there is an apple half-rotten, of which one cannot say that the half not yet rotten is rotten, even if it soon will be. When a Catholic turns heretic, there must be a more or less long process, full of contradictions, and of which God alone can have the complete measure. The Church could adequately defend herself against such confusion by means of the Inquisition, but in our time firstly the name and then the thing were gutted. It changed its name to "Holy Office" and then "Congregation for the Doctrine of the Faith," a sign accompanying its change from iron guard of the Church to a paper tiger!

Fr. Schmidberger ended his conference with a swift overview of the Protestant influence on the course of the Council and its final documents, and drew the conclusion that the Christendom split by Luther between truth and error was reunited by the Council Fathers – not in truth, but in error!

The last conference of the first half of the Congress was given by the second Italian layman to speak, Professor Dalledonne on "The undermining of Thomism at the Council." With clarity he sketched out the essential irreconcilability between Thomism on the one hand, meaning the theology and philosophy of St. Thomas Aquinas based on being and adopted by the Catholic Church for nearly 700 years down to Vatican II as her own system of thinking, and on the other hand immanentist humanism, the system of thinking of the neo-modernists of Vatican II whereby not objective being but the subjective interior of man is the measure of reality.

With traces of passion the Professor denounced the various ways in which the neo-modernists, in a phrase of Italy's national poet, Dante, "refuse to consent to the contradiction" between their subjective systems and objective Thomism, pretending that St. Thomas can be absorbed into their Newthink. Imagine a dealmaker between one man saying two and two are four and another saying they are five, who would propose a reconciliation – whereby two and two would be four and a half! Such mental insanity is everywhere today, it lies at the heart of Vatican II pretending to mix Catholicism with Newthink, and Professor Dalledonne was wholly justified in edging his denunciation with passion. Who on earth would drive cars or walk over bridges built on the idea that two and two are four and a half? Newthink is deadly!

On Thursday January 4 began in effect the second half of the Theological Congress, to which only a second letter can do justice. Suffice it to say for the moment that participants in the Congress left well contented.

Meanwhile January remains the month of the Holy Family, which explains the two enclosures. On brown paper as usual is some reader reaction, a letter written by two teenagers to console the dinosaur who complained one year ago in this letter of being somewhat lonely in his pre-historic attempts to take up the slack in defense of old-fashioned ideas of woman and family. In truth, he is not that lonely. He knows of many girls and women in the United States courageously backtracking in a Catholic direction. He says Our Lord will reward them

On pink paper is a Pope, Leo XIII, defending family towards the end of the last century by defending Christian marriage, which is the supernatural bond necessary to hold together the natural family. For instance, "Let married couples turn to religion for strength to carry their crosses," he says, in paragraph 50 numbered according to the recent edition of Leonine Encyclicals, published by TAN Books out of Rockford, Illinois, and highly recommended. Leo knew our world, 100 years ago!

Finally, the seminary may lose the farmer and his family, presently looking after the seminary's 140-acre farm. The advantage is proximity to the Mass. The main disadvantages are lack of any Catholic school for children, and the reluctance of a seminary to socialize! Let anyone interested get in touch with the Rector.

Nixon's Career: A Liberal View and a Catholic View

NIXON, THE LATEST film of the controversial American film director, Oliver Stone, is interesting but confusing. Richard Nixon, President of the United States from 1968 to 1974, was a decent man, but like many decent men today, he built on sand and then could not understand why everything collapsed around him. At the risk of seeming to be Stoned, let me attempt to cast some Catholic light on recent history.

Let us see, in turn, firstly the basic facts of Nixon's career; secondly, the prevailing liberal view of those facts; thirdly, Oliver Stone's view in Nixon, and finally a Catholic view.

We begin with the bare outlines of Richard Nixon's career. Born of a Quaker family in backwoods California in 1913, and making his career in the law, he rose to national prominence in the USA by the part he took in the famous trial of the late 1940's, incriminating the eminent US Government official, Alger Hiss, as a Soviet spy and perjurer. This prominence made of Nixon, when the Republicans recaptured the White House in 1952, President Eisenhower's Vice-President for eight years, until 1960, when he ran himself for President, and was narrowly defeated by J.F. Kennedy.

For a while he retired from public life, but in 1968 he made a comeback, ran for President again and was elected, thus inheriting from President Lyndon Johnson the major problem of the Vietnam War. This war Nixon prosecuted with vigor. He was re-elected for a second term in 1972, but around the election campaign he came to learn of a secret raid that had taken place on Democrat election headquarters in Watergate, D.C., and over 1973 the Democrats with the help of the media so succeeded in implicating him, despite his denials, in the Watergate break-in, that in 1974 he was forced to resign as President. For his remaining 20 years of life he played honorably the part of elder statesman.

As for the liberals, secondly, they hated Nixon with a passion. Alger Hiss was a darling of theirs, because he was, for instance, one of the architects of their United Nations Organization, a key piece in their Brave New World Order, and so they never forgave the backwoods Quaker for his valiant contribution to the unmasking of Alger Hiss as a traitor. Really, they did not believe collaboration with the Soviets to be treachery. To this day, they believe it to be the only way forward . . . Hence when Nixon came back from defeat at the Presidential polls in 1960 to victory in 1968 and again in 1972, the liberals turned on him the full force of their vile media to make him into one of the United States' most unpopular politicians of modem times, especially by their harnessing – or creating – of popular revolt against the Vietnam War.

Truth to tell, Nixon as President had carried out a number of their policies, notably the fraternisation with Mao and Communist China, and with Brezhnev's Russia, but no doubt Nixon did not bend enough to their will. Their crusade brooks no resistance. Now whatever happened at the Watergate break-in was no crime at all when compared with the Presidential delinquencies currently being hidden or glossed over by the media, but these same media so hammered and hammered and hammered at Watergate that Nixon was hounded out of office. Yet when Nixon died, the liberals pretended they had loved him all along!

Now Oliver Stone, thirdly, does not accept this liberal vision of Nixon as being the inadequate instrument of a wonderful system. True, Stone does not seem to appreciate Nixon's anti-communism, but to Stone's credit, he does know there is something deeply wrong with the system. In his film JFK he blamed President Kennedy's assassination on "the industrial military complex." In Natural Born Killers he scourged the media in particular as promoters of society's disintegration. In Nixon, Stone evokes a shadowy "Beast" controlling the United States from behind the scenes through the CIA, the Mafia, Wall Street, etc. . . .

For while Stone presents Nixon's downfall as being at least partly the result of a lack of honesty which had become habitual in his climb to the top of the system, nevertheless the main cause is the system itself. Thus Nixon is shown as having been driven by ambition to climb from humble and honest origins to the highest office in the land he loves, only to find at the top that the system is not under his control, and so the land slips out from under him. In a climactic scene (which did happen in real life), Nixon is shown going to meet a group of young Vietnam War protesters in, significantly, the Lincoln Memorial, shrine of the President of national unity – there Nixon and the youngsters share their belief in Lincoln's ideals, so why should the Vietnam War be tearing them, and Lincoln's land, apart? Answer of Stone, "the Beast," which controls the United States and was insisting that the war continue.

But is the "Beast" the real problem? No doubt the "Beast" exists. For the liberals may be past-masters at ridiculing as "conspiracy nuts" people who believe that the modern world is run by a conspiracy – after all, who wants to admit that they are being led by the nose by secret masters? But the fact remains that only an idiot believes that Lee Harvey Oswald killed President Kennedy, and when Oliver Stone says there is a Power Behind the Scenes, he is only saying what several US presidents themselves have said, e.g., Woodrow Wilson.

But is the "Beast" the real problem? Supposing Oliver Stone or whoever could pull it out of its lair into the light of day and kill it off, would our problems be over? Rather, is it not true that if the people then still clung to their liberalism, preferring illusion to reality, they would perpetuate all the conditions necessary for the "Beast" to come back to life in the same shadows? "Please deceive us! We love the rotten way of life you give us! Please pretend you are not there, and we will pretend also!" Ultimately, the "Beast" is rather product than producer, of the people's turning away from God. Let us return to the Lincoln Memorial.

For, fourthly, from a Catholic point of view, is not the good President Lincoln the problem rather than the solution of the clash between the anti-Communist Nixon and the anti-Vietnam War youngsters? Lincoln, alternately praised as Savior of the Union and Savior of the American Revolution, was indeed savior of a revolutionary union, which is, if Catholics think about it, such a contradiction in terms as only Protestants could found and only Freemasons could Constitute. No doubt Abraham Lincoln personally was in many ways a wise and venerable man. But did he ever discover the contradiction on which he was building? Might that partly explain his deep melancholy? He was not a shallow man.

Poor non-Catholics! The better they are as men, the more they strive to build up good on their false principles, the more sad is the collapse of their efforts. For love of his land, dear Nixon lashed out at its communist enemies, but then that revolutionary land mutated beneath him, revolted against his anti-communism, and hung him out to dry. He fought his way to the top only to find when he got there that the country for which he had done it no longer existed. As for the youngsters, they were proud of their achievement in discarding Nixon and his like, but where did their brave revolution get them? – the nirvana of grunge, abortion, driveby shootings! Those youngsters look back with nostalgia on the 1960's, when they actually still believed in revolution . . . God is just, and He is not mocked.

But if Catholic principles matter, and matter like crazy, then where was the worst betrayal of those 1960's? Was it not from inside the Catholic Church, where, from the top downwards, the humanist Revolution, instead of being denounced as darkness, began, with Vatican II, to be glorified as light? If Catholic priests took prominent part in the anti-Vietnam War parades, and if their superiors did not efficaciously forbid them to do so, how could a poor Richard Nixon keep his head on straight? Nixon and Lincoln were, typically, destroyed by the Revolution they did so much to serve.

Dear Catholics, let us think, let us think hard, let us think clearly, and then for our own souls, for our families and for this beloved land of the United States, let us pray the Rosary to obtain light, and let us in no shape, size or form praise darkness! And men, if you think that what the SSPX teaches on these questions is not what the Catholic Church teaches, then come on the Doctrinal Session this summer, Winona, July 16 to 20. You might be surprised!

Influences of Vatican II

O UR LORD JESUS Christ is God, His one and only Catholic Church is infallible – how then can the normal teaching authority of that Church, the Catholic bishops in their dioceses spread throughout the world, go wrong in the Faith, and if they do, how must the Catholic people react? That was the major question for our times tackled by Fr. Philippe Marcille, SSPX priest stationed in France, when the second half of the Society's Congress opened in Albano, Italy, two months ago, to continue the study of problems posed for the Catholic conscience by the Second Vatican Council: how can a Catholic in the name of the Faith resist the authority instituted by Our Lord for the defense of the Faith?

For indeed in 1870 the wholly Catholic First Vatican Council taught that infallibility belongs not only to the Pope teaching solemnly "ex cathedra," but also to the Ordinary Universal Magisterium, i.e., to the Catholic bishops teaching in their dioceses throughout the world. However, ever since the mass of Catholic bishops either taught or tolerated heresy in the Arian crisis of the fourth century, it has been obvious that diocesan bishops cannot be followed blindly, even if they are in union with the Pope, because at that time Pope Liberius also faltered.

Fr. Marcille explained that God's protection of His Church cannot allow such crises involving the bulk of the bishops and the Pope to go on for too long, otherwise the Church would be destroyed, which is impossible. But the question remains, what must Catholics do in such a crisis? Fr. Marcille replied that what the scattered bishops teach infallibly is to be recognized by its oneness, precisely because scattered bishops will normally teach scattered things, so only under divine guidance will scattered bishops teach one thing, especially in different ages.

If then Catholics notice the bulk of diocesan bishops even in union with Rome to be changing the Faith, as in the Arian crisis, then they must keep to what was taught "always, everywhere, and by everybody," because that teaching is locked into the past and can no longer be tampered with. Then Catholics must resort to any Catholic bishop clearly keeping that Faith for all further aid they need, up to and including the consecration of bishops necessary to ensure the continuance of faithful priests, if religion's very survival is threatened, if the local bishop is powerless, and if there is no hope of help from Rome. Fr. Marcille quoted several examples from Church history.

The question of the teaching authority of the bishops in general was followed by that of Vatican II in particular, upon which the judgment of Fr. Pierre Marie, editor of the French Traditional Dominicans' quarterly magazine, *Le Sel de la Terre*, was quite severe. Proceeding in logical order, he examined first whether the Council documents come under the Church's extraordinary or ordinary infallibility – not under extraordinary infallibility, he argued, because both Pope John XXIII and Paul VI explicitly said the Council was making no definitive declarations; nor under ordinary infallibility, both because (see above) the Church's bishops were no longer scattered at Vatican II, but gathered together in such a group as to expose them to group pressures which could and did falsify their judgments; and because the bishops of Vatican II presented none of their doctrines as requiring definitively to be believed.

Nor, Fr. Pierre Marie went on to argue, are these doctrines even part of the Church's authentic (i.e., ordinary, non-universal) teaching, because the bishops expressed no intention to hand down the Deposit of the Faith, on the contrary their spokesmen (e.g., Paul VI) expressed their intention to come to terms with the modern world and its values, long condemned by true Catholic churchmen as being intrinsically uncatholic. Therefore, concluded Fr. Pierre Marie, the documents of Vatican II have only a Conciliar authority, the authority of that Council, but no Catholic authority at all, and no Catholic need take seriously anything Vatican II said, unless it was already Church doctrine beforehand.

The next three conferences dealt with influences upon the Council coming from France, the United States and Germany. Firstly, Fr. Benoit de Joma, Society District Superior of France, presented the thinking on the Church of Fr. Yves Congar, the French Dominican priest, made Cardinal by JP2, who had an enormous influence on Vatican II. As far back as the 1930's Congar was working out the distinction between the Church as visible hierarchical institution confined to baptized "Catholics," and the Church as an invisible mystic body reaching out to include all mankind.

Now in truth, Christ did tell His Apostles to go to all nations, but they were not to go to them without teaching them His doctrine and giving them His sacraments, starting with baptism (Mt. 28: 18–20) – that is true ecumenism. But the ecumenism of Vatican II, following

Congar, suggests that God works through all "churches" to save men, that men have supernatural grace by their mere nature, that merely by being a human being one belongs to the true Superchurch of the cosmic Christ, now emerging in a New Advent, announced by Congar like a new John the Baptist, and in which the God of the Universe – who is he? – will be revealed. Heaven help us!

Next the influence of the United States upon the Council was presented by your servant. This conference may soon be appearing in *The Angelus* so there is no need to go into detail here. The conference showed firstly how religious liberty is the key ingredient in the "spirit of America"; secondly, how this world-conquering spirit clashed with the Catholic Church in the last century; thirdly, how that spirit finally conquered the bulk of the Catholic churchmen at Vatican II when they approved of the *Declaration on Religious Liberty*; lastly, how the spirit of that document and of the Newchurch is in perfect harmony with the Masonic spirit of America. Heaven save the United States and Mother Church from Freemasonry!

The influence of German theologians upon the Council, especially that of Fr. Karl Rahner, was presented by a Swiss priest stationed in Germany, Fr. Niklaus Pfluger, Rector of the Society's Seminary at Zaitzkofen in Bavaria. Like Congar, Rahner wished to overcome the division between grace and nature: grace, he held, is built into man's nature, so all men are saved, non-Christians are all anonymous Christians (i.e., saved by Christ, but unaware of it), and non-Christian religions are all means of salvation. So the Catholic Church must get together with them by ecumenism.

Under Pope Pius XII, said Fr. Pfluger, according to a familiar pattern, these grave errors were disapproved of and held in check, but as the Council dawned, so Rahner's moment came. Appointed theological expert to the Council by Pope John XXIII himself, he was of all "experts" the best prepared and the most often quoted. At the Council's first three sessions, 1962, 1963, 1964, Fr. Rahner personally exercised enormous influence upon the Council Fathers and among its theologians. When for instance a classical text on the sources of Revelation was proposed for discussion on the Council floor, it was Rahner who prepared an alternative "ecumenical" text, following which, in the decisive week of Nov. 14 to 21, 1962, the Council Fathers swung leftwards once and for all. Even experts disagreeing with Rahner had to admire his increasing prestige, while the progressives would drop everything "to listen to the genius of a master."

Yet by the fourth session in 1965, Rahner was no longer so active in the Council. "The Council is boring," he wrote in a letter in October of that year. No doubt he had done his work. The Church had been changed.

With Thursday's final conference by the Italian layman, Dr. Carlo Agnoli, the Congress was reaching to the heart of the evil influences on Vatican II: "Freemasonry and the Council." From 1738 to 1958 the Catholic Popes steadily and repeatedly condemned Freemasonry as the central source of the particular evils of the modern world. With ample references and documentation, Dr. Agnoli proved that the common source of the novelties and errors of Vatican II was Freemasonry, whose main tool was Pope John XXIII. He concluded with several arguments (amounting in the case of Freemasonry, he said, to proofs) that Pope John XXIII was himself an initiated Freemason. There is not space enough in this letter to do justice to the importance of this conference, so we pass to the two conferences of the final day of the congress.

Professor Romano Amerio, Italian lay author of a masterly account of modern errors, *Iota Unum* ("[O]ne jot or one title shall not pass of the law" – Mt. 5: 18), spoke on "The dislocated teaching function of the Church after

Vatican II." He explained how, following on the Council, the bishops and even the Pope, have abdicated the function entrusted to them by God of laying out the one unchanging, supernatural Doctrine of Jesus Christ, and are instead giving their personal views. By thus falling in with the modern world, JP2 is dissolving his papal authority, which holds the Church together by proclaiming that Christianity is not just the fulfillment of all men's religious feelings, but the revealed word of God.

In place of this one Divine Word, we are given today a multiplicity of theologians' opinions, contradicting one another, resting on no stronger authority than their own human thinking. Thus the mind is broken up, and love, love, love takes over. But in the beginning was the Word, not love, because Love (God the Holy Ghost) proceeds from the Word (God the Son), because there can be no love of something not first known by some word. Without the Truth, minds rot; and rotten minds follow rotten hearts. Holy Father, tell us Christ's Truth!

The sixteenth and last conference of the Congress was given by the Society's Superior General, Bishop Bernard Fellay, on the speeches made by Archbishop Lefebvre on the floor of the Council. Surveying the series of these speeches (published by the Angelus Press in book form as I Accuse the Council), Bishop Fellay noted how the Archbishop's style changed as the Council wore on: if at the beginning he used diplomatic phrases smoothly rounded like the head of his crozier, by the end he was attacking and defending vigorously with its pointed tip!

The Archbishop spoke at the Council mainly on Communism, on collegiality, on the Church in the world, but most often on Religious Liberty where he must have sensed the worst error of the Council. The Archbishop's warnings are as relevant today as they were 30 years ago, said Bishop Fellay, because everything he said was based on Catholic Tradition.

To conclude the whole Congress Bishop Fellay quoted words spoken by the Archbishop concerning the Constitution "*Gaudium et Spes,*" but which the Bishop re-applied to Vatican II as a whole: "This so-called pastoral Council is neither pastoral nor catholic: it does not feed men or Christians with the evangelic and apostolic Truth, nor has the Church ever spoken in this way. This is a voice we cannot listen to, because it is not the voice of the Bride of Christ, nor is it the voice of the Spirit of Christ. The voice of Christ, our Shepherd, we know. This voice we do not know. The skin is sheepskin, but the voice is not the shepherd's, perhaps it is the wolf's."

Dear Friends and Benefactors, continue to pray quietly and steadily with an unshakable trust in God. Vatican II will eventually be washed out of the Church's system, and the Catholic Church will emerge again more brilliant than ever. For this holy intention amongst others let us offer our Lenten penances.

Patrick Buchanan's Campaign

W HAT HAPPENED A few weeks ago to derail Patrick Buchanan's promising campaign to win for sanity the nomination as Republican Party candidate for the Presidential election due to take place here in the United States at the end of this year?

Old-fashioned Catholics were interested, because Buchanan is a Catholic who likes to attend the Tridentine Mass, whose convictions include many Catholic principles, for instance love of his country and an uncompromising refusal of abortion, and who has the courage of his convictions.

Moreover his bid for the Republican nomination began very well. When in the opening races of the campaign he ran a close second in Iowa and then won in New Hampshire in February, then, in US politics long stifled by the two party system ("There's not a dime's worth of difference between the two parties," said Governor Wallace back in 1972, and he was shot for his pains), a lot of Americans, and not only Catholics, felt they had been given a whiff of oxygen, and their long dead interest in politics stirred with a tremor of hope. At last, a real man daring to address real issues.

But two weeks into March and it was virtually over. As soon as Buchanan's chances of winning the nomination became serious, the media swung into action with a truly extraordinary campaign to denounce and discredit Buchanan as an "extremist." The campaign worked. Masses of couch-potatoes dutifully voted as their media told them to vote, and Buchanan has been effectively eliminated.

For himself, this elimination must be a grace in the sense that if he had come much closer to real power, he would also no doubt have been shot, whether wounded like Wallace and Reagan, or killed like Robert and John F. Kennedy. "Democracy" is for couch-potatoes. Our secret masters play hardball.

On the other hand Buchanan's elimination is very grave for the United States. In his candidacy God gave the country a real chance to repudiate abortion amongst other horrors of liberalism, but the country turned the chance down. How many more chances will the United States be given? There comes a time when the only mercy left to God to send down upon a nation is fire and brimstone, because divine terror will bring at least a few souls to their knees, whereas nothing else will save any souls at all. That time is fast approaching for the apostate nations of the West. So let Catholics profit from Buchanan's "failure" to understand at last where the real problem lies.

The real problem lies not in any personal failings of Buchanan, as though, for instance, he could have won through if only he regularly attended SSPX Masses – he already stood for far too much Tradition. (Similarly with President Nixon. A few readers of this letter two months ago complained of its being too kind personally to that "crook," "liar," etc., but that kindness was meant to highlight that if he was removed from the Presidency in 1974, it was not because he was a crook, but because he was not enough of a crook.) Buchanan's very integrity and manliness make him unacceptable!

Similarly the problem does not lie in any supposed mistake of Buchanan's February-March campaign, as though he could have broken through if only he had, for instance, appealed more strongly to the women voters, or pensioners, or whoever. Give or take this or that issue, friend and foe alike realized what Buchanan means, namely God and country as opposed to godless internationalism, and this is what they voted for or against, the large majority against.

For instance one might have expected Protestants of the "religious right," surely believers in "One nation under God," to support this valiant candidate for God and country, but in the important South Carolina primary of mid-March, the "religious right" battalions were mobilized to swing the election against Buchanan, because he is Catholic. In other words, one nation under God, yes, but only if he is not the Catholic God. That is why the very best of Protestants (I could quote several honorable names) are powerless – powerless – to help the USA.

Nor then does the problem lie in the two-party system, as though the system can be saved if only Buchanan will start a third party, which is what many of his ardent followers hope. This is not because of the two-or three-party system in itself, but because of what it and democracy mean to present-day people, namely that not God, but man, is God. The fault lies, if you will, not in democracy as such, but in today's democrats. Thus democracy could work if all the people recognized a God above them and honored His Law in all their democratic dealings, but that is emphatically not the case with people today.

For instance at Senate hearings on an abortion question held in Washington, D.C., a few years ago, a Chicago pro-lifer declared that above the US government, above the US Senate and House of Representatives, is God and His Law. A young Senator promptly denied this, and the consensus of the other Senators present was behind him! And there must have been countless such incidents throughout Western democracies over recent years.

But this is shocking only at first sight. For in the dear young Senator's mind, who is God and what is religion? It is, of course, a Sunday morning "Sound of Music" affair! Then of course he is right in saying that the US Government is more important and has priority! Given religious liberty in the "land of the brave and home of the free," in which even Catholic Cardinals have glorified the principle whereby God may say you cannot have false gods but the State says you can, how could the dear young Senator think other than that real religion is the U.S. government?

The young Senator's problem is that so many Catholics he meets are not Catholics, but Sound-of-Musicians, and here is where Buchanan's real problem lies. The country he loves was built on the skids and Catholics have not protested, so it has had nothing to stop it from sliding to perdition ever since. See the enclosed salmon-colored flyer, which is the key to many a letter from the seminary. In fact, from the time of Henry VIII, the English-speaking world has been on the skids. Since then brave individuals like Patrick Buchanan (plus or minus Richard Nixon) have attempted to stop the slide, but – and here is the rub –EITHER they get out of the mainstream, OR they go down with it. The mainstream is decadent and doomed.

If only it was not so! If only the system was not at war with God, and God with the system! Can I not console myself that it is deep down a wonderful Constitution, the best ever thought up by man, and if only we could get good men back into office, why, the mainstream could be reversed?

My dear friends, Americanism and Vatican II are great helps to set up that consolation, but the truth of the matter is that even if by a triple miracle Buchanan was nominated today, elected tomorrow, and not shot the day after, still he could not straighten out the United States, because the people are too far gone in putting man over God, and they would, interacting in vileness with their media, never have Buchanan or anyone else putting God back over man. Political solutions are inadequate for religious problems. The people must turn back to God, and the "God" of the Protestants will not do.

If only it was not so! If only I could be on good terms both with God and with the mainstream! How much easier life would be! What a nice picture! A huge speaker on each corner of my party-raft drifting downstream blasts out that the hills are alive with the sound of music – my friends and I smell an increasingly unpleasant stench of sewage in the water, and ahead of us, is that the thunder we hear of a great waterfall? My friends, turn up the speakers! Sprinkle more smell-killer! The party is to go on forever!

Dear Catholics! The one thing we must not do is let anyone around hear from us, or see from our example, that religion can be pushed into a nice sweet little compartment from where it pours forth its sentimental perfume upon a way of life damned by God and doomed to destruction! To stand up to that way of life may cost us more than blood, sweat, toil, and tears, but such may be the cost of getting to Heaven.

"But your Excellency, being a real Catholic today hurts too much, it is difficult!" Yes, I know. Just a few days ago there came here terrible news of a young Novus

Ordo priest from an Iowa diocese who had been offering the Tridentine Mass for a group of souls (having nothing to do with the Society of St Pius X). The more these souls responded, the more the diocese hounded him, for instance took away his car until he could see only one way out. He disappeared from view, until he was found a few weeks later in the hotel room where he had taken his own life. Now parents are apparently blaming those Tridentine souls, while the diocesan officials will be saying they were right all along – you see, he was crazy!

God, have mercy upon us all! Catholics, think long, think hard and think clear. Do not think that any problems are serious except those involving heaven and hell, the state of grace and mortal sin, and to those problems do not think that there are any other solutions than those of God, Jesus Christ, and His one and only Catholic Church. If God is allowing the world to get into such a mess, it is only to let it drive us back to Him, not to let it drive us from one form of godlessness to another. See again the enclosed flyer. All He asks of us in this situation is to give witness to the Truth, as did His divine Son, and the harder that may become, the greater will be our reward, which will last forever. We have no honorable alternative!

Dear friends and benefactors, the seminary is well, thanks be to God and to your continuing support, which, when I think of these letters, I admire! Eight new American priests should be ordained here at Winona on Saturday, June 22, by your servant. And no fewer than 18 of last autumn's 22 new seminarians are still here in pursuit of the Catholic priesthood. Come to the ordinations to show Our Lord how much you appreciate having seminarians and priests after His Heart, and He will protect all you have, and give you more.

Bishop Bruskewitz & the SSPX

POOR ROME! IT cannot swallow the SSPX down, nor can it spit it out, as another United States bishop is presently learning. How well God built His Church!

It is now getting on for two months since Bishop Fabian Bruskewitz of the diocese of Lincoln, Nebraska, threatened to excommunicate in mid-May Catholics still belonging to any one of twelve different organizations, ten of them liberal, two of them the SSPX and its local chapel in Lincoln. Of the liberal groups five are Masonic, two pro-abortion, one pro-euthanasia, and two pro-women priests and a married clergy, etc. . . .

By daring to remind these liberals that they are worthy of damnation, the good bishop caused quite a flurry in the national media. Non-Catholic liberals in our all-inclusive world objected to the very idea of excommunication, while Catholic liberals have themselves convinced that even if excommunication is a good idea, it cannot be deserved by themselves. On the other hand many decent Catholics rejoiced that at last a diocesan bishop was taking action to clean out the stables.

However, when the bishop added to his list of ten liberal groups the two so-called Traditional Catholic organizations, then nobody who thinks could take him seriously. So from the beginning his bombshell went off like a damp squib.

Cynical Nebraskans say he was only seeking publicity and advancement from Rome in the first place. Other Nebraskans say he is sincere. Experts in Conciliar tactics might say he was imitating Paul VI by condemning liberals and anti-liberals together, so as to keep the Conciliar balance. But all such speculation as to Bishop Bruskewitz's personality or motivation is only of secondary interest. What matters is the principles involved. The Catholic Church runs on principles, not on personalities, because it is principles that make Catholic personalities, as too few Catholics realize.

Nor then is it a mere question of the SSPX. If Bishop Bruskewitz crippled his own initiative by including in his condemnation the SSPX and its local affiliate, it is not because the Society is of any significance in itself, nor because it consists of saints and wise men (Please do not laugh. Thank you for your co-operation), but because members of your Society, with all their sins and shortcomings, nevertheless are Society members because they profess those principles upon which alone a Catholic excommunication can be based. Hence by including Society members in his threat and so condemning their principles, the bishop was cutting the ground from under his own feet. This is what needs to be proved.

As Bishop Bruskewitz wrote to a friend of ours, he included the SSPX in his condemnation because it is "disobedient" to Rome and to himself, while he, no doubt, is "obedient." But what characterizes this Rome which he "obeys" and which the Society "disobeys"? No doubt the Second Vatican Council, without which the Society would never have risen up to resist. But what is at the heart of this Council making the difference between the Society and Rome? Notably, religious liberty. For if Rome were to return from the Vatican II principle of liberty for false religions to the old principle of toleration for them, with all that that return would entail, the Society would have lost the large part of its reason to exist, whereas if Rome abandoned many other Conciliar ideas, but not religious liberty, then the Society would still have a major reason to exist. Then what is the relationship between religious liberty and excommunication?

The Conciliar principle of religious liberty declares that the State has no right to coerce men in matters of religion. Prior to the Council, the Catholic Church always said that the State may abstain from coercing men in matters of religion, but it always has the right to use its power prudently to protect the Catholic religion and to suppress the public exercise of false religions. The difference between these two positions may seem small, but it is in fact enormous, like the difference between God being God and man being God. Which in turn needs proving.

If God is the Lord of all creation, then He is God also of the State, which is not outside of creation. If God is Lord of the State, then it too must, as State, worship and obey Him, in other words the State authorities must, as State authorities, protect and prudently promote His worship by His one true religion, as part of the duty of all creatures to render to their Creator what is His due. Therefore every State on earth is, as such, bound to use all prudent means, including the force at its disposal, to favor the Catholic religion. God is God, and Catholicism is, since Jesus Christ died on the Cross, His one and only true worship.

On the other hand if, as Vatican II declared, the State is bound to respect the dignity of the human person by leaving men free in the State to practice publicly false religions as they desire, then the State's first duty is to the freedom of man, and only after that comes any duty it may have to the God of the true religion. In other words, that State is no longer under the God of all creation, or, God is no longer the Lord of all creation. If there is a true religion, it no longer imposes itself on men but comes begging as some inferior for their lordly consent, on an equal footing with all false religions. In effect, man is God and "God" becomes some whining wimp.

Now modern man may, born and bred in liberalism, have a special difficulty in grasping that these are the real consequences of that religious liberty on which his nations are virtually founded, because he is dazzled by his own dignity. But in fact there is no comparison between the God of the Old Testament and the "God" of Vatican II, and the God of the New Testament is identical with the former, not with the latter! So this true God who thundered on Mount Sinai, who thrashed the money-changers out of the Temple and who demands that men practice His one religion and that States favor it accordingly, is obviously capable of driving false members out of His true Church. It makes complete sense that this God will excommunicate bad Catholics.

But how can the "God" who out of respect for human dignity makes no demand that the State bring pressure to bear on man's choice of truth or error, suddenly require that His Church bring pressure to bear? It is the same man with the same dignity confronting the same choice between the same truth and error. If the State, and "God" behind the State, must come cap in hand to beg consent to the Truth from such a man, how can this "God" and his "Church" do other than beg, cap in hand? How can this whining "God" who has no thunderbolts for the State, suddenly have them for his "Church"?

Deep down, liberals have no sense of the true God or of the true Church because they have lost grip on Truth.

"What is Truth?" asked Pontius Pilate, and put Barabbas alongside Jesus. Similarly Bishop Bruskewitz puts believers in the one Truth amongst Freemasons, abortionists, euthanasians and women-priesters. How can he be surprised if neither intelligent Catholics nor intelligent liberals take him seriously?

For if the Society deserves to be punished for its stand, then there is no Truth and no true God, but only a miserable makeshift "God," who then can have no thunderbolts for Freemasons, women-priesters or whoever. On the other hand if abortion and euthanasia deserve to be smashed, then there must be a Truth and a true God who on occasion uses thunderbolts, but in that case the Society which, against modern Rome, believes in such a God, cannot deserve to be excommunicated.

In brief, either God is God, or man is God. If man is God, then the Society is wrong, but there can be nothing wrong with activities of man such as euthanasia and abortion, and there can be no basis for condemning them. On the other hand if abortion and Freemasonry are damnable, then there must be such a God as the Society exists to proclaim, in which case it cannot be condemned.

Modern Rome was cleverer (and more crooked) than Bishop Bruskewitz when it singled out Society members as a target for excommunication, instead of crucifying them between thieves, but even when they were singled out, the "excommunication" of July 1988 bounced off, because God lends none of His force to measures condemning His Truth or its (until now, by His grace) faithful spokesmen.

That is why Rome will in a few days most probably hang Bishop Bruskewitz out to dry, which is why he were better to have said nothing in the first place. Dear bishop, try next time condemning the delinquents without the Society! Then you will be a real hero to all real Catholics, and then you will have thrown a real bombshell! In the meantime we must pray for Rome, because that is where Bishop Bruskewitz's real problem lies. Pray for the Pope to lead him in consecrating Russia to the Immaculate Heart of Mary. That is what the true God has decreed as the first step necessary to save Church and world.

Meantime, let us thank Him for His gift of the SSPX, despite its human deficiencies. And enjoy in the enclosed *Verbum* the commemoration in verse of Archbishop Lefebvre's enormous achievement. Objectively, no language could be noble enough to say worthily what he did.

The Unabomber Manifesto: Is It Relevant?

A FASCINATING DOCUMENT was published recently in the United States in two easily available books written about the case of a serial killer – the famous or notorious "Unabomber," hunted by the US police over the last 18 years for his killing by postal bomb of three men and injuring of several others, and perhaps at last tracked down this April in the State of Montana.

The document is his Manifesto, nearly 100 closely printed paperback pages, laying out in 232 numbered paragraphs and 16 notes a closely argued attack upon our industrial-technological society. It was, he says in paragraph #96, to get his message before the public "with some chance of making a lasting impression" that he resorted to bombs and killing.

Now Catholics know that the end can never justify the means. However important the Unabomber's message, nothing gave him the right to maim and kill innocent victims in order to get it before the public. So this letter may discredit itself by apparently crowning his terrorist means with success if it considers seriously his message, totally mocked and discounted on the contrary throughout the rest of one, probably both, of the paperbacks.

But I reply, firstly – again – principles are more important than personalities, and the message is, strictly, for good or ill, independent of the messenger. The author of the Unabomber's Manifesto might have since become a Saint without its contents being changed by one word. Secondly, if one stops and listens to some of the delinquents, real or supposed, protesting against modern society, like the Unabomber, film director Oliver Stone, or many rock musicians, e.g., Pink Floyd, then without accepting that their ends justify all their means, one cannot help having a measure of understanding for their resorting to such desperate means. Modern man is in the more deadly trouble for having his ears blocked by a seemingly impenetrable complacency!

"Yes, but Catholic bishops have no business rummaging in such gutters!" Dear Madam, do you wish to save your rebellious teenagers' souls? I am sure you are well aware that if you talk to them of St. Ignatius of Loyola or St. Thérèse of Lisieux, you do not even get to first base. But just breathe the name of Pink Floyd, and see how their ears prick up! This is our world, and there is no other in which we have to save ours souls! If only the honorable professors and respectable bishops were tackling the questions tackled by the Unabombers and the Oliver Stones, then your children might look up instead of down, but since nobody "decent" seems to address their concerns, who can be surprised if they feed from the gutter? Rock music is one long, unheard, scream for help!

Then let us firstly consider the problem raised by the Unabomber which paperbackers and all similar technophiliacs would rather run a mile than face, because they have no solution (Pink Floyd has no solution either, but at least he faces the problem). And secondly let us indicate the Catholic solution, because if a problem is human and serious, the true Church of the true God cannot not have the solution. We begin with the Unabomber's argument, here cruelly condensed from the 232 paragraphs which he says are already too brief for the subject (my own section numbering):

1) Modern society is destroying human dignity and freedom by its industrial technology. A symptom of this destruction is the modern left-winger, or "Leftist," a type of man recurring in numerous protest movements today. Often himself belonging to no minority group, yet in the name of a variety of such groups he attacks Western civilization with a hostility betraying his lack of real compassion for the supposed victims. Nor can his revolt be so real against society when he wishes to integrate them into it!

2) In truth, the industrial-technological system, I.T. or IT for short, makes it so easy for men to satisfy their basic needs of food, clothing and shelter that man's equally natural need to attain some goal by serious effort on his own part remains widely frustrated. Also family, or any such small-scale loyalty natural to man, is necessarily disrupted by the large-scale commitment required for IT to function. So IT destroys family values. Similarly the host of rules and regulations imposed by IT's functioning stifle man's acting on his own part to attain real goals, which is his real freedom.

3) Nor can any minor adjustment or compromise reconcile IT with freedom, both because IT has to regulate human behavior closely in order to function at all, and because all parts of IT are interdependent. Moreover men's desire for IT and IT's benefits have for a long time been proving stronger than men's desire for freedom, for a variety of reasons, so that the advance of IT seems to many people to be irreversible. For instance, the use of a motor car was originally optional, but it so changed

the layout of cities that now it is obligatory. Therefore IT will be stopped by no small-scale reform but only by wholesale revolution.

4) The clash between IT and human freedom is highlighted by IT's present pursuit of ways to tame "wild" behavior. Control of schooling, control of parenting, drugs, psychotherapy, neurology, genetics, eventually brain-engineering, etc., are all forms of manipulation by which IT will (if it can) re-engineer the very nature of man to fit IT. Presently more and more humans are rising up in revolt against IT, but if IT prevails, not even IT's rulers will have much freedom to move, whereas if IT is smashed, there may be chaos, but at least humanity has another chance, and the chaos may cause less suffering than IT's continuance will.

5) For if IT survives, then the future looks grim. Either, for the sake of efficiency, machines will be in total control and no man will be free. Or an elite will run the master machines, either so as to eliminate the masses so that a few are in control while the rest are dead, or so as to domesticate the masses so that the few are chained to the machine while the rest have no freedom or meaning in their lives. If IT survives, whichever way, man will have had to be re-engineered beyond all recognition!

6) However, IT is not unstoppable. The positive alternative is WILD NATURE, free of men, or with wild men. Wild nature is non-technological, it is beautiful, it takes care of itself, it permits survival living (One may have toothaches, but rather toothaches than IT!). The means of IT's overthrow are a revolution not merely political, but economic, technological and worldwide, for IT cannot be overthrown piecemeal. Above all, let our revolutionaries have the one clear goal: IT must go! All means to achieve that goal can then be pragmatically adjusted.

7) Finally, let our revolutionaries not mix with leftists who are anti-individualists as IT is, and so will only oppose IT in order then to use it against everybody else. Also, leftists habitually collaborate in revolutions with non-leftists only to double-cross them later. Leftism is totalitarian by nature, in fact it is a substitute religion, the need to believe in which will make even decent followers condone the most indecent crimes from their leaders.

I hope the brevity of this summary does not prevent readers from discerning a sharp mind tackling a real problem. Say what one will about the advantages of the present industrial-technological system of living, it is doomed as long as it rides roughshod over the deepest needs of human nature. This the Unabomber senses very clearly (sec. 2), as he sees very clearly the falsity of the solution by leftism (secs. 1 and 7), which is why the leftist media have no love for him as they would have if he were one of theirs.

On the other hand as a child of the IT society and a product no doubt of an IT education (or rather, non-education), the Unabomber has an inadequate grasp of human nature, which prevents him from getting it correctly in focus, in two ways. Firstly, he centers the problem on man's loss of freedom (secs. 2 to 5), which is why the only positive solution he can come up with is a return to wild nature with no, or wild, men (sec. 6)! Shades of baby seals, hug-a-tree and ozone! He is falling back into leftism's pathetic conclusion that the only pollution is men! ("I can keep the kitchen wonderfully clean – just let nobody have any more meals"). Archbishop Lefebvre said to go back to the country, not to the wilds. (The man picked up in Montana had gone back to the wilds. That is not a solution.)

Secondly, when the Unabomber seriously considers the possibility of IT prevailing (sec. 4), and argues that it is stronger than men's desire for freedom, he underestimates the need of human nature for "freedom," and man's power to resist whatever thwarts his deepest needs. In a marvelous passage by another author considered indecent by some because he also faces indecent modern problems, Dostoevsky has his anti-social worm of a hero (in *Notes from the Underground*) declare that 19th century materialism may so swamp and drown man in comfort and prosperity that only bubbles still reach the surface, yet man is so "cussed" that against all reasonable calculation and self-interest, against every prediction, just to assert his free will, he will rise up and destroy every shred of that comfort and prosperity, maybe reducing himself to misery, but remaining a man and not a machine.

The Unabomber should read Dostoevsky and all the great Russian authors, because then he might no longer feel the need to kill in order to get his message over. True, the Antichrist will swamp hordes of men in corruption, but still his IT will not have been able to re-engineer human nature. Still the human spirit will rise, even if only in a handful of Christians – "Behold, I am with you all days, even to the consummation of the world."

What then is the Catholic solution to this problem of the machine, so clearly sensed by the Unabomber and become so difficult today that it evokes the end of the world? "Seek ye first the kingdom of God, and all these things will be added unto you," which includes the putting of machines in their correct place. Secondly, man must be put second after God, above machines and money. Especially children must be put before machines and before money. And thirdly, Catholics must realize that if they think IT is wonderful or even just irreversible, they have a virus in their thinking which threatens their Catholic faith. The Unabomber's Manifesto is neither crazy, nor irrelevant to their salvation. Industrial technology is neither wonderful, nor even, absolutely speaking, irreversible.

Dear friends and benefactors, the heart and soul of the problem in the world around us is still the sin within us, as it always has been, and against sin we continue to give battle at the seminary by means of the Ignatian Spiritual Retreats, this summer for men from June 26 to 29 and from July 8 to 13 (places still available), and for women from July 1 to 6 (waiting-list only).

The Retreats provide fuel for the spiritual war, while ammunition is provided for men by the Doctrinal Session, running this year from July 16 to 20, and covering basic Papal Encyclicals, covered before but always needing to be covered again, with an excursion into a contrary encyclical from a recent Pope. Places available, sign on! Audio and video tapes are available for purchase of last year's Doctrinal Session, as per the enclosed flyer. Machines can serve truth!

Last month a flyer was enclosed with this letter on behalf of St. Mary's Academy and College in St. Mary's, Kansas. To entrust your children or teenagers to the priests, nuns and teachers at this SSPX facility in the heart of the United States, is one serious way of protecting them at least partly from the world around them in their vulnerable years, and of ensuring that they get to know and often to love their Catholic Faith. Let nobody pretend that St. Mary's is a problem-free paradise, because the spiritual war in and around us lets up never and nowhere, but at least in St. Mary's, the school is allied with the Catholic family against the world, instead of being allied with the world against the Catholic family.

THE KEY TO ROCK MUSIC – FROM 1864?!

Sensible men will do the most senseless things . . .

And one even comes upon this sort of thing all the time: there constantly appear in life people of such good behavior and good sense, such sages and lovers of mankind, as precisely make it their goal to spend their entire lives in the best-behaved and most sensible way possible, to become, so to speak, a light for their neighbors, essentially in order to prove to them that one can indeed live in the world as a person of good behavior and good sense. And what then? It is known that sooner or later, towards the end of their lives, many of these lovers have betrayed themselves, producing some anecdote, sometimes even of the most indecent sort. Now I ask you: what can be expected of man as a being endowed with such strange qualities? Shower him with all earthly blessings, drown him in happiness completely, over his head, so that only bubbles pop up on the surface of happiness, as on water; give him such economic satisfaction that he no longer has anything left to do at all except sleep, eat gingerbread, and worry about the non-cessation of world history – and it is here, just here, that he, this man, out of sheer ingratitude, out of sheer cussedness, will do something nasty.

. . . just to show that they are not machines.

He will even risk gingerbread, and wish on purpose for the most pernicious nonsense, the most non-economical meaninglessness, solely in order to mix into all this positive good sense his own pernicious, fantastical element. It is precisely his fantastic dreams, his most banal stupidity, that he will wish to keep hold of, with the sole purpose of confirming to himself (as if it were so very necessary) that human beings are still human beings and not piano keys, which, though played upon with their own hands by the laws of nature themselves, are in danger of being played so much that outside of the calendar it will be impossible to want anything.

Men would pull the universe down with curses . . .

And more than that: even if it should indeed turn out that he is a piano key, if it were even proved to him mathematically and by natural science, he would still not come to reason, but would do something contrary on purpose, solely out of ingratitude alone; essentially to have his own way. And if he finds himself without means – he will invent destruction and chaos, he will invent all kinds of suffering, and still have his own way! He will launch a curse upon the world, and since man alone is able to curse (that being his privilege, which chiefly distinguishes him from other animals), he may achieve his end by the curse alone – that is, indeed satisfy himself that he is a man and not a piano key!

. . . even go mad, to show they have a will of their own.

If you say that all this, the chaos and darkness and cursing, can also be calculated according to a little table, so that the mere possibility of a prior calculation will put a stop to it all and reason will claim its own – then he will deliberately go mad for the occasion, so as to do without reason and still have his own way! I believe in this, I will answer for this, because the whole enterprise seems indeed to consist in man's proving to himself every moment that he is a man and not a sprig! With his own skin if need be, but proving it; by troglodytism if need be, but proving it...

—Fyodor Dostoevsky (1821–1881), *Notes from the Underground*, Part I, Section 8

Has the SSPX Lost
Its Charity?

"CHARITY" IS A word both used to name the greatest of virtues, and misused to name a multitude of sins. Where this confusion comes from is worth examining on the occasion of a recent letter from a Catholic in Florida.

He writes: "Please answer rumors that the Society of St. Pius X, its seminaries and its schools, have lost their charity and are so harsh, judgmental and filled with animosity towards the Conciliar Church that they are becoming a cult. Defensive and fearful of the outside world, they are with their spirit of 'Thou shalt not' falling into the opposite extreme from Vatican II."

To this question Our Lord himself gives the immediate and practical answer: judge by the fruits. It is certain that the SSPX is at present a major source of priests ensuring the continuance of the Traditional Faith, worship, and sacraments. It must constantly be judged from their actions whether these priests are keeping or losing their Catholic balance. Thus on June 22 here in Winona upwards of a thousand Catholics were blessed with brilliant sunshine for the largest ordination of priests to be held yet at the Society's seminary in the USA, but it is only as these priests begin to circulate in Florida and wherever else they are sent, that Catholics will be able to judge for themselves whether the Society is taking on the spirit of a cult.

However, behind that practical and unfailing answer to the rumors, there hangs a more general question, concerning which there reigns a great deal of confusion in people's minds today: What is true charity? When do people fall into extremism? What does it mean to be judgmental? What is a cult?

The confusion arises ultimately from the clash between two opposite worldviews: the ancient Catholic worldview whereby God is God, and the new humanistic (Judeo-Masonic) worldview whereby man is God. By whatever Catholic Faith Catholics still have, they read life according to the first worldview, but from the apostasy of the nations built up all around them over the last few centuries by the Judeo-Masons, they come under a fierce pressure, of which they are often unconscious, to reread life according to the second worldview. From the mixture of the two contradictory worldviews comes the confusion.

For if God is God and men are His creatures, designed by Him to merit in this brief life their eternal happiness with Him in the next, then in order for men to get to Heaven they must be given not what they think they want, but, whenever the two things differ, what they really need, and it is God who will have laid down what men really need. On the contrary, if man is God, then men are the divine measure of anything they need, and all their wants are to be satisfied as divine wants, even if they constantly change. From these two sources come two quite different ideas of charity.

Thus on the one hand, if God is God, then reality is as He made it and not such as men would remake it. Now in reality all love or desire must follow some knowledge, for nobody can love or desire what he in no way knows. This is common sense. For instance: She: "I want to go shopping." He: "Yes, honey, but for what?" She: "I don't know, but once I get to the shops I will find out!" He: "Oh, my hard-earned dollars!" She knows, and so can want, the delights of shopping in general, but it seems she cannot desire anything in particular to go shopping for until she knows it by seeing it in the shops. Some knowledge must go ahead of any love.

Now charity is a love, in reality a supernatural love of God, and of neighbor in and for the love of God. "Supernatural" means that in reality charity is above any natural strength or powers of man, in its origin and in its object. As to its origin, it can come to a man from God alone. No man can, by his own merely human efforts, acquire or increase his own charity. As to its object, charity loves God not just as man can love God naturally from the world of nature, but as God is in Himself, infinitely high above all possible realms of mere nature.

It follows that ahead of this love must go such a knowledge. That knowledge (in the broad sense) is supernatural Faith, having for its origin God alone, which no man can give himself by his purely human efforts, and having for its object the supernatural God as He is in Himself, way above the highest idea that man's mind can naturally form for itself of the Maker of the Universe. But how then can man's mind have any such idea of God? Only by God's revealing Himself as He is in Himself, for instance "One in Three and Three in One," a revelation which nothing obliged God to grant to men, but which He did in its fullness bestow on men through His Incarnation, when the Second of the Three Persons took flesh, and for one human lifetime walked as a man amongst men.

Now the essence of what Our Lord Jesus Christ confirmed naturally and revealed supernaturally to men in that lifetime is summed up in the Creeds of His one Church which all lay out, more or less elaborately, the same essential truths. And the above-natural knowledge, or gift of mind, by which a man assents to those truths, is the Catholic faith, which is not just a cozy glow in my breast, but a knowing assent in my mind to a quite determinate set of truths, namely the Faith laid before my mind by that instrument of God which is His one and only Church.

From all of which it follows that if God is God, then only a believer who enjoys that fullness of the knowledge of God which is the Catholic Faith, can possibly have that fullness of love which is true charity. Catholics may, alas, have the Faith and not have charity; non-Catholics may also not have the Faith and yet – above all by an imitation or a heritage of Catholicism – have a semblance of charity, but true charity necessarily requires beforehand assent to the Catholic Faith, at least implicitly.

That is why believing Catholics are remarkably united amongst themselves by their Faith (did not Our Lord say that men would recognize His disciples by their love for one another?). That is why dissension amongst Catholics is so scandalous. That is why the Catholic Faith is so important, and why heresy destroys charity. Heresy matters! That is why Catholics are in duty bound to love non-Catholics towards Catholicism, but cannot love them independently of Catholicism. That is why, if God is God and took flesh as Jesus Christ, the modern churchmen's ecumenism, whereby non-Catholics are to be loved with – and even for – their non-Catholicism, is intrinsic nonsense.

On the other hand, if man is God (or if God matters as little as religious liberty would have Him matter), then we have a very different picture of "charity."

If I think I know man as man to be the highest being, then I can only love man as man as the highest being. But man as man is full of error, pride, weakness, and sensuality. Therefore the new "charity" will love man with and for the error and vice that are his ruination, because these are what he clings to. What kind of love is that?

At the back end of our poor 20th century, it takes the following form: when all Christendom held the Catholic Faith, the natural effect was a universal love amongst men which made life as relatively cozy as it can be made in this valley of tears, so that in today's after-glow of Christianity, when most men have lost all idea of the Faith, still they remember the cozy effects of all-round love, and so want to enjoy them. Hence modern "charity" – a mushy warmness towards all my fellow human beings, regardless of their beliefs, and with no desire to get them out of their errors or vices. That is the Judeo-Masonic version of love amongst men, coming from the rejection of God and leading to the abjection of men, and which, when it infects churchmen, produces today's "ecumenism."

But notice how, if true charity or love amongst men depended on the true knowledge of God, the cozy effects amongst men cannot long survive the loss of that knowledge of God. That is why today's after-glow of Christianity is fast fading, growing cold, and why today's mushy "charity" is rapidly turning into mutual alienation and hatred amongst men. That is why the most tolerant of liberals yesterday have – incredibly! – swallowed down today the most intolerant expression of "politically incorrect" with which to brand those who disagree with them, and why tomorrow the most "charitable" of men will swallow down the next Satanically clever ticket with which anyone will be discredited who still believes in God.

So, to get back to our original questions, true charity towards men is that love of neighbor proceeding from a Catholic knowledge and love of the true God who created him for Heaven, whereby we wish to our neighbor every good by which he can get to Heaven, for the greater glory of God and for the salvation of his soul and body which will otherwise burn eternally in Hell.

Then "extremism" as a word of blame cannot be applied to anyone who does all he prudently can to save his neighbor's soul. It can only be applied to someone who either so exaggerates one part of the Faith against another as to dislocate the foundation of charity, or mistakes charity by using such means to save his neighbor's soul as serve only to alienate him. Similarly being "judgmental" can only mean making judgments on people which are out of line with the Faith or counter-productive in the saving of souls (but let it be remembered that it is by no means always the apostle's fault if the Gospel is rejected!). Finally, the word "cult" might be used for any worship or practice offending against the Catholic Faith or practice of the Church in the saving of souls, but it cannot be used for the teaching or doing of whatever the Catholic Church has always taught or done.

So, to answer the rumors from which our friend in Florida set out, he must ask, when they pass him by again, in exactly what such and such a Society priest – or any priest – is departing from Catholic Faith and practice. If the departure is real, which he can examine for himself by checking it against 2,000 years of Church history, then the harsh words apply. But if the departure is only apparent, or is a calumny, then our friend should reckon he is falling foul of misunderstandings of "charity." If God is God, then there is such a thing as sin, and sinners must only be loved despite their sins, not with and for them.

Dear friends, you have seen us through another peaceful and successful school year here at the seminary, culminating in the ordination of nine priests, about whom you can read in next month's *Verbum*. We owe great thanks to God, and many thanks to yourselves. Please continue your support, however little.

May God grant us to put our trust in Him, and not in the machinations of men, or their pieces of paper!

The Charity of St. Pius X

CONCRETE EXAMPLES OFTEN convince people better than abstract principles. Last month we argued about the difference between apparent and real charity. Let us this month give a notable example, which teaches many other lessons besides, from the beginning of this century.

A book appeared recently in French (it may or not appear one day in English) entitled, *The Conduct of Pius X in the Fight Against Modernism*. It contains the French translation of a document from 1950 which served in the Process of the holy Pope's Beatification and Canonization, to examine and clear away "certain objections concerning the conduct of the Servant of God in the victory over modernism."

The objections bore on three main points, but they all come down to the accusation that he lacked charity. The answer, proved by the documents quoted in this book, is that Pius X was full of charity even towards the Liberals that he rebuked and held in check, but to understand this real charity requires, as argued last month, the real Faith (no love without prior knowledge), which is why Liberals, because they do not have the real Faith, neither understood then, nor understand now, the charity of Pius X.

The first of the three points was Pius X's attitude towards Catholic journalism. Then as now, between the integral Catholics on the one side and worldly Liberals on the other, there were inside the Church all shades of Liberal Catholics, or Catholic Liberals, seeking to soften the antagonism between the Church and the modern world. When it came to the press, the Liberal Catholics encouraged the Catholic press (or part of it) to gain readership and influence amongst Liberals of the world by muffling their Catholic convictions and ideals, and by "tolerating" Liberal errors. No, said Pius X, rejecting this so-called "penetration press": "The truth needs no disguise; our flag must be unfurled; only by being straightforward and open can we do a little good, resisted no doubt by our adversaries, but respected by them, in such a way as to gain their admiration, and little by little to win them over to the good." (Letter of October 20, 1912, to Fr. Ciceri)

This distinction between a truly Catholic press and a semi-liberal press is necessary by way of background to understand the second of the three objections to Pius X's beatification: his conduct in the major controversy that raged in early 1911 in the Church in Northern Italy between Cardinal Ferrari of Milan and Monsignors Gottardo and Andrea Scotton of Breganza, brother priests and editors of a review called *The Rescue*.

This review they had founded in 1890 with the encouragement of Pope Leo XIII, who became a regular reader, to alert Catholics to the special dangers then current of scientism (an exaggerated trust in modern science) and hedonism (the unbridled pursuit of pleasure). So when Pius X became Pope and in 1907 issued his great Encyclical letter *Pascendi* against an even greater danger from within the Church, the treacherous heresy of modernism by which churchmen, while preserving all outer appearances of the Faith, sought to transform

Richard N. Williamson

its inner substance by adapting it to modern godlessness, it was natural for the Scotton brothers to rally to the defense of the Pope's cause. Alas, such clarity and courage were rare in the supposedly Catholic press, which dismayed Pius X by its general lack of understanding and support. So in 1908 the Scotton brothers received from Pius X through his Secretary of State a warm note of encouragement.

Now they may not always have been prudent or measured in the vigor of their attack upon modernism, but they were relying on public facts and inside information when in 1910 they declared that in the Seminary of Milan there was "a seed-bed of modernism." Cardinal Ferrari of Milan was indignant: how dare a Catholic journal so impugn the honor and integrity of the Seminary with its Professors and Superiors, and the Diocese with its Cardinal? The "good" Cardinal was convinced that there was no trace of modernism in his seminary or diocese.

However, when he complained about the Scottons to Rome in January of 1911, Cardinal De Lai replied on behalf of Pope Pius X that howsoever it might be in the Milan Seminary, the evidence indicated that there was not a little modernism in the Milan diocese, and even if the Scotton brothers had been excessive in their manner, still the present danger to the Church from modernism and the media was not the moment to come down hard on real defenders of the Faith like the Scotton brothers.

In February the Liberals seized upon this dispute between churchmen to create an uproar in the media, which made Pius X call upon all concerned to stop the polemics. However, towards the end of February, Msgr. Gottarao Scotton gave an interview to the press which made Cardinal Ferrari again complain to Rome, in the hope that Rome would silence the Scottons.

Again Cardinal De Lai replied that the Scottons were no doubt at fault, but could not the good Cardinal of

Milan see that what the uproar was really about was not modernism in the Diocese of Milan, but the resistance of the anti-modernists? The Liberal Catholics wanted to smash the Scottons in order to hear no more of world and Church being irreconcilable.

In early March, the two Msgrs. Scotton wrote separately to Rome that they would do anything they were asked to do to repair their fault, while Cardinal Ferrari wrote to Rome amongst other things in defense of the Liberal Catholic paper of Milan, *The Union*, which he sensed was being called in question. At the end of March, Pius X himself took up the pen to write to Cardinal Ferrari.

Like Cardinal De Lai, the Pope admitted that the Msgrs. Scotton had been excessive in their manner, but he said that they had been provoked, not perhaps by any doctrinal modernism in the diocese of Milan, but certainly by a widespread practical modernism. In other words, good doctrine might be taught, but it was loosely applied. And Pius X gave the example of the Milan clergy fully supporting *The Union*, a newspaper which he said left many things to be desired from a truly Catholic point of view, while the same clergy wished to exterminate *The Rescue*.

On April 3 Cardinal Ferrari replied to the Pope, more or less justifying the attitude of his diocese towards the Catholic Liberal paper, *The Union*, but on April 14 the Cardinal took a further astonishing step: less than three weeks after the Pope had written to him personally with a list of founded complaints against *The Union*, the Cardinal gave an address to the theology students in the Milan Seminary in which he vigorously defended *The Union*, and said that this was in accordance with the will of the Pope!

When this address came into the hands of Pius X, he was scandalized and so deeply hurt that he said none of

the many other hurts of his pontificate could be compared with it: "Imagine a Cardinal who on Good Friday,
with a quiet conscience, deceives so many poor clerics,
who tomorrow will go throughout the Diocese spreading their Archbishop's ideas as though they were the will
of the Pope; tell me if my grief does not call for compassion, because 'I know not which way to turn,'" he wrote
to his faithful Cardinal De Lai, who passed on the letter
to the Cardinal of Milan.

The latter replied with a flood of tears. He is heart-broken to have offended the Pope. He is humiliated. He will
be saddened to the end of his days. He begs forgiveness.
He never meant to hurt the Pope. He never said a word
disrespectful to the Pope, etc., etc. . . . As for the address
to the seminarians, he never meant it to be copied down
or published. All he meant to say was that *The Union*
should go on improving. There had been no significant
scandal in the Diocese. He was ready to take back anything he said, and would come to Rome if necessary.

When Pius X read this letter, he replied that there had
in fact been great scandal in the Milan diocese because
the Cardinal's defense of *The Union* had been clear and
clearly understood. Let the Cardinal correct the scandal
by conveying the Pope's real thinking to all concerned,
but let him not come to Rome.

This last instruction was intended to calm the agitation, so that the controversy might die a quiet death, but
the Liberals turned it into a refusal of the Pope to listen
to his Cardinals! Thus when on the death of Pius X Cardinal Ferrari went down to Rome for the Conclave to
elect his successor, to an Italian senator remarking on
the people's emotion and veneration for the deceased
Pope, the Cardinal sternly replied: "Yes, but he will have
to give an account to God for the way in which he would
abandon his bishops in the face of accusations being
made against them"!

Truly, as Msgr. Benigni remarked, Cardinal Ferrari had understood nothing.

Dear readers, I cannot tell if from such a brief summary of the controversy laid out in 60 pages of the book, you have been given enough to understand this verdict of Msgr. Benigni (center of the third objection to Pius X's conduct which it will take another letter to relate). I can only assure you that from the documents themselves Cardinal Ferrari looks like a classic case of the Liberal sickness of our times: a man who is as convinced that he is Catholic and charitable, as he is blind to what the Faith and charity really mean (II Tim. 3: 5).

And the disease had reached up to the level of the Cardinals at that time, but Catholic health still came from the Pope. What do you imagine happens when the disease reaches the Pope?

We had the answer a few years ago when the Pope beatified Cardinal Ferrari. Fact.

Dear readers, how can the Lord God get through to our wicked and perverse generation? Surely only by an overwhelming chastisement.

Pray steadily. Pray quietly. Pray the Rosary. Pray unceasingly, says St. Paul. There is only prayer left, said Padre Pio, who died in 1968. And take heart from the enclosed *Verbum*. These nine new priests are an answer to prayer. God will not abandon us if we do not abandon Him.

The 150ᵗʰ Anniversary of La Salette

THIS MONTH, SEPTEMBER of 1996, September 19ᵗʰ to be precise, is the 150ᵗʰ anniversary of the great Apparition of the Mother of God to two peasant children at La Salette in the mountains of eastern France in 1846. The so-called Secret of La Salette, made public by Mélanie Calvat in 1858, is the greatest single portrait of modern times given to us from Heaven, for now and down to the end of the world. That is to say its importance. Here is the apocalyptic backdrop against which each of us today has to play out the salvation or damnation of his soul. By all means read or reread the Secret on the flyer enclosed.

Of course there are souls that will smile at the mere mention of the Mother of God appearing in modern times. Surely such superstition is disappearing with the peasants it was good for, they say. But Catholics know firstly that as our religion raises us up into a unique familiarity with Heaven, teaching us to say to God "Our Father" as no other religion teaches (Gal. 4: 6; Rom. 8: 15), so it also brings down Heaven familiarly upon earth, especially our Heavenly Mother, who has appeared in all centuries to bring souls to her Son, especially in dangerous times like ours. And secondly Catholics know that despite fierce and continuing opposition, the Apparition and Secret of La Salette have been fully approved by the competent Church authorities, so that we are in no danger if we take them seriously. On the contrary, the danger consists in making light of them, or denying them.

In fact, the message of La Salette was a gigantic corrective, or update of Revelation, in the heart of the last century when churchmen especially were in danger of being seduced by modern "progress," or by the liberalism then really getting under way. The fierce opposition, then as now, came from the liberal churchmen preferring to be up-to-date with the world than with the God from whom that world was and is moving away. As Archbishop Lefebvre said, the Church battle in the 19th and 20th centuries is essentially the same.

That is why it is so important for readers to absorb from the Secret of La Salette the mind of Heaven for our own day. For while, for the good of our souls, much in the Secret remains mysterious, nevertheless much is becoming clear, for instance the famous statement that Rome will lose the Faith and become the seat of the Antichrist (column 4). To give flesh and bones to this awful scenario put before us by the Mother of God, let us turn to a modern observer of the Church scene, quite independent of the SSPX, Malachi Martin.

Now here is a man that not everybody trusts, for reasons best known to himself, as far as I can tell, and of which God alone is the infallible judge. But if one judges recent sayings and writings of his as they stand (which is how the Holy Office used to bind itself to judge), then surely they can be commended for throwing much light upon our darkling scene. For the set of audio tapes he issued last year (*The Devastated Vineyard*) and the book he published this year (*Windswept House*) contain terrible accusations against modern churchmen, but there is no trace of bitterness or anger, hardly even of sadness. The spirit remains Catholic, flowing with "the milk of human kindness."

The Devastated Vineyard is a set of three tapes entitled "The Judas Complex," studying the infidelity of the mass of today's bishops; "St. Peter's Successor," examining the question of Pope John Paul II; and "The Essence of Catholicism," proposing action that ordinary Catholics can take when bishops and Pope are failing to defend their faith.

As for the bishops, Malachi Martin says that with a few praiseworthy exceptions, difficult though it is to admit, a solid block of the Catholic bishops in North America (USA and Canada) no longer believe, they no longer have the Catholic Faith. Otherwise they could not behave as they do. How could they drink back "consecrated" wine like at a cocktail party and forbid people to kneel for Communion, unless they no longer believed in the Real Presence? How could they rejoice in altar girls, female administrators and female Eucharistic ministers unless they had ceased to believe in the male priesthood? How could they fail to resist abortion unless they had come to share the abortionists' view that a fetus is a blob of tissue and not a baby? And so on. The bishops' non-Catholic behavior is simply explained by their loss of Catholic Faith.

Malachi Martin says this loss of faith goes "way back somewhere." These bishops may even never have had the faith. In any case their access to high office only confirmed their lack of faith. The "Judas Complex" is Malachi Martin's name for these bishops' taking sides with the world against Jesus in order to get Jesus to be less demanding and more reasonable. There is now a tight bond between the US Catholic bishops and the US Government, which gives the bishops favors they want. Also the bishops do not want to upset those state officials and officers with whom they go to dinner, play golf, etc. The bishops do not want to be confronted by fellow club members being indignant at, for instance, the pro-lifers calling them baby-murderers, and so on. Also the New World Order has a necessary part for the bishops and Church to play as stabilizers of society, so the bishops are happy to go along with the planned replacement of Christ's priesthood by social worker "priests" who keep people happy, manage the plant and the money, and in general make everybody feel good.

So these bishops are far from disappointed, in fact they are delighted by the disappearance of the old out-of-date Church, they persecute true priests and they hate the real Mass with a hatred coming straight from the heart of Satan. When, oh when, asks Malachi Martin, are the "decent conservative Catholics" going to wake up to the fact that the Catholic Church structure is no more, having been snuffed out somewhere between 1965 and 1995?

All of which raises in Malachi Martin's second tape the question of JP2. How can Christ's own Vicar be happily presiding over such an incredible collapse? Firstly Malachi Martin insists, claiming inside knowledge of JP2's election in 1978, that he really is Pope, and that Catholicism without whoever is Pope is not Catholicism. Nevertheless, JP2's ecumenism, and disbelief in the necessity of the Catholic Church for eternal salvation, set a very real problem.

Malachi Martin begins by guessing why Christ might have chosen Cardinal Wojtyla for His Vicar. He imagines our Lord saying to himself at the Papal election in 1978, "My Church is rotten. But if I put in Cardinal Siri of Genoa as Pope, he will fight the rot so that it will in fact go on longer, whereas if I let in Cardinal Wojtyla, the rot will go faster and I can start rebuilding sooner."

Not that the rot is a good thing, nor that Christ can will evil, but he can will to permit evil for a greater good, and in the meantime all Catholics are entitled, even obliged, to resist the rot as best they can.

Then Malachi Martin discusses at length three weaknesses of Pope John Paul II: firstly, he is in philosophy not a Thomist who goes by the inner reality of things, but a phenomenologist who goes by their outer appearances or relations. Secondly, he is from Poland and suffers from that excessive tolerance or broad-mindedness which down history has been a weakness of Poles. And thirdly he is a geo-politician who dreams and makes dream-trips around the world, while the reins of the government of the Church in Rome are seized by his enemies, now pressuring him fiercely to resign.

In brief, Catholics can expect to suffer much at the hands of such a Pope who will neither vindicate them nor protect their religion. Under him, they can expect no good to come out of Rome, only misdirection and imperfection. However, that does not prevent them from defending their own faith, in fact Malachi Martin says that a whole underground Church is being set up independently of the official bishops or Rome, and I think he is referring to a network alongside of, or in addition to, the SSPX. Which is normal. Abnormally normal, but normal. There is a God, and lies remain lies.

This dark picture of Pope and bishops and Rome, which we know from Our Lady of La Salette to be a feature of the end times, is corroborated, even darkened, in Malachi Martin's recent book, Windswept House.To tell harsh truths about the state of the Church in Rome and North America today, he has chosen to write a novel, partly for audience appeal but perhaps mainly for self-protection. If for instance he dared to publish as naked fact all that precise detail of the enthroning of Satan inside the Vatican in 1963 by a double ceremony linking

Rome and South Carolina, one wonders how long he might be left to live, and the same might be true for horrendous details of Satanism and the vice against nature he depicts as being rampant among the upper and lower clergy in North America. As it is, he and anybody else can say, "It's only a novel."

But the novel is built around a very real-life struggle for the heart and mind of the "Slavic Pope," between a handful of loyal Catholics on the one side, and on the other side a global conspiracy of Roman prelates and world politicians scheming to incorporate the Catholic Church structure, but not faith, into the New World Order.

There are fascinating pages in the novel on the mentality of these prelates, deciding that if Mother Church can no longer lick the Process of History, then they must join it; fascinating debates also between an older priest justifying at all costs the Slavic Pope's failure to defend the Faith, and a younger priest who cannot let the failure pass. Devotion against Doctrine. A debate going on in Malachi Martin's mind. He has up till now sided with Devotion, whereas the SSPX sides with Doctrine, but in the conclusion of *Windswept House* is Malachi Martin at last tilting towards Doctrine?

In the third tape of *The Devastated Vineyard*, Malachi Martin's solution was still Devotion. After scanning in the first two tapes the collapse of bishops and Pope, he begins his third tape by surveying the collapse of Christian civilization. The nations no longer acknowledge Christ. In no government of the world do Catholics hold sway. The protective walls are broken down. Wild animals prowl and devour. The police, the F.B.I., the military, the State, the big Corporations, now devour the people instead of protecting them. We are lonely, unhappy, and see no light at the end of the tunnel. Wall Street can collapse, the world economy is shaky, all parts of the world are in contention. The ancient civilization is like dead, being replaced by a new way of life which is feckless, rich, dirty, glamorous and self-satisfied.

As for the Catholic Church, it has been undone by the undoing of its devotion, what St. Paul called piety, expressed in devotions. And Malachi Martin has beautiful things to say about those devout practices of Catholics which were the hallmark of our religion, and which made Heaven and earth so familiar to one another. With their deliberate extinction according to a satanic plan, the Catholic Church and Faith have been extinguished in the people's hearts and minds. For instance, how can a person receive Communion worthily unless he has some devotion to the Person of Our Lord? Impossible. And that is why, to destroy the Church, a "powerful and dirty alliance" of servants of Satan, inside the Church in Rome and outside, are working together, to silence for instance the Mother of God as she tries to make her voice heard at La Salette, at Fatima, at . . .

All of which external influences throw an extra obligation upon parents, concludes Malachi Martin, to safeguard their children's faith. The truth is still out there, and accessible, but to find it, people must want to find it. Parents must search out true priests, the true Mass, the true sacraments. They must believe in that eternity, to prepare for which we have only this life. "This is it!"

Now Catholics who think with the SSPX might wish Malachi Martin would draw his conclusions tighter but it takes time for people to realize that the necessary line of defense of the faith is the "extremism" of Archbishop Lefebvre. Meanwhile Malachi Martin must he reaching a range of souls that the Society cannot for the moment reach, and with many truths close to the heart of Our Lady of Salette.

Catholics, beware! The same Devil who sand-trapped so many bishops, priests and laity in mid-19th century, as Our Lady of La Salette warned, sand-trapped many more in mid-20th century, along the same lines, and he is prowling about to do the same to ourselves. Bing Crosby Catholicism was deadly for the Faith of tens of millions! We must watch and pray and listen to Our Lady, if we wish to save our souls.

Asia and England

WHEN THE BRITISH Empire spanned the globe, the British Navy had a recruiting slogan, "Join the Navy, and see the world." For several years now the SSPX has spanned the globe, and this summer I made, at the request of Headquarters, my third trip around the world, to visit Asia and England.

Of course such traveling has been made immensely easier by the enormous (and usually safe) airplanes which were unheard of in the heyday of the British Navy. How the world is changing! And, unless the machines are destroyed, that change is necessarily in the direction of world unification, which if it does not gather with Christ, is bound to scatter with the Antichrist (Lk. 11: 23). Scattered, or dispersed, is exactly the word now to describe the souls following Christ (Zech. 13: 7; Mt. 26: 31).

Through Asia, relatively few souls as yet have found their way to the old Mass celebrated by priests of the Society in seven different countries. For instance in South Korea and Japan, both countries with order and discipline sufficient to put in the field a mighty modern army, only a hundred or so Catholics profit by the monthly visit of the devout young Society priest, Fr. Onoda, himself from Japan. It is mysterious how God can allow so many souls for so long to live without the Light of the World (Jn. 8: 12). One can only say, men have free will. For instance, Japan had a famous harvest of Catholic martyrs in Nagasaki, just 400 years ago next year, and Korea had a similar harvest, less famous but more numerous, about 140 years ago. But now of course by the principles of ecumenism, Rome is encouraging Japanese and Koreans to rejoice in their Shintoist and Buddhist cultures respectively. Dare one say it? The heart of Asia's problem lies in Europe. It may be "politically incorrect" to say such a thing, but that has nothing to do with whether it is true. "Politically correct" – "Politically incorrect" – stuff and nonsense!

The numbers are more encouraging in the Philippines where several hundred Catholics now attend Mass in our two main centres, in Manila and Iloilo City. But then the Philippines are a Catholic country because it was colonized by Spaniards back in the sixteenth century, as the warlike Koreans and Japanese never were. Then is it so good to be warlike? Is it so bad to be colonized?

Answer: if Heaven exists, then the only true measure of war or of colonization or of whatever, is Our Lord Jesus Christ. Conversely, if Heaven does not exist then Our Lord does not matter, and if Our Lord does not matter then only standards of this world apply, and you have an intellectual, moral and spiritual free-for-all. Either Our Lord, or chaos – He leaves us our free will to choose.

My next stop was Singapore, where a Society priest visits three times a month some 60 souls grouped around a faithful Indonesian family. It cannot be easy to keep the Faith in this unique modern city-state. The population is predominantly Chinese, but following their English-educated leader of many years, Lee Kwan Yew, they are such skilful practitioners of modern materialism that they are, according to some reports, an experimental site for the New World Order, which will try out there devices like kinds of plastic cards that are being planned for the entire world.

So in earthly terms, Singapore is well governed, but as for souls . . . ? Mr. Yew would surely reply, "That is their own affair. We do our part by guaranteeing freedom of religion." And how else will he have in his prestigious English university learned to govern? But meanwhile his countrymen's souls are being sucked into the glamorous quicksands of materialism. Asia's problem lies where the materialism came from – Europe.

Similarly in Sri Lanka, my last stop in Asia, the large island-state off the southern tip of India, where just recently the SSPX set up a house with two priests to sustain a valiant rearguard action, as Catholicism on the island gives way to a steadily more aggressive Buddhism, for instance on the part of the government. But are the Buddhists the problem?

Our two colleagues meet with old missionary priests from Belgium or France who arrived in Ceylon, as it was then called, soon after the Second World War. Apparently, these poor men are completely discouraged. Because of the Buddhist government taking away the fruits of their labors? Not essentially. Rather because the ecumenism of Vatican II has, as Archbishop Lefebvre said it would, cut the heart out of Catholic missionaries' sacrifices and labors by pretending all religions have such value that it hardly seems any longer worth converting anybody to Catholicism! And since this ecumenism comes down from the Pope himself, either these poor men question the Pope or they break their hearts. Mostly they break their hearts. Such was the Catholicism (e.g., "Better in Hell with the Pope than in Heaven without him") they learned in Europe before the Council. The accusing finger points in the same direction.

But what a state Europe finds itself in today! The last stop on my world tour was my own country, England, where for the first time in many years, I spent nearly two weeks. Most of those two weeks were given over to a seven-stop tour of Confirmations, which afforded me the pleasure of seeing how much in quantity and extension the work of the Society has been built up by our colleagues in England over these years.

But England, oh, England! There is a good priest here in the USA who regularly rebukes me for being anti-American. Dear Father, ask our District Superior in Britain if I ever blasted America while I was there on this last visit! (What would be the point?) On the other hand, ask him if I did not more than once suggest that Traditional Catholics in England are shadowed by that old English fault of maintaining the prestigious outer forms while neglecting the inner substance.

Dear Father, if this letter keeps attacking Americanism, it is partly because the soft heresy of Liberalism killing souls all over the world has, since Vatican II and its decree on Religious Liberty, been mutating along Americanist lines, partly because this letter is written in America mainly for Americans, the best of whom can understand, and do profit by, a home presentation of the worldwide error.

Of course there may be souls that pray without too much thinking. May the Lord God hear and bless their prayers, and may they think at least enough to keep on praying, because our world needs prayer more than it needs anything. But the future of Church and world surely belongs to those souls that pray and think as well, because who that does not think can understand what is coming, or imagine how to put it together again afterwards? So may the Lord God doubly bless souls that both pray and think.

There are such souls in the United States, for whom this letter is mainly written. Also in England, only I have no idea how many, as I am not stationed there. But this last visit makes me suspect, if it is any relief to you, Father, to hear it, that as often as over here I attack Americanism, so often if I were stationed over there I would be tempted to attack that deadly English pride which pretended at the Reformation to put the Lord God on an Anglican leash, proceeded to build an Anglican empire that established Liberalism all over the world, and now runs the same risk of putting on a leash, however charming and elegant, the Lord God of Catholic Tradition!

Heavens, dear friends! How we all of us need to be put on a diet of the Old Testament prophets! The Lord God is "a consuming fire," the chalice of His wrath is brimming over, nay, flooding over, and we wish to make sure that He does not exaggerate? We make the angels weep.

Dear friends, somebody once said the Lord God must love beetles, since He created so many varieties of them! Similarly He must love our doing our ordinary daily duty, since there is so much of it. Surely our going to Heaven will depend much more on our ordinary deeds faithfully done, than on any extraordinary deeds. Said Pius X, "Let everyone do his duty, and all will be well." Simple and obvious words? When all is said and done, also profound words.

Let us quietly pray, steadily pray, amongst other intentions for the United States, or England, or whichever is our country, especially for Mother Church, and let us do our daily duty, and that is enough, and it is immense. For the rest, God only requires of us to put our trust in Him.

On Americanism

THERE IS A can of worms I want to open yet again, because these worms do untold harm to Catholics' innards without their even being aware of it. The can of worms is religious liberty.

To reopen the can may be hurtful, but it is made necessary by, for instance, the recent article of a Catholic writer here in the United States of America knocking down with one hand what she builds up with the other, because even while hating Vatican II she believes in one of its key errors, namely religious liberty. Since this writer Understands Otherwise Catholic doctrine, let us call her U.O. and press on with the arguments.

U.O.'s self-contradiction appeared earlier this year in an article criticizing Dr. John Rao's lecture on "Why Catholics Cannot Defend Themselves," an overview of which was sent out with this letter last year. You may remember that Dr. Rao argued that the collapse of the Catholic Church over the last half-century was to be blamed on Catholics having been conquered by pluralism, meaning the widespread modern acceptance of freedom for all different religions to co-exist in peace (religious liberty). For, once a mind holding a single Truth like Catholicism accepts plural truths, its grip on that single Truth is bound to be loosened until it can lose the Catholic Faith. As Dr. Rao said, this disintegration of Truth by pluralism can be especially seen in the United States of America, where the pluralism originally imported from Europe so flourished that it was re-exported to Rome for the Second Vatican Council, to be spread from there by the Church all over the world.

The objection of U.O. to Dr. Rao's analysis is essentially twofold. Firstly, in general, U.O. distinguishes pluralism in the Church, or in the supernatural domain, from pluralism in the State or in the natural domain. Now of course, says U.O., to accept a plurality of truths in the supernatural domain is out of the question for Catholics who know there is only one religious Truth; but to accept a plurality of faiths or religions in the natural domain of the State is not only "in the modern systems of democracy an absolute necessity inasmuch as it secures the peaceful co-existence of diverse religious communities," but also it is a positively good thing because, for instance, "a free competition of different Christian religions . . . has worked well in asserting the absolute superiority of the Roman Catholic Church over all other Christian sects."

Thus, secondly, in answer to Dr. Rao's accusations against pluralism in the United States of America in particular, U.O. replies that "the excellent Christian social order of the U.S. Republic brought forth the most prosperous Christian nation in modern times, simultaneously giving the impetus to the wonderful growth of the Catholic Church in this hemisphere."

On these two points, general and particular, U.O.'s thinking is as common amongst American Catholics as Dr. Rao's thinking is rare. Nevertheless, Dr. Rao is right, and U.O. is in self-contradiction, or, Dr. Rao is Catholic and U.O. is Liberal. Since general governs particular, let us start with her first objection.

To answer Dr. Rao's accusation that pluralism is what paralyses Catholics, she distinguishes Church pluralism, which she admits would indeed undo Catholics, from State pluralism, which she says Catholics should not only accept but also rejoice in. But this distinction rests upon the separation of Church and State, which is a Liberal principle constantly condemned by the true Church. Her distinction wants to place that separation in the mind. Thus in the upper or "supernatural" part of my mind, she wants plurality of truths to be unacceptable, whereas in the lower or "natural" part of my mind, she wants plurality of truths to be acceptable.

But, as Mother Church knows and teaches, that is not how truth works, nor how a truthful mind works. That is only how a divided mind works. Either truth excludes error both in the upper and lower parts of my mind, or it excludes it in neither, but it cannot exclude it in one and not in the other, except in a divided mind. But as the Truth is one, so the mind seeks to be one, so the divided mind is unstable and will seek stability in unity.

Therefore if I refuse Church pluralism but accept State pluralism, one of two things will happen: either by believing firmly that plurality of truths is unacceptable in Church I will arrive at the Catholic position that it is equally unacceptable in the State (although the State will only coerce error if that is both possible and, for the salvation of souls, in the circumstances, prudent); or, being a liberal convinced of the wisdom of pluralism in the State, I will, like so many U.S. Catholics, in effect pay merely lip service to the Catholic Church being the one and only true Church. Of such Catholics (who include too many "Traditionalists") it can be said that their real religion is not their Catholicism, but that which really holds their minds and their lives together, namely their liberalism or Americanism.

Richard N. Williamson

A good illustration of a sane man's natural refusal to split his mind, and hence of the unnaturalness of Liberalism's Church-State split, was to be found in *The Angelus* article of July 1995 by Edwin Faust. During his Pennsylvania boyhood in the 1950's, he wrote, "few then considered that God and country might be at enmity," especially as they were both enemies of Communism. "Bred of an ignorance of history and abetted by Americanist sentiment, that habit of the Catholic mind that blinds itself to conflicts between the Faith and the Republic was taking shape in me. Later, when these conflicts became apparent, they gave rise to cynicism. My mind seemed a collection of beliefs like so many pieces of a puzzle that failed to fit together. As is the case with many young people new to the habit of self-reflection, the weight of contradictions bore down on me and I wanted to rid myself of all I had been taught to that point and begin again" (my underlining).

Along the same lines, to exclude error from the Church but not from the State, as U.O. proposes, is a contradiction that will usually be resolved, given original sin, in favor of error being admissible in both. In vain U.O. hates Vatican II, when the split she proposes between Church and State pluralism contains all Vatican II in a nutshell!

It also, as Dr. Rao claimed, turns men's minds to mush. Here is how. To be different at all, different religions must contradict one another on some point of doctrine (notably the divinity of Our Lord Jesus Christ, or the divine institution of His one Catholic Church). If then the State is to treat all religions alike, the State will encourage in its citizens' minds contradiction, at least in questions of religion. But if contradiction in religion does not matter, then truth in religion does not matter. But if truth in religion does not matter, how can religion matter? (And if truth in religion does not matter, what truth matters? The mind is mush, sentiment is all.)

The United States' founding President, George Washington, wanted religion, any religion, to back the new nation's morals. But how can a religion of doubtful truth back anything? Men's minds do not work that way. To give backing, religion must have truth. But the State which is pluralist in religion undermines the truth of all religion.

Thus God's having over the last 40 years been driven out of the USA public schools is not, as the decent patriots following George Washington claim, despite the First Amendment, but it is, as the indecent but logical liberals claim, because of the First Amendment. Decency is in the long run no match for logic. Principles matter. So if the Founding Fathers bequeathed to the Republic that they founded decent instincts but liberal principles, the contradiction might last for a while, but sure enough, principles in minds eventually prevailed and the Republic is inexorably disintegrating. If Americans now wish to save anything of all that was truly decent in their Republic, they must refound it on integrally Catholic principles.

That is why, to come to U.O.'s second objection, she is only superficially right when she claims that "the excellent Christian social order of the U.S. Republic" gave "the impetus to the wonderful growth of the Catholic Church in the hemisphere." That "wonderful growth" had a mighty collapse in the 1960's, because Catholic bricks were held together not with Catholic mortar but, as Edwin Faust suggests, with Liberal sand. Then was that "wonderful growth" so wonderful? Or, is Bing Crosby "Sound of Music" Catholicism Catholic?

Objection: the 1960's Church collapsed worldwide, not just in the USA Reply: true, all nations were rotten with their own rot, but firstly, it is surely more profitable on this side of the Atlantic to tell of the form the rot took on this side of the Atlantic, and secondly, as Dr. Rao (a New Yorker) truly says, the virus of pluralism originally imported from Europe (England) to the Americas was re-exported from the United States to Vatican II. The essential problem is doctrinal, not national, but because the United States happened to be founded on religious liberty, the problem in the USA is accessorily national as well as doctrinal. Hence a local name for the virus is "Americanism."

So U.O. is superficially right in saying that the US social order promoted Church growth, but Dr. Rao is profoundly right when he says that the pluralism underpinning that social order undermined the Catholic Church. U.O. will surely object that Leo XIII in Longinqua Oceani praised the US social order, but that paragraph of Leo XIII must be read in context, and taken together with everything else Leo XIII wrote on these questions, notably in his great encyclical on "Liberty," roundly condemning religious liberty, separation of Church and State, freedom of the press, etc., etc.

Leo's encyclical on liberty is also presented and explained in the videotapes of the Winona 1996 Doctrinal Session, together with three other basic encyclicals to present the Catholic Popes' clinical diagnosis of today's ills. Surely profitable Christmas presents.

FAQ on the Future of the Church & the SSPX

AS THIS CALENDAR year draws to its close, we are only the space of three years from the third Millennium after Christ. Now Christ does not change, but the times they are a-changing, dramatically. The 1990's are no longer the 1970's when the SSPX began, still less are they the 1950's which, from before Vatican II, look to us today like another world. What then might the 2,000's be? Here are several certainties and a few guesses, in answer to questions coming mostly from readers:

Q: Is the crisis in Church and world showing any signs of letting up?

A: No, on the contrary. And grave though the world crisis is, the Church crisis is incomparably worse because the Catholic Church is meant to be the salt of the earth and the light of the world. As that salt loses its savor, so it is trodden underfoot (Mt.5: 13), and as the light grows weaker, so the world is plunged in darkness. Towards the end of Prof. Romano Amerio's careful and profound analysis in *Iota Unum*, published in 1984, of the errors constituting this crisis of the Church, he wrote that if it is true that the nature of the Catholic Church is now being overthrown from within, "then we are headed for a formless darkness that will make analysis and forecast impossible, and in the face of which there will be no alternative but to keep silence."

Q: *Do you agree with this dark judgment on our future?*

A: Not entirely. The nature of the Church can be neither changed nor overthrown, nor can truth be at a loss to analyze error, nor will the truth be silenced. But the Professor is well expressing how without precedent the darkness is that is engulfing the Church.

Q: *Can you give a few examples, at various levels of the Church?*

A: From top to bottom:

- For instance, the Pope has recently re-enforced the key dogma of secular humanism by declaring that evolution is "more than just a hypothesis," or theory. He is wildly wrong. The theory of evolution is today discredited as unproven by more and more real scientists, i.e., scientists who respect reality.

- Next down, inside the Vatican "a very powerful group" of top-level churchmen celebrate Satanist rituals, according to the well-informed Malachi Martin. (For parallel horrors in the Old Testament, see Ezechiel 8.)

- As for Catholic bishops, as an American ex-diocesan priest told me who is speaking from hands-on experience, conservative bishops who are not modernist in their ideas run into head-on trouble if they try to confront the heresy, immorality, irreverence, etc., rampant in their dioceses, so to lead a quiet life they compromise, which eats away their character, making them finally into caricatures of bishops.

• As for young priests who are traditionally minded, according to a conservative American Catholic magazine one year ago, they hold onto the Faith as best they can, feeling as though they are "waiting for the cavalry to come," but then they find themselves stabbed in the back by, for instance, Rome's approval of altar-girls, all of which leaves them to conclude, "There ain't no cavalry."

• So the laity are being prepared by flyers from, for instance, the Archdiocese of St. Paul and Minneapolis, for "Sunday Celebration in the Absence of a Priest," SCAPs in English, ADAPs in French ("Assistance Domininicale en l'Absence d'un Pretre"), and thus the Catholic Church worldwide is being ruined (No Mass, no Church, bragged Luther).

Q: But how can God be allowing His own Church to fall to pieces like this?

A: Because He chooses so to leave to His churchmen their free will that those who serve the Church well will greatly merit, while out of the evil wrought by the rest of them He has from eternity planned to bring forth a greater good. Out of the present purification of the Church, or end of her 5th Age, will come the Triumph of the Immaculate Heart of Mary, which looks like being the Catholic Church's last and greatest peaceful triumph (6th Age) before her final and most terrible persecution under the Antichrist (7th and last Age).

Q: So we are not today living in the days of the Antichrist?

A: No, but we are living in days very like them, because just as the long-drawn out 5th Age of Apostasy (from Luther to today) is now finally corrupting the long-drawn out 4th Age of Christendom (the 1,000 year Middle Ages), so the swift 7th Age of the Antichrist will corrupt the swift 6th Age of Mary's Triumph. Today we are living through "the end of times," in Greek "kairoi," not "chronoi," i.e., the end of 2,000 years of opportunities for Gentiles to enter the Catholic Church, but after this end of times (5th Age) there is still a way to go to the end of the world (7th Age). If you think this "end of times" is painful, pray not to have to live through the end of the world!

Q: But how much longer will this "end of times" drag on?

A: That is God's secret. Longer, I fear, than we might wish. Some Catholic prophecies speak of a virtual eclipse of the Church, but that seems not to have happened yet. Her structures are still, apparently, standing. The darkness should then be darker yet before dawn.

Q: But can one be sure that there will be a dawn?

A: Absolutely. Back in the 17th century the Sacred Heart told St. Margaret Mary that His enemies will be overthrown just as they think they are on the brink of triumphing. Certainly the Judeo-masons consider they are today very close to total world control. The astonishing thing is how much use Our Lord will make of mere men to overthrow them. It will be a wonder to watch: like St. Joan of Arc, only on a much grander scale. But we must pray more, for God to intervene.

Q: Meanwhile, do you not think the darkness is such as to have taken away our Popes? Is it not logical to think that recent Popes have been so bad that they cannot have been popes at all?

A: I think it is logical only if you exaggerate papal infallibility, as do both liberals and sedevacantists. Both say, popes are infallible and recent popes are liberal. The sedevacantists conclude, therefore these "popes" are not popes. Oscar Wilde said, sentimentality is the bank holiday of cynicism (prolonged holiday today!). Similarly, sedevacantism is the reverse side of liberalism. Admittedly, this is the Church's worst crisis ever. Nevertheless, Church history indicates how far Our Lord can go in allowing His Vicars to err while He works around their errors to prevent them from destroying the Church. True, the pope leads the Church. But the Church is greater than the pope. Sedevacantists are like liberals in almost reducing the Church to the pope.

Q: But if the SSPX refuses sedevacantism and recognizes that these liberal popes are popes, how can it disobey their orders?

A: Because the Catholic Church is greater than the pope, and so when a pope by word or deed (1) disserves the Church (2) gravely, then for the sake of the Church, i.e., out of a higher obedience to God, Catholics may, and sometimes even must, "disobey" the Pope. But the disservice must be (1) real, i.e., to "disobey" we only have the right if we are right, and (2) it must be grave, i.e., Catholics should not even seem to break Catholic unity unless there is serious cause. Neo-modernism is serious cause.

Q: But if you "disobey" the Pope, how can you still recognize him as Pope?

A: Because the pope can make serious errors without ceasing to be pope. The liberals follow the pope when he is right and still follow him when he is gravely wrong. The sedevacantists refuse to follow him when he is wrong and refuse to follow him (do not recognize him) when he is right. Catholic common sense follows him when he is right and refuses to follow him when he is gravely wrong, but that need not mean not recognizing him as Pope.

Q: But how can the SSPX set itself up to pick and choose when it obeys or "disobeys"? How can mere Catholics sift words and deeds of popes?

A: Because mere Catholics have nearly 2,000 years of Catholic Tradition available to them by which to judge when any Catholic, from pope down to layman, is serving or gravely disserving the Church. The presumption is always in favor of authority, but if an angel from heaven brings me some new doctrine other than that which Catholics have always received, then I must anathematize or reject that angel, teaches St. Paul, word of God (Gal. 1: 8). And if I may and sometimes must reject an angel from heaven, all the more may I and sometimes must I reject a pope on earth. And how can I tell when I must do so, except by sifting his doctrine in comparison with what the Church has always taught? If I am right, I have the right.

Q: Well, might you believe in the "Jovite" solution, that there has been a secretly and divinely consecrated Pope?

A: No. The Catholic Church has to be visible (How could God oblige on pain of damnation men to adhere to a Church they could not see?). The Church might consecrate bishops secretly, for special reasons, for instance of persecution, but in no way could the Pope be appointed secretly on whom the whole Church depends. His appointment must be visible, even if, in the near future, it may in some way need to be miraculous.

Q: Then what do you see concerning the next Conclave to elect a Pope? Malachi Martin is saying that, "short of a miracle," John Paul II will die or be replaced within a year by someone who will co-operate with the New World Order and with their agenda of control of population and education.

A: Surely the next Conclave will significantly darken the Church. John Paul II may have such faults as Pope as to at least partly excuse the distress reaction of sedevacantism, but just let sedevacantists see John Paul's successor! Then they may think JP2's was an angel in comparison! They must admit that it is to John Paul's credit that (as Malachi Martin tells us) the globalist churchmen want him out of the way, pushing him to resign if he will not die. Inadequate though he may have been as Pope, objectively speaking, things are set to be worse without him. It is possible to imagine the See of Rome becoming truly vacant.

Q: Why? Do you think the next conclave to elect a pope will not be valid?

A: Possibly. An invalid election has certainly been made easier by one of the recent changes in the rules for electing a pope. From 1179 until earlier this year a two-thirds majority of the Cardinals voting was required, but now a pope may be elected by a one-vote majority, making his election potentially as dubious as any one of the votes electing him. Did the liberals now in power in Rome make this change to facilitate the election of one of their own men? Or do they envisage undermining the one-man rule of the Church, instituted by Our Lord, because an individual man can always let himself be moved by God's grace to block their plans, whereas some more or less democratic substitute like a Cardinals' Committee will always be subject to control by themselves? Interesting speculation.

Q: But would not such a dissolution of the papacy be the end of the Church?

A: Such an eclipse of the Papacy would surely bring on the virtual eclipse of the Church mentioned earlier. But man proposes, God disposes. Just suppose a globalist pope is dubiously elected at the next conclave, thanks to the unwisely loosened rules. It is easy to imagine a parallel with the introduction of the Novus Ordo missal in 1969. Back then, a Catholic had to love the Mass to take the trouble of examining the legislation supposedly mandating the new missal, but if he did take the trouble, sure enough, he found the legislation was so flawed that the new missal is not in fact mandatory. Similarly tomorrow, it may take a Catholic who loves the papacy to question the new "pope" acclaimed by the vile media and accepted by nearly all "Catholics," but if, thanks to the new rules' looseness, the election will have been a fraud, God will have left enough evidence for souls of good will to see clearly that it was a fraud.

Q: But is that not all sheer speculation?

A: Indeed. However it is certain that the New Mass legislation put Catholics to the test back in 1969, and most were found wanting, and that is a pattern being repeated in this crisis of the Church. The liberals are masters of the appearances, and Catholics who content themselves with appearances are letting themselves be constantly deceived. The Lord God wants substance from us and not just appearances. Only those who really seek the truth will find it.

Q: Are you saying that the mass of Catholics today do not truly love God? How dare you?

A: Look at the fruits. How many "Catholics" to-day behave – actions speak louder than words – like Catholics behaved 50 years ago? On the contrary, how many "Catholics" today behave just like their Protestant or secular humanist neighbors? For instance, are not abortions statistically as common against Catholics as amongst non-Catholics?

Q: *But if Catholics were so good 50 years ago, how are they so bad today?*

A: Maybe they were not that good. Here is how an American Catholic wrote to me of Catholicism as she knew it before Vatican II: "In the 1940's and 1950's emotionalism, or devotion, was our religion. It filled our churches for Mass and Novena services. Our Church on Grand Avenue had seven or eight novena services every day and as one service emptied out, the line was backed up in the street to get in for the next service. Yet with all of that we were not practicing our religion. Protestants gave better example than we did, especially in the parking lot after Mass . . . I understand now how saccharine all of this was."

Q: *Do you think that that is a fair description of pre-Council Catholicism?*

A: Judging by the fruits, I am afraid so, to a great extent. How else could the Church have so collapsed in the 1960's? Our Lord quotes "the great commandment in the Law" thus: "Thou shalt love the Lord thy God with thy whole heart, and with thy whole soul, and with thy whole mind" (Mt 22: 37). Catholics cannot afford to be sentimental, like the post-Protestant culture all around them. If they are, the Devil will snatch their minds to mislead their souls.

Q: *Do you see a danger of "Fiftiesism" amongst what are called "Traditional Catholics" today?*

A: Yes, alas. The same causes produce the same effects. The same modern world that made so many Catholics of the 1950's give the appearances and their sentiments to God while they gave the substance with their minds to the Devil, is with us today, all around us, even more so. After all, ever since Protestantism, to give the appearances to God and the substance to the Devil has been the classic way of resolving the tension between them as they struggle for our souls. Hypocrisy is the hallmark of the Age of Apostasy – "I know thy works, that thou hast the name of being alive: and thou art dead" (Apoc. 3: 1). In the 1900's it was modernism. In the 1950's it was Neo-modernism. In the 1990's and 2000's the Devil is sure to be finding new ways of our giving the appearances to "Tradition" while our minds and hearts go dancing with the world. He has no shortage of devices up his sleeve, where the Fraternity of St. Peter and the Indult Mass came from.

Q: *Then nobody should attend the Indult Mass?*

A: The Indult Mass, like the Fraternity of St. Peter, has the official Church's approval for one purpose only, to keep respectively Mass-goers and vocations away from the SSPX, in order thereby to separate them eventually from their Catholic Faith. For a mouse to try nibbling the cheese off a mouse-trap without springing the trap is at best a risky affair.

Q: *But what about souls on their way out of the Novus Ordo? May they not attend the Indult Mass?*

A: You are right. What neo-modernist Rome designed as halfway houses into the Novus Ordo can serve as halfway houses out it. Thus for someone in the mud at the bottom of a well, a niche in the wall halfway up is halfway to the sunlight, but for somebody out in the sunlight that same niche is halfway down to the mud.

Anybody in the sunlight of the Tridentine Mass untrammeled by neo-modernist Rome needs his head examined if he climbs down to the niche of the Indult Mass, halfway down to the mud of the Novus Ordo.

Q: *But does not Michael Davies say that attending the Novus Ordo Mass fulfills one's Sunday duty? And that Archbishop Lefebvre said the same thing?*

A: When Michael Davies says it, it is because he claims that the officially promulgated Novus Ordo Mass cannot be intrinsically evil, otherwise the Catholic Church would be defectible. When Archbishop Lefebvre said it, he meant that the Novus Ordo Mass is objectively and intrinsically evil, but Catholics unaware of, or disbelieving in, that evil, because of the rite's official promulgation, may subjectively fulfill their Sunday duty by attending the New Mass. The third Commandment says, thou shalt keep the Sabbath holy, not, thou shalt attend a semi-Protestant Mass.

Q: *Then how do you answer Michael Davies' argument that if the Pope had officially promulgated a sacramental rite intrinsically harmful to the Faith, then the Church would have defected, which is impossible, because the Church is indefectible?*

A: That is a delicate question, but see nine answers back, concerning the legislation which "enforced" the new rite of Mass: it appeared mandatory but it was not. Now the doctrinal ambiguity and the disciplinary looseness (opening to wide alternatives) intrinsic to the new rite are bad enough to condemn it as intrinsically evil for a sacramental rite, but they are not bad enough to undermine the Church's indefectibility so long as they are not mandatorily imposed upon Catholics. (It is sometimes fortunate that at least in their theory liberals are not given to commanding!)

Richard N. Williamson

Q: But Michael Davies says the SSPX has no competent theologians.

A: He is quite right that the Society priests (and bishops) have almost no doctorates or licentiates from the official Church in philosophy or theology or canon law. However, they do have, following Archbishop Lefebvre, a sense of the Catholic Faith whereby they grasp the gravity of this crisis in the Church requiring old rules to be applied in new ways, beyond most books of theology or law from which those doctors studied whom Michael Davies appreciates. After all, had those doctors grasped the crisis, would it be here? Some of them to this day say there is no crisis! Learned men can be blind!

Q: But should not the SSPX at least be in dialogue with Rome?

A: You cannot dialogue with persons who share none of your basic principles. Right up until the spring of 1988 Archbishop Lefebvre charitably assumed that the Roman churchmen wanted to defend the Catholic Faith of souls, and so he engaged for thirteen years in hand-to-hand discussions with them, but when in the summer of 1988 their actions made it clear beyond doubt that the unchanging Faith of souls was not their concern, then he gave up discussing, and took definitive action to guarantee the Faith's interim defense, God willing, until Rome comes to its Catholic senses. The disagreement had finally showed itself to be too basic for dialogue to be continued.

Q: So the SSPX wants Rome to return to the old religion, so to speak. What does Rome want of the SSPX?

A: Ask them. Our understanding is that they want us to blend into the new religion of the New World Order.

Q: Well, a conservative Catholic magazine here in the USA said that the SSPX in ten years will not be so stoutly affirming papal primacy, and that the SSPX will probably not then be intact.

A: Time will tell. If the SSPX is faithful, the magazine will be wrong on both counts.

Q: The magazine also said that it would take only one of the SSPX leaders to break ranks and join Rome for the SSPX-Rome division to come to an end.

A: How little the magazine understands! The division is not personal. The problem is not between leaders personally. In 1988 an outstanding Traditional leader, Dom Gerard of Barroux, went over to Rome. He made Archbishop Lefebvre weep, but the problem was unchanged. If the Pope and the Cardinals were to come back to the fullness of the true Faith tomorrow, the Judeo-masons would simply start all over again to capture the Vatican for globalism the day after. Conversely, if all half dozen or so present SSPX leaders were to go over to Rome, like Dom Gerard, the best of the SSPX priests and laity might weep but they would refuse to follow. And if all men were, extraordinarily, to abandon the Truth, then Our Lord says the stones in the street would cry out (Lk. 19: 40). The problem is neither leaders, nor politics, nor egos, nor canon law, nor personalities, nor diplomacy, nor misunderstandings, nor lack of dialogue, but the clash between, on the one side, the Way, the Truth and the Life, and on the other side the Father of lies, Satan. Men may shift in that clash from one side to the other, but the clash is eternal and it is not matter for any kind of conciliation.

Q: So be it. But then would not the SSPX strengthen its position by gathering together all Traditional priests?

Richard N. Williamson

Why can't we have unity? Why can't Traditional priests stop fighting one another?

A: Because Catholic unity requires not only the Faith but also authority. As Fr. Calmel said at the onset of the present crisis, any such association "which would profess to be OF the Church but would be neither diocese, nor archdiocese, nor parish nor a religious order . . . would be artificial, man-made and foreign to the established and recognized groups within the Church. As with all groupings, it would be faced with the problem of leadership and authority and all the more acutely the larger it was. It wouldn't take long for it to be faced with the question of authority; being artificial (and thus not an association according to nature or grace) it would find the question of authority insoluble. Rival groups would soon arise . . . Conflict would become inevitable and between these rival groups there would be no canonical means to put an end to this conflict nor even to conduct it." Traditional Catholics would be wise to be grateful for the remarkable degree of unity given to them worldwide by the Faith they share, and to cease complaining of the lack of unity caused by the lack of authority. Let them pray for the Pope and for the Church's hierarchy, and as for the rest, let them endure what they cannot cure.

Q: Then the situation is hopeless?

A: No, says Fr. Calmel, because we know Our Lord will be with His Church to the end of the world (Mt. 28: 20). So even if Church hierarchical authority is steadily being eroded, he says, still each of us at our own level, priest or nun or layman, should exercise what authority he has in order to form bastions of sanctity on however small a scale. These bastions should stay in touch with one another to prepare for the Church's revival when it pleases Our Lord, but they should not seek to form worldwide organizations "which would find the problem of leadership insoluble."

Q: *But our struggle is very lonely. Can we not then co-operate with good Protestants, for instance in the fight against abortion or against corruption in politics?*

A: Be careful . . . Abortion and today's corrupt politics are poisoned fruits but not the poisonous roots of the Great Apostasy, which began with Protestantism. So however good the best of Protestants appear on the surface, deep down they are part of the problem, which is why they are apt to turn to politics as a solution. Sin is the problem. Grace is the solution. The only grace is of Jesus Christ which comes to men essentially through the Catholic Church. No intelligent Catholic will today spend much effort on any action which does not more or less directly rebuild the Catholic Church: "bastions of sanctity (supernatural)", like family, mission, chapel, school, parish, such as the Catholic Church has always built. The Church has also built Catholic States, but that supposes a sufficient number of enlightened Catholics, which we do not have today. Now to form such Catholics! That is action worth attempting! Order doctrinal audio or video tapes from the seminary to start study groups going. How can men demand action, or look for action, without having first thought out what action is really necessary? For instance to kill abortionists might be tempting as action to take, i.e., to remove grave enemies of the State when its competent authorities refuse to remove them. But the disorder of citizens taking the law into their own hands normally disrupts society more than the continued activity of such criminals. Catholic action needs to be well thought out.

Q: *Do you mean a Catholic can never resort to force? Not even if the State violates his family, as wicked States are more and more threatening to do?*

A: The Church has always taught that a man has the right (and maybe, but not necessarily, the duty) to use proportionate force to repel violence or the threat of violence against the person, honor, property of himself or those for whom he is responsible. If a modern State closes in on a man's family, it is that man's responsibility before God to judge whether his using that right is a lesser evil than not using it. In any case, force is not always wrong, especially not defensive force. Therefore there is nothing wrong in owning weapons to be able eventually to exercise such force.

Q: *And supposing homosexuality or divorce break in on the family?*

A: Each case is different and must be handled individually, especially today when the general breakdown of morals means that people may not be subjectively aware of what they are objectively doing. However, God's law does not change and all men have a God-given conscience, and it is no kindness to souls to put cushions under their bad consciences. To be kind to divorce means being unkind to lawful marriage, which means being unkind, yes, to children, who are the ones who suffer from the breakdown of lawful marriage. Similarly to condone homosexuality, one of the four sins crying to Heaven for vengeance, is, objectively, to mock Heaven or to mock God, and it is to help to undermine society, the survival of which depends, obviously, on the normal exercise of the reproductive function.

Q: *But why is society so important? Is it not the individual that matters?*

A: Yes, but God made the human individual to live in society so that if society breaks down, all the individuals suffer. In fact the common good overrides the individual good, as men recognize when they sign up to fight and maybe die for their country. But liberalism makes the individual sacrosanct, which is why we have for instance all these absurd "rights" and lawsuits turning society into dissociety all around us. There is a common good which I undermine by being kind to guilty divorcees or to unrepentant homosexuals. Catholics get "charity" all wrong if like everyone around them they ignore the common good.

Q: *Then Professor Amerio was right after all – let us relapse into silence?*

A: It is true that our circumstances are very difficult, but God does not ask us to conquer, He asks us to give battle, and then He, as St. Joan of Arc says, gives the victory. If in His inscrutable wisdom He has given to Catholics of the 5th Age to fight a 500-year rearguard action, which may soon be over but is not over yet, then that is what it is appointed for us to do. Had Catholics not fought during that half-millennium, it would have been over much sooner, but they would not have gained Heaven. We need not keep silence until it is forced upon us. Truth carries. So each of us in his own station in life must give witness to that unchanging Truth of Our Lord Jesus Christ which we have received from the Church and which alone can save our souls for eternity. Martyr and witness are in Greek the same word. We should not be surprised if living our lives to give witness to the Truth seems equivalent to a martyrdom "Blessed are ye when they shall revile you, and persecute you, and speak all that is evil against you, untruly, for my sake; Be glad and rejoice, for your reward is very great in heaven. For so they persecuted the prophets that were before you." (Mt. 5: 11,12)

Dear friends and benefactors, take plenty of courage, and have a Happy Christmas and New Year. Remember the men's 5-day Exercises here at the seminary from December 26 to 31, as usual, and remember the seminary audio and video tapes for Christmas presents, or presents at any time of year, to get the Church's Truth into circulation.

Pink Floyd's "The Wall"

O NE GETS USED to anything, but nevertheless the music of youngsters in modern Western society is an alarm bell ringing off the wall. In case any readers are comfortably asleep, let them be rudely awoken by a few moments' study of a classic "Rock" album, so that in this month of the Holy Family we can think of what Catholic parents should do.

The rock album in question, Pink Floyd's "The Wall" appeared in 1979. It made quite a stir at the time, even achieving a kind of cult status. The Pink Floyd group is still well-known, making concert tours nearly 20 years later, and numbers from "The Wall" are still played regularly on Rock radio. So "The Wall" has achieved classic status amongst thirty years' worth of Rock albums.

What interests us here is the words of the album, which are made available with the Compact Discs. As for the music, it seems to me not wild, although it breaks into a heavy beat at regular intervals. Above all, it serves the words well, which is what one would expect from a "classic" – these musicians have a message, and their music gets it over. As with – from the sublime to the ridiculous – plainchant, polyphony, Wagner or Frank

Sinatra, the words inspire the music and the music weds the words.

That is why, even if it were true that most fans of Pink Floyd (or of Rock in general) listen to the music without caring for the words – I do not believe it is true, but even if it were – still the words are of central importance, because they are what inspired the music that gets to these youngsters. Tell me what music you like, I will tell you who you are. Tell me the words set, I will tell you the music setting.

Nor may adults excuse themselves from taking seriously the words of, for instance Pink Floyd, on the grounds that these musicians merely make the kind of music that makes lots of money. Of course Rock can make its stars into millionaires, but money is never the ultimate explanation, the question being merely pushed one stage further back – why does this kind of music and not that kind make so much money? Answer, because it is "hitting the spot," it is filling a need.

Nor may adults dodge the accusation that Rock flings in their face, by saying that skilful managers like Brian Epstein of the Beatles see an opportunity to exploit, and merely create the kind of music to exploit it. For indeed musicians are creators, and all down history they have created new kinds of music. But they do not create in a vacuum. What they create is to a considerable extent shaped by what they sense in their audience. Brian Epstein did not create the Beatles out of whole cloth, but out of the vibrations he was picking up from British youth in the early 1960's, and it is because he read the vibrations correctly that the Beatles achieved such fame and wealth.

No. If Pink Floyd also achieved fame and wealth, then Western adults, if they care at all for their youth, must pay attention to the message. Surely the message is, precisely, that the adults do not care! "Rock music is one long, unheard, scream for help," readers of this letter were told last June. Let us take a look. We were unable to obtain in time copyright permission to reprint the lyrics of the 27 songs making up "The Wall," but here is the message of the first 14 songs, which form like a sequence. (The remaining 13 songs are in similar vein.)

(1) The artist tells us he has cold eyes which are part of a disguise. He is obviously at war with the world. (2) Sure enough, modern life may look good, but it is as cold and deadly as thin ice. (3) The artist's father disappeared early from his life, leaving only a snapshot behind. (4) The artist's school teachers were cowardly sadists. (5) His school education was a waste of time (famous lines – "We don't need no education, Teachers, leave the kids alone"). (6) He turns to his mother, who promises to comfort him, but as far as he is concerned, her mothering him means her smothering him. (7) The politicians promised a brave new world, but they lied. There is no blue sky. (8) As for the activities with which most people seek to fill their empty lives, they are a restless waste of time. (9) The artist seeks refuge with any "cold woman" in the "desert land," but in fact (10) the woman he is with means nothing to him. (11) Yet he longs for his girlfriend, but she is running away because, as he freely admits, he only wants her there in order to be cruel to her. (12, 13) In brief, all people around are nothing but bricks in the meaningless build-up of the wall of modern life which alienates and divides people from one another. Conclusion – (14) – this life is good for nothing but to be departed from, a song which has inspired God knows how many young people to take their own lives ("Good-bye, cruel world").

Adults! Wake up! In Western society suicide has become a leading cause of death amongst youngsters – what do you think that means? That we have a wonderful way of life that in all history no civilization on earth has equalled? What is unequalled in all history is so many youngsters singing and dreaming of suicide! Youngsters!! Suicide!! Adults!! Wake up!! They are crying out!! You have got something desperately wrong!!

Understand me rightly. I am not saying that the musicians who make up the group Pink Floyd are saints, nor that youngsters who revel in Pink Floyd are faultless while all the fault is on the side of the adults. As a colleague commented, the revolt behind these songs has something satanic about it, for instance when it sees no more in mothering than smothering (6). No doubt, if these musicians and youngsters think they are only being sinned against and not sinning, they are under a youthful illusion.

But, again, for oldsters to dismiss their revolt as a mere passing stage which they need to grow into and grow out of as part of modern life, is a serious error which the oldsters will pay for, for instance by being euthanized. The revolt against everybody and everything that is expressed by Pink Floyd is so against nature and so unhappy (e.g. 11) that one cannot believe such a mass of youngsters as make stars of Pink Floyd would choose it as a way of life if they had the choice. But the Western materialism inspiring this revolt was chosen for them, by generations and generations of adults that went before them, who, as they grew up, settled for the satisfactions of age-old pride and sensuality made increasingly available by that materialism.

And no doubt it is true that many Pink Floyders in turn will settle for these ever more available satisfactions (say, coach tours of the North Pole in luxury-heated buses). But woe to them if they do! Nature will not be defeated in this rising war against her. She will take a terrible revenge. She is already taking it, in the suicide rate of the young, but worse is to come. The young are right to protest. There is much more involved in Pink

Floyd than just juvenile revolt. Thank Heaven the young are protesting! Their protest is a call from our common human nature which we are violating. Our way of life is rotten. There is a precious spark that is extinguished each time a youngster gives up protesting and joins in building "The Wall," or, as Augustine would have said it, helps raise the city of Mammon against God.

Then what do Catholic parents and adults do? First and foremost, render unto God what is God's. Treating God as though He is of no importance is the heart and soul of the problem. Parents, adore God, love God, give the example of practicing the one true religion of the one true God, with all your mind and with all your heart, in the home. Make the presence of God there as natural to souls as oxygen is to the bodies. Pray the family Rosary, with father kneeling in front, or doing whatever he needs to do to be seen leading his family towards God.

Secondly, parents, concern yourselves with your children. They are your real wealth. God bless you for not having contraceived them or aborted them. But when they are born, your glorious responsibilities are only just starting. Today's world teaches you well how to look after their bodies, but you must take at least as much care of their souls. From the earliest age teach them to pray, teach them to control themselves, to think of Jesus, to make sacrifices, to think of others, to respect and obey you, their parents. They are not in any way your equals.

Love them, but discipline them. Never discipline without love, but also never love without discipline. Give them always good example. They will watch what you do much more than they will listen to what you say. Give them your time. They are more important than your bank accounts. One soul, one world, one eternity. Give time especially to adolescents, who are today desperate for adult counsel, guidance, advice. Adults have lost the art of listening to them! That is why they turn to one another and to the Pied Pipers of Rock. And the Grim Reaper reaps a grim harvest!

Give to your children at all ages instruction. You are their elders. You do know better. Teach them not only their Catholic Faith, but also life. The natural is carrier of the supernatural. No carrier, no carried. Children have to grow up for this world as well as for the next. Teach them a Faith for living and living in the Faith, not some cultish sentimentality which they will toss out the moment they meet the real world. Teach boys handskills, teach girls handcrafts, because "The devil finds work for idle hands." Let children not just eat and go to Mass. Keep their minds and hearts occupied all day with good things, according to their varied talents, so that the Devil will never find a vacuum waiting to be filled by him.

Lastly, keep television and the computer to a minimum in the home. The problem is not primarily the filth so easily available on each of these machines, serious though that is, and more than enough reason to ban both. The real problem is that machines cannot teach people to be people. Only living souls can form living souls. Better, for a child, a live reading than a dead video, as such. Better, to learn life, a live farmyard than a dead cupboard of Nintendo games. The subject needs a letter of its own.

There is also little space left to present the magnificent Pastoral Letter enclosed, by Cardinal Siri. Here is the severity, balance and wisdom of a great churchman tackling what he saw to be a rising threat then, which has turned since into a disaster raging out of control.

Lord, give us back such churchmen! And let us men be men, as You meant us to be, let the dear women be women and let children be children, throughout the New Year, and our nature will be in that much better posture to carry Your sanctifying grace.

It Always Comes Back
To Disregard of God.

W^{E ARE IN} trouble. Dead trouble. Listen to this. In our dear little Midwestern town of Winona, in woodland adjoining the parking lot of a supermarket at the foot of the Seminary's own hill, through this way-below-freezing winter are living in cardboard shacks a dozen teenage children! What?? Yes, our Seminary Secretary (whom many of you know on the telephone) went on a visit of mercy just before Christmas to see with her own eyes the children and their shacks. What on earth?? Why on earth??

It is not a material problem. As one of the woodland girls, 12 years old, told Mrs. Mehren: "My parents said to me, 'We give you everything you can possibly need, so if you don't like it, you can leave!' I left." One 16 year-old boy has been in the woods for three years, and can see no future for himself ("Good-bye, cruel world"?). But no doubt the children still prefer warm hearts in cold shacks to warm houses with cold hearts. Man does not live by central heating alone.

But are not such children an indisciplined exception? Indisciplined maybe, but they are more and more the rule. Check out your own town. The police in Winona know. They regularly go in and break up the shacks, but the children promptly rebuild them! As for lack of discipline, it is all too easy to dismiss these children as indisciplined. Why are they indisciplined? Because they have never felt any warmth or meaning behind any discipline they have known. Human beings need to feel human. Human beings need to feel human.

The point is well made by a New Ager of all people, editorializing in the January issue of a little Midwestern monthly sent to me because it says what this letter was trying to say last month about the message of the Rock group, Pink Floyd. I quote: "The song 'A Brick in the Wall' . . . was a haunting message of alienation ("We don't need no education, we don't need no thought control") . . . It was not just about an education system . . . It was about not listening. It was about treating children as programmed robots moving along a conveyor belt headed toward the job market. Adults didn't get it then and, unfortunately, they still aren't getting it now that they are in the midst of an even more evolved breed of children who will not tolerate the system as it now stands . . . Educators are drugging kids to keep them in their chairs in the classroom. Instead of changing the 'system' to meet the needs of students, they change the students to work within the system . . . "

Do readers remember who was the last person quoted in this letter as saying exactly that, only he said it for adults as well as children, namely people being fitted to technology instead of technology being fitted to people? It was the Unabomber. When "sane" people are crazy (inhuman), it seems to take "crazy" people to be sane (human).

Of course children need discipline, and Rock musicians for instance are indisciplined by principle, but again, why? It is easy to dismiss "grunge" music (a recent kind of Rock) with a description like this one appearing in last November's issue of the Mindszenty Report: "Grunge music for the unenlightened has no melody, sounds something like a 20-car pileup on the freeway at rush hour and is executed by very thin young men with blank stares and wardrobes from a skidrow flea market . . . " But one must ask: have the wise elders of such decent Catholic publications as the Mindszenty Report taken the full measure of phenomena such as "grunge" Rock which they so brilliantly dismiss? Do they see any serious problem at all in the king of "grunge" Kurt Cobain's being idolized by millions of teenagers even as he blows his own head to smithereens with a shotgun? "Where's the outrage?" was the title of the Mindszenty Report article. "Where should the real outrage be directed?" is the question good Mindszentians should be asking. There are today thousands of decent citizens and dozens of decent organizations denouncing the filth rising all around us, but how many of them are asking the right questions? Decency is not enough, especially in Catholics. What future do even decent men have when their youth are resorting to shacks and shotguns? Euthanasia – if they are lucky.

Of course problems of youth are no more nor less than symptoms of problems of adults. To your materialistic and outwardly despairing Rock musician corresponds exactly your materialistic and inwardly despairing businessman (cf. T.S. Eliot's "Wasteland"), and between them, of course, the family falls to pieces. Alas, decent businessmen convince themselves that the ever-rising stock market, economic prosperity and technological progress prove that democracy with separation of Church and State and religious liberty are the founding principles of the most wonderful way of life ever known to man.

To such adults the Lord God keeps sending wake-up calls. For instance here in the United States we have had over the last few years an unprecedented series of floods, fires, heatwaves, snowstorms, droughts, earthquakes, all kinds of natural disasters to get men's attention, but self-satisfied materialism seems to be stuck in the businessmen's mouths like a baby' pacifier: Federal Disaster Relief will fix the problem. Our Government can see off these so-called "acts of God." In fact our Government replaces God, who is just a sugar-daddy that should be content with the candy graciously given to him on Sunday morning by our religious liberty.

That is how "decent" businessmen think, and they include all too many "Catholics." But the Lord God of Hosts has news for them all. He exists, and He is immensely patient, but He does not play games, and He is not replaced by Government. Witness the bombing of the Alfred E. Murrah Building in Oklahoma City, Oklahoma, on April 19, two years ago, as presented in the enclosed *Verbum*.

"Oh dear", I can hear readers say, "here we go into politics again!" No, we are going into the religious problem behind politics, which is the modern nations' making of politics into a substitute religion, and of their government into a substitute god, because they have turned away from the True God.

"But can't you give us some spiritual uplift instead of the dreary world which we have all too much of?" The uplift should be from the sugar-and-spice "God" of Sunday morning to the real Lord of Lords and King of all days of the week, to whom all politics and politicians are subject, and who blinds apostate nations with the media they trust and scourges them with the governments they pretend to put in His place.

"But why drag up the Oklahoma bombing which is nearly two years old?" Because for people who pretend to respect practical facts and scientific evidence, here as it happens was a clear case of a crime engineered to betray the people and covered up by the media to deceive the people. Let all readers stop thinking now we have government by the people or for the people. Modern democracies are a sham. The system is not working. Our help is in the Lord God alone. The system is in the hands of traitors by a just punishment of God.

"Then you are a conspiracy nut!" Logically, whoever believes in the system cannot believe any conspiracy controls it. But the great advantage of the Oklahoma bombing (as opposed to, for instance, the rather more complicated JFK assassination) is that for anyone who takes the trouble to examine the evidence, it is as clear as can be that those who are presented in public as having committed the crime, cannot possibly have done so. The real criminals have been hidden from view, unless of course the Murrah Building columns fell down all by themselves. They were certainly not blown down by the public van bomb.

"But who except right-wing terrorists would have any motive for such a crime?" Whoever thought to profit by it. Our secret government sought to stampede public opinion and Congress into passing "anti-terrorist" legislation to help clamp the One World tyranny upon the American people. It also sought to get its public President re-elected in 1996 (as happened) after his party did so poorly at the polls in 1994. He himself told a journalist that between those dates it was the Oklahoma bombing that turned his bad fortune into good fortune.

"'Secret government'! What nonsense! We are living in America!" If you wish to believe the Murrah columns fell down by themselves, you will believe it. "Conspiracy nut" is an expression flowing from the liberals' conviction that their way of life and government is far superior to anything that went before it. Let us suppose that what went before was open tyranny. Oklahoma demonstrates we now have secret tyranny.

"You are just being anti-American once more!" All nations today are going the American way, but that is not the fault of Americans, it is the nations' own fault. The problem is worldwide apostasy which it takes a Catholic to understand, but which any historian knows neither originated in, nor runs deepest or guiltiest in, the United States.

"But your anti-Americanism is killing the apostolate!" Anti-liberalism scares off many liberal Catholics today, but uncompromising Catholics are the only hope for tomorrow, be they only a handful. Church and world depend on such Catholics.

"Well, I don't want to know. I prefer my God and my country to be made of sugar and spice and all things nice." Then skip the Oklahoma article, and stick to sugar and spice, but do not be surprised if your children walk out on your world of lies, and even turn the shotguns on you! It is already happening more and more. Wake up!

Nor will the "fix-it" mentality fix the problem, any more than it would fix the children in winter shacks. Here is the fix-it mentality as expressed in a recent newspaper magazine article on the future of the United States. "We perceive our civic challenge as a vast, insoluble Rubik's Cube. Behind each problem lies another problem that must be solved first, and behind that lies yet another, and another, ad infinitum. To fix crime we have to fix the family, but before we do that we have to fix welfare, and that means fixing our budget, and that means fixing our civic spirit; but we can't do that without fixing moral standards, and that means fixing schools and churches, and that means fixing the inner cities, and that's impossible unless we fix crime."

Poor non-Catholics! What darkness they walk in! But Catholics know that that vicious circle is broken into by attendance at the real Sacrifice of the Mass. There they learn to make real sacrifices for their spouses and children (not just "quality time" – hypocritical horror! But quantity time for one's nearest to make them dearest). Then marriage, children and the family recover, and with this seeking of the kingdom of God and His justice, the recovery of all things we really need is added unto us (Mt. 6: 33). So the follow-up question which the decent Mindszentians should be asking is, "Where is the nearest true Mass?"

Dear friends, please do not swamp the Seminary secretary with offers of blankets for the shack children, but please do pray for their souls, and do give time and your human heart to some youngsters within range. Our Lord died for every one of them!

A New "Concentration Camp"

ALRIGHT, YOUR EXCELLENCY, if you are so smart at diagnosing the world's problems and the problems of modern youth, what do you propose to do about it?

I have a wild idea. An idea for a camp to help young men to concentrate. In other words, a concentration camp. Here it is.

Next to the Seminary building is a convent building originally put up by the Dominicans for Sisters who would help look after the material needs of the Dominican priests and novices. It has eight cells upstairs and all rooms needed for independent living downstairs. On an experimental basis for one school year, either autumn '97 to summer '98 or autumn '98 to summer '99, I am thinking of inviting eight or ten selected young men to spend a school year in the convent learning English grammar and literature, music, history, Euclidean geometry and Latin.

The young men would be around 18–20 years of age. They would be chosen for their capacity and readiness to learn the best things which an old-fashioned Cath-

olic education used to teach, but which almost no education teaches any longer. Therefore they would have
no interest in accreditation or the modern world, or degrees, whether on pieces of paper rectangular or shaped
like a frisbee (frisbees are circular pieces of plastic, the
throwing of which through the air constitutes one of the
major occupations of students at most higher institutes
of learning in the USA today).

These young men would begin the day by attending
Mass. Lessons would follow until midday. After lunch,
there would be two hours of manual labor, preferably in
the seminary fields. Late afternoon another lesson. Evening, supervised study. The young men would be essentially self-motivated and self-disciplined. They would
keep elementary house rules, e.g., no smoking, no television. At the end of each month they would be entirely
free to leave the whole thing behind them, but if they
chose to stay, they would have to submit to the demands
made upon them for the next month.

At year's end they could apply to enter the seminary if they wished, but there would be no obligation
or pressure whatsoever in that direction. Nobody can
unwillingly serve God. On the other hand the seminary would undertake to cover all costs of board and
tuition (unless that attracted the wrong young men),
because our world will more and more desperately
need humanly oriented human beings. The seminary
would calculate that to put even only half a dozen
young men into circulation with their heads set for
one school year straight on their shoulders, would be
a worthwhile investment. Mother Church is generous.
Money would not be wasted, but nor would it be the
problem.

"With their heads set straight on their shoulders . . . "
Much could be said about the six subjects chosen above
for the concentration camp's curriculum . . .

Firstly, to learn the grammar of one's native language is the very beginning of learning how to think. Since the New World Order's secret masters want nobody to think but themselves, wisely for their purposes they have eliminated the learning of grammar from all school systems they have taken care to control. Let Our Lord's servants learn this much natural wisdom from His enemies by giving high priority in schools to the mastery of grammar in the native language. Catholics must think.

Close after English grammar comes Latin, the staple diet of boys' schooling yesterday, but despised today when boys are not meant to become human or to think. As to the thinking, Latin is a language of which the venerable age and the complicated but logical structure exercise the mind rather more than do modern languages. So it requires from pupils a higher proportion of thinking to memory work, and from teachers – extra advantage – proportionally less correction work.

However, with Latin the thinking is always linguistic and so human thinking, as opposed to the inhuman thinking called for by the sciences, mathematics or computers. These work in quantity, which militates against quality. Computer education is a contradiction in terms. But Latin at the outset forces a boy to discern for instance subject and predicate, which is a distinction flowing from the very structure of the human mind. Also Latin always works in human terms, e.g., "the slave killed the queen" (pure opera soapae), as opposed to "$H_2+O = H_2O$." Then again these human terms work towards access to all-time classics of humankind : Cicero, Ovid, Virgil, Horace, etc.

Finally these Latin classics are at the root of Western civilization. By divine Providence, pagan Rome provided the central launching pad of the Catholic Church. Pagan Romans were the raw material of the first Roman Catholics. So the study of Latin gives access, as no other study can do, to the natural lifeblood of our supernatural Faith. Only three languages were nailed to the head of Our Lord's Cross. Latin was one of them.

The mention of literature brings us to the third component of the projected concentration camp's curriculum: English literature. Once more, the world around us has it all wrong. "Eng. Lit." as it is called in modern universities has become there a monster like the rest of the so-called "humanities," engendering students who chant "Hey, hey, ho, ho, Western culture's got to go." This is understandable, because they are being given no serious reason to value that culture, because the Catholic Faith from which over centuries it came, and the one true God of whose creation it tells, are being rejected by the students' so-called teachers in favor of an all-embracing fantasy coming from hell and leading back to hell via the Antichrist. That is why Catholic parents must be extra careful today in committing their children to "humanities" in modern "universities."

On the contrary in our concentration camp, the centuries of "Western culture" would come flooding back into their own. The history, music and literature of those centuries show to youngsters, as nothing else can, how the Gospel fits in concrete life, because that "culture," for centuries taken for granted, gave in stories, pictures and music all kinds of models for thinking and living in accordance with our God-given nature, which was a good start towards being able to live in His grace.

Now that culture is being taken from us by the masters of the New World Order pushing upon us their substitute stories, pictures and music to seize our imaginations, minds, and souls: cinema, television, newspapers, advertising, MTV, Rock. Human nature cannot do without stories, pictures and music. He who controls the stories, pictures and music controls the men. That is why the concentration camp would be full of Catholic history, Shakespeare and Mozart.

Note, Catholic history, because non-Catholic history deserved to be dismissed as "bunk" by Henry Ford, just as the desiccated horror of deconstructed "Eng. Lit." deserves to be thrown out of all schools. History has been deconstructed by the will to rule out of it Jesus Christ. It has been written back to front to get rid of Him. On the contrary the five-volume *Puritans' Progress* recently published by the Angelus Press is a valiant initiative to rewrite American history front to back. "Historia magistra vitae", said the Latins. History rules life. He who writes the history books writes the future.

As for the importance of music, does any reader of this letter still need persuading? Ideally, concentration camp inmates would perform music rather than just listen to the wealth of good music available on tape and disc, because, again, live music is human whereas tape and disc are mechanical. So inmates would surely be obliged to sing as well as to listen to the great instrumental composers.

Finally Euclidean geometry would teach the young men to think logically. Euclid is almost pure logic, without the technicalities of Major, Minor and Conclusion, but with all the substance, and with clear diagrams as the working matter. Today's schools have succeeded in disconnecting even mathematics and geometry from reality! Whole systems are constructed upon the fantasy that parallel lines meet, or that minus numbers have square roots! Heaven help us!

And so at the end of such a year, the young men might seem unfitted for today's world, but they would be that much better fitted for reality. It is all very well to say that education must go with the times and fit the computer model. Reality says that these times and that model do not fit human beings, so will not work. Human beings are not machines. The world is still run today by men who understand human nature, however horribly they misuse that understanding. Witness that little book of 100 years ago which was a veritable blueprint for our century's horrors, including the disabling of the Catholic Church. The concentration camp would help restore the Church by putting the start of some real Catholics back into circulation.

However, there is a major difficulty. Where do we find a master for the camp? As a colleague said, he must be a combination of Socrates, General Patton and Michael Jackson! Socrates for the ancient wisdom, General Patton for the camp discipline and leadership, Michael Jackson for the ability to get through to young men of today, who can be something of a breed apart. Does anybody know of such a man? In my imagination he is a Catholic widower, ex-military, presently sidelined, withering from frustration at being unable to do any real teaching, who would love to have access to a mini-dozen red-blooded Americans to teach them for the love of Christ a dose of reality, regardless of what he or they would do the year after. To heaven with career, resumes or, since I have Scottish blood, salary!

Can anybody think of such a man for one experimental year? If the Lord God wishes the experiment to take place, a man will be found. If not, the seminary goes quietly on its way, and relies on others to restore "opera soapae." Man proposes, God disposes.

May He have mercy upon us all, may He protect and guide us, and may His Mother keep us all safe under her mantle.

The Resurrection: An Historical Fact

A PRIL THIS YEAR falls wholly in the season of the Resurrection. Let us consider for a moment this foundation stone of our religion.

That the human material body of Our Lord, having been nailed to the Cross and separated by death from His human soul, and laid in Joseph of Arimathea's tomb – that this very same body rose reunited with His soul, and re-emerged alive from that tomb, is a historical fact – F-A-C-T – as easy to prove now as it was then, to any reasonable mind not blinded by prejudice. Nor does this proof require that somebody should already have the Catholic Faith. On the contrary, this proof is a foundation stone in anybody's mind on which to rest the Faith.

Thus when St. Peter summoned the Jews of Jerusalem to do penance and be baptized in the name of Jesus Christ (Acts 2), he did not argue that they should believe in Christ in order to believe in the Resurrection, on the contrary he argued that the evidence for the Resurrection (Acts 2: 32) was the strongest argument for Jesus being the Lord and Christ in whom therefore they should believe (Acts 2: 36, 38).

Now Peter appealed in this speech firstly to a knowledge of the Old Testament which most Jews then had but which most Catholics no longer have, and secondly to the living eyewitnesses of the risen Lord, who have long since died. Yet still we can say that the Resurrection is a fact as provable now as it was then, independently of the Faith. All that is required is a minimal recognition of the realities of human nature and human history.

There are two main arguments, one positive from the behavior of Our Lord's friends, the other negative from the behavior of Our Lord's enemies. Let us take the positive argument first, from the behavior of the Apostles.

When Our Lord allows Himself to be captured in the Garden of Gethsemane, they do not behave like heroes, they all run away (Mk. 14: 50–52). When Our Lord is crucified, only one of them is, with a group of women, standing by him (Jn. 19: 25,26). When the Apostles meet together on the evening of the day of the Resurrection, they meet behind closed doors, "for fear of the Jews" (Jn. 20: 19). And doubting Thomas not being with the other ten on that occasion refuses to believe that Jesus appeared live to them, despite their manly testimony (Jn. 20: 25).

This is not the picture of a pride of apostolic lions, ready to spring upon the world and conquer it for Christ. On the contrary we see what we would expect, a group of ordinary decent men, dismayed by the capture and brutal death of their beloved Master, and wholly discouraged.

Yet 50 days later we see them, led by Peter, setting out upon that conquest of the civilized world for Christ, launching the 300-year process of the conversion of the Roman Empire, which is a historical fact. That extraordinary process, of lifting a whole corrupt empire to the heights of a sublime but demanding religion, can only have been launched by an original core of deeply convinced men. What turned a draggle of downcast fisher-men into such world-conquerors? The conquest is histo-ry. What can be the human explanation?

It is not enough to say that unscientific fishermen of 2,000 years ago would have accepted any pious non-sense, whereas we moderns are more hard-headed, etc... Doubting Thomas demanded, precisely, scientific evi-dence and f-a-c-t-s that he himself could touch. And he was given them (Jn. 20: 27). But just imagine that he re-ally was given them. Is that not exactly the turn-around moment when a dispirited backwoodsman begins turn-ing into a world-conqueror? St. Thomas became the Apostle of India where he was martyred, where his body rests to this day, where the Church he founded lives on in the southern part of the subcontinent.

Given the facts of history and stubborn human na-ture, could anything less than the repeated, direct and personal appearances, spread over 40 days, of the Lord risen from his terrible death, explain the transformation of these men, which we know must have taken place? And even then the descent of the Holy Ghost upon them at Pentecost was still necessary. But that descent made them, like Peter, irresistible witnesses to the fact of the Resurrection (Acts 2.)

But there is a second argument, a negative argument from the behavior of the Jews. These were then as now, with noble exceptions, implacable enemies of Our Lord. They do Him the honor of hating Him and all His fol-lowers, because He takes away their "place and nation" (Jn. 11: 48). The world is to be run their way, and God has no business to be interfering with their supremacy. So they had the Gentiles crucify Jesus Christ, and thought thus to have put an end to their problems.

But here comes Peter with his band of Galileans back into their stronghold of Jerusalem, glorious Sion, and based on that absurd business of the body of Jesus getting out of the grave, Peter is stirring up the whole problem all over again. In the heart of Jerusalem! And he is making thousands of converts to the Nazarene, as they call him. This must be stopped (Acts 2, 3, 4)!

Now, if Peter is basing his argument on the Resurrection, then to stop his nonsense once and for all, would not the best way be to discover Jesus' body and triumphantly produce it in public? ("Sorry, Peter, dear fellow, but . . . ") And is it likely that Annas and Caiphas were any less rich, determined, intelligent, cunning or powerful than their successors are today? In which case, with such a strong motive to find the body of Jesus, can we doubt they would have found it if it was there to be found? In which case, if, as is obviously the case, they failed to stop Peter in his tracks, can there be any other explanation for their failure than that the body was nowhere to be found by human beings because it had been raised from the dead by God?

In brief, whether we think of Our Lord's friends or His enemies, the gigantic success of the Christian religion can be accounted for only by the Resurrection of Our Lord from the dead being a hard, hard fact. To say otherwise is to deny history or to deny human nature.

But then comes a pernicious objection: "Ah, but who needs to ARGUE the basis of our beautiful religion? The Faith is above mere arguments. It is all so lovely, and the more lovely for being believed without reasoning."

The objection is pernicious because it seems to put the Faith high above reason, where it belongs. However, in fact it disconnects the Faith from reason altogether, and makes the Faith a matter of sentiment or feeling. But men naturally know that truth is in the mind, not in the feelings. Therefore on this reckoning the Faith will cease to be true, and the Church will be turned into a mere NIF factory (factory of Nice Internal Feelings).

So the question is not whether the Resurrection makes me feel good or not, because that depends upon whether it is true or not, which is an entirely different question. The whole of Christendom is sick with the notion that religion is a matter of feeling, not truth. Mushy minds never made martyrs. Now Protestantism has long been rotted with "feelings," but the drama is that since Vatican II, countless "Catholics" suffer from the same disconnection of religion from reality. But men will always insist in the long run on living in reality – they have to – so if religion is disconnected from it, it is religion that will go out of the window. The present collapse of the feely-feely "Catholic" Church is right and proper.

So the historical fact of the Resurrection is a truth accessible to reason, working from a knowledge of history and human nature, which all men share. Thus the Catholic religion is not just my personal preference, but it has a grip and a claim on all men's minds, and by their minds, on their lives. "He that believeth not shall be condemned" (Mk. 16: 16). How could this be so if belief were all just a matter of NIFs?

The Doctrinal Session to be held at Winona this year from July 22 (NB, not 21) to 26 inclusive will hammer relentlessly at minds to present the Popes' teaching on liberalism, ecumenism, communism, secularism and neo-modernism, errors all of them descended from feely-feely Protestantism.

One month beforehand priestly ordinations are due to take place at Winona this year on Saturday, June 21, and one month afterwards the SSPX is making an 80th anniversary pilgrimage to Fatima (1917–1997) in honour of the Immaculate Heart of Mary. If the Society's 1987 pilgrimage to Fatima helped obtain the grace of the Episcopal Consecrations in 1988, what grace for the Society and for the Church might God have appointed to be obtained by the 1997 pilgrimage?

May the Mother of God obtain for all of us Catholic minds and Catholic hearts!

Woes of Modern Education

I CAN SEE why so many of you related positively to the idea put forward in this letter two months ago, of a concentration camp for young men (even if it was to be at most a one-year experiment) – there is a crying need for old-fashioned education of the kind that the Catholic Church always used to foster.

This is because the public and secret masters of the New World Order are fabricating a new human nature. Man, made in the image of God, they are making over in the image of man, especially through education. The result is that the very thought, let alone the effort, of saving one's soul becomes more and more alien to people, especially youngsters. You rightly wonder how your children and grandchildren will get to Heaven.

From a friend of mine working in a prestigious academy in the USA, here is an alarming portrait of how the situation is evolving. From his knowledge of schools he works back to the influence of computers, and he concludes with an assessment of the effects upon people in general. All I have done is give an order to his quotes:

> In the last two years the whole class-room experi-
> ence has changed. There is a whole new breed of stu-

dent out there. They are not really students, because they have less and less interest in studying. One or two of my colleagues have taken alarm at the change but most of my colleagues are happy with it because it means they no longer have to teach. Something has happened and adults do not know what it is.

Young people now react to nothing, they do not connect. I find it increasingly difficult to connect with them, and much of the time they make me uncomfortable, because their reactions are so twisted, so inhuman. They are horrified by nothing. Horror creates in them glee. Less and less sparks from them any human reaction. The three-letter word (s_x) has become so commonplace that only violence can still get the juices running. Violence does interest them.

It is all very unnerving. It cannot go on. They cannot hold down jobs, so jobs become unreal, and they seek an underground existence. The urges of the human heart (which are still in them), being so misunderstood, will come out in massive mutual suicide in the streets. It's the end.

I do not blame them. It is not their fault. Where do they see around them anything that anybody would die for? For instance, not one student I know of made one comment on last November's elections in the USA, because they know it is all empty and fraudulent.

What in fact do they see around them? People not living, but sleep-walking. Zombies, getting into a machine to go to work, working on a machine all day long, recreating with a machine at night. That is not living, and the youngsters know it. Yet such people are consumed with pride and rear up indignantly if anyone points out to them that they are not living.

I do not blame the machines, because machines are only machines, but I blame the adults who make life out of their machines, especially in recent times, out of the computer. The adults are making reality virtual, and the mass mutual suicide in the streets will be a form of that virtual reality. If I live my life watching screens, then the eyeball becomes a screen, and whether I create a world, or zap the world, on screen or in life, it's all the same.

Let us reflect for moment on the nature of these flashing screens. Cinema is already bad insofar as it is only half human. It manipulates minds by dead images. There is no live exchange between performer and audience, there is nothing real. Television is worse with its 100 channels of junk, after so much promise when it first appeared. But worst of all for human purposes is the computer which is just as mechanical and passive as television, only the passivity is better disguised.

For instance, by accessing the library, television, video-store, newspaper and magazines, the computer gives me an illusion of omniscience, of knowing everything. But information passively accessed is not the same thing as knowledge actively assimilated. Children are the smartest users of computers, but they do not use them for knowledge.

Similarly, by empowering people to buy their groceries, do their job, go to school, etc., without moving from their chair, the computer can make them feel omnipotent, all-powerful. But this mechanizing of human contacts isolates people still more from one another. The new language generated by computers seems likewise rather for quasi-ritual initiation than for human communication.

Of course these machines can serve well if they are kept in their reasonable place. But in real life they seem to undermine that reasonableness of the users which is needed to keep them in their place. Take my colleagues for instance –

They are losing interest in the subjects they teach, for computer toys. There is a new toy out every two months. I mistrust the computer, but even me it pulls in. You play with it. My colleagues seem chained to their computers so that if the computers go down, they can be seen staggering and wandering down the school corridors like souls in Hades. Then the computers come up again, and the E-mail pours in once more: instant sending, instant receiving, instant reacting, but no time to ponder. No stopping to think. No thinking. Images replace ideas.

The computers can be seen acting in real life like a narcotic, an addiction, a form of slavery. And – we come back to education – the US President talks of wanting computers in every class-room! The way education is now going, it will create zombies who know nothing except how to push buttons!

For as the screen creates the child, so the child becomes like a machine. Human beings are turning into machines, asking to be programmed, all happy to be spouting the same nonsense! It is this willful ignorance of the human heart and of its fundamental needs which is generating the violence. The God who made that heart for Himself is not mocked.

As for Traditional Catholics, what Faith they have in this God does give them a handle on their own hearts and their children's needs, but to the extent that they do not live wholly by their Faith, to the extent they live like everybody else by their environment of machines and computers, they are not fully living, they are in a state of schizophrenia, torn between Christ and the culture of the Anti-christ. But if they are torn, they are at least still half-alive!

Dear people! They come to me in our Chapel with some question or other they think I can answer. I build a case to answer their question. They stare at me. Three weeks later they are back with the same question. It is as though brains cannot absorb any more. Ideas seem to have lost any power to effect how people think or live.

The problem is profound. Something significant has happened to the way the mind works and absorbs information. The flood of images on screens naturally follows the collapse of ideas – and the collapse of words to express them – but I think it also helps to cause that collapse. It is an unparalleled catastrophe, an enormous frustration, but few can see what has happened, or sense its magnitude.

Ideas being discredited, any integral vision becomes very difficult. We are like into a new world. The crisis is much deeper in the 1990's than in the 1970's, yet most people are unaware of it. We are into a whole new set of problems out there.

Dear friends, the Bill Gates of hell need not prevail. As Archbishop Lefebvre wisely reminded Society priests a little while before he died, the doctrine, sacraments and Church instituted and left to us by Our Lord Jesus Christ cannot go out of date, or lose their efficacy. Upon one condition: that they be the real doctrine, sacraments and Church. The breakdown of the idea started with Protestantism's breakup of the Truth.

In the home there must be the Rosary. If the family prays the Rosary, not only are family members in communion with one another as human beings, but they are also communicating together with God, which is to cater for the deepest needs of their human being. The Rosary is a sure way of accessing the God who is not mocked, but who is also not inaccessible.

A wicked world may be seeking to set up more and more obstacles between Him and ourselves, but God remains the Master. If there is the least good will on our side, nothing can stop His grace from rolling over any roadblocks, and even if there is not good will on our, side, it can still roll over them.

> 8. If I ascend into heaven, thou art there: if I descend into hell thou art present. 9. If I take my wings early in the morning, and dwell in the uttermost parts of the sea: 10. Even there also shall thy hand lead me: and thy right hand shall hold me. 11. And I said: Perhaps darkness shall cover me: and night shall be my light in my pleasures. 12. But darkness shall not be dark to thee, and night shall be light as the day: the darkness thereof, and the light thereof are alike to thee.

(Ps. 138)

Is Deep Blue Human?

I T IS ASTONISHING what nonsense even supposedly intelligent people can write about computers so as to credit them with quasi-human qualities. This is mainly because they have such a low view of human beings. Materialists who believe only in matter, and their kissing cousins, evolutionists, have almost no idea what a human being is.

Let me give for instance the argument of an article written last month by a nationally renowned columnist here in the USA. It concerns the recent one-game victory by chess computer Deep Blue in its six-game rematch played one month ago in Philadelphia against world chess champion, Gary Kasparov. The article is called "Be Afraid," and it concludes that mankind must fear an evolution of computers from victory over Kasparov to victory over the human race! Here are the bare bones of the article, in four propositions:

1. In the second game of the second match, "Deep Blue" played in a way (apparently) more human and less mechanical than ever before, thus not only defeating but also unnerving Kasparov.

2. This is because the computer was stronger than Kasparov in chess strategy, where normally humans

are stronger. Thus Deep Blue seemed to have risen from mere calculating to real thinking, from mere quantity to quality, from mere brain to mind.

3. Similarly Deep Blue looked as though it was breaking free of mechanical determinism insofar as its makers could not tell what move it would make in any one situation, because its 32 computer nodes each with 16 co-processors could talk to one another in such different orders that it would give unpredictably different results: said one of the makers, "We can never know why Deep Blue did what it did."

4. Thus Deep Blue demonstrated in early May that computers have moved up the first stage on the evolutionary ladder from merely mechanical determinism to non-determined action, and, given that integrated circuits have only been around for 40 years and microprocessors for the last 30, then we can reasonably expect that computers will soon make, as human beings did, the second step, from non-determined thinking to fully intelligent freedom! Mankind, move over!

Now our columnist might not like his argument to be so cruelly shrunk, but he could not deny that here are its bare bones. Let us take each of the four propositions in turn:

Firstly, however much Deep Blue may have "appeared" (sic . . .) to be moving humanly instead of merely mechanically, it remains obvious that the computer was still only doing what it had been programmed by its designers to do. Outside that program it absolutely could not move. Kasparov won the first match because he discovered a weakness in the computer's programming (pawn structure), and being human was free to adapt his own play accordingly. On the contrary the computer could not be adapted until after the first match was over, when no doubt its human designers freely corrected it, to Kasparov's grief in the rematch. Brute force of millions of lightning calculations is still the computer's only internal strength. To defeat a Kasparov still requires external manipulation of that brute force by other humans.

Secondly, however much Deep Blue may have "seemed" (sic) to have risen from brute calculation to real thinking, from quantity to quality, etc., in reality any such rise is only an illusion, or, such a violation of common sense as only evolutionists are capable of. Since when, if I buy 20, 50 or even 50,000 cans of beans at the store, do they turn into a joint of beef by the time I get home? Since when, if I add oceans to oceans of water, do they make one piece of land? Since when if I pile up billions of unthinking apes, do they make one thinking man? As though quantity, if only big enough, will jump into a change of quality or of substance! As though mechanical circuits, if only I connect up enough zillions of them, will make an unmechanical thought! Idiocy! But then evolutionists, like our columnist, are (witting or unwitting) idiots. For them, apples slide into oranges all the time!

Thirdly, however much Deep Blue "looked as though" (sic . . . are you beginning to feel sea-sic?) it was breaking free of determinism, of course it was doing no such thing. To conclude from the designers' no longer being able to observe their machine's determinedness to the machine being undetermined in itself is as idiotic as to say the moon has no other side because I can never see it! Any randomness of Deep Blue's complications is only relative, or apparent. If in one and the same situation it can give different results, that is only because it is designed to be able to do so. Its determinedness is only relatively unobservable. Absolutely, Deep Blue remains determined.

Fourthly, to add to the fancy of Deep Blue's having risen to – sorry, having seemed to rise to – undeterminedness, the fancy of its rising from undeterminedness to full intelligence, is to double the stupidity. But then our columnist's wits are addled by his belief in just such an evolution on the part of man himself. After all, if man evolved from mineral to vegetable to animal to humanoid, why can't the mineral machine do the same? Poor columnist! He may ape all the mindless fools in creation, but he is still going to answer at God's judgment seat for the misuse he has made of his God-given intelligence!

The human being ranks high in God's graded creation, because of all material creatures man alone is also spiritual. Amongst spiritual creatures he ranks low insofar as he alone is also material. Above him are the purely spiritual angels. Beneath him are the purely material creatures of the animal, vegetable and mineral categories, in that order.

> Now through all these grades of creation, rank is by more or less spirituality climbing out of matter. Lowest minerals have no semblance of life, whereas the highest minerals (e.g., amino-acids?) seem close to life. The lowest plants are little more than mineral, the highest (e.g., fly-catchers) seem close to animal. The lowest animals (e.g., starfish?) seem little more than plants, the highest animals are those constantly credited by the media with intelligence. The lowest human beings behave little better (even, worse!) than animals, the highest seem angelic. And the angels again are graded towards God.

However, while the highest of the lower in God's creation thus always touches on the lowest of the higher, still each main category is unmistakably distinct from its neighbors, and no creature can belong to two such categories. Thus every plant has life in itself which no mineral has; every animal has sensation which no plant has; every human being has intelligence which no animal has; no angel has a body which every human being has. Nor is there any scientific evidence whatsoever to prove that any creature has ever moved from one category to another, on the contrary there are masses of evidence for every creature's being fixed in its category.

So Deep Blue is mere mineral, will remain mere mineral, and has not in it a grain of life, let alone of intelligence, nor will it ever have. So with its zillions of electronic circuits it may be able, in a game that suits it like chess does, to overtop the calculating capacity of the strongest of human players, but it is still intrinsically incapable of one truly intelligent or free thought, because it is totally material and all its operations are locked in the determinedness of matter. To be a match for the free Kasparov, Deep Blue had to be programmed and reprogrammed by a team of spiritual and free chess and computer experts.

So the machine is and always will be a mere instrument of human beings. The problem remains inescapably the human beings, or, whatever fouls up human beings, which in any serious sense is always sin, which is always human beings fouling up their relations not firstly with one another but firstly with God.

So what we need to be afraid of, dear columnist, is not a take-over of mankind by Deep Blue, but rather the human beings who are liable to misuse the powers of Deep Blue, because, amongst other reasons, columnists completely misrepresent to them their own spiritual nature and the material nature of Deep Blue. There is no way in which men will behave like angels if they are equated with machines!

Nor will they always behave like angels even if they are treated like men! Here at the seminary we have just had a stormy month of May. A priest who had been a professor here for nearly four years precipitated his own expulsion for combined subversion and disobedience at the beginning of the month, because, it seems, he thought the moment had come when his own project for the apostolate, ripening within his mind for the last ten years, could no longer be advanced from within the seminary. So instead he manipulated his departure.

The gravity of his condition as an incorrigible dreamer was not immediately apparent when he came to Winona, firstly for three years as a seminarian and then as a professor. On the contrary, his out of the ordinary talents rendered for a while considerable service to the seminary and to seminarians, as they had been brought here to do. But now it seems that he was driven by his dream all along. Alas, each time he meets with a reality check, he will be sure it is the fault of reality.

But who can help loving Peter Pan? When this 34-year old priest left the seminary behind him, he took with him one priest and two seminarians, and since then another half dozen seminarians have left, at least for the time being, and some of those who are still here have stardust in their eyes and tears in their hearts. It can be painful to grow up!

Dear friends, pray for these two priests that they come to their senses before they have to be expelled from the SSPX, and pray to lose no more of your priests to their dream, which they themselves indicate may end up back within the Novus Ordo establishment. Let no more fantasies of the Devil be allowed to distract or divert our seminarians or priests from the seeming treadmill of labor appointed for our sanctification by Our Lord in his vineyard!

This week we shall be consecrating the seminary to the Sacred Heart of Jesus, at a little shrine we are constructing in a prominent place. The seminary belongs to Him. May He continue to have mercy on it as He had for the last month! And thank you especially for the help of your prayers over the same time period.

Hamlet's Lesson for Modern Man

IN THE MIDDLE of April a number of seminarians and seminary professors took the opportunity to see a local production of Shakespeare's famous play *Hamlet*, done (quite well) by the college at the foot of the hill. It was a grand reminder that the solutions of Our Lord Jesus Christ are organic to modern problems, neither mere bandaids to be stuck on the surface, nor optional extras we can do without. From when He came into the world, real problems have no other solution.

But why should any Catholic be interested in *Hamlet*? What does Our Lord have to do with the theater, or with literature? Indeed he appears to be irrelevant, because modern "literature" has pushed Him to one side. But in fact nobody is more relevant, because that very pushing aside is what governs what we call "literature." Let *Hamlet* serve here to show how work on Monday to Friday, culture (or Literature) on Saturday and religion on Sunday is not a workable way of life!

Two recent films of *Hamlet* with Mel Gibson and then Kenneth Branagh in the leading role remind us how any male actor of standing wishes at least once in his career to play the part. The famous British actor, Sir Lawrence Olivier, played the part five times and on his deathbed expressed the wish to play it again. This is because the play speaks in a special way to modern man.

Yet there are almost as many different interpretations of the play and of its central character as there are different producers or actors. How can this be? Firstly, Hamlet is the broadest character that Shakespeare ever portrayed, uniting in himself so many diverse elements (philosopher, "courtier, soldier, scholar," cynic, poet, clown, etc.) that whoever plays the Prince of Denmark must choose which elements to leave out, because he cannot fit them all in. Corresponding to this elusive central character, the play as a whole expresses some conflict so deep that it can surface in a variety of different ways. Shallow conflict, only one issue. Deep conflict, many possible issues. Hamlet is in fact riddled with conflict, or contradiction.

For illustration, let us take Shakespeare's famous heroines. In *Julius Caesar*, Brutus turns aside from his loving wife Portia, and comes to grief – no contradiction. Othello tramples on his innocent Desdemona and comes to grief – no contradiction. King Lear spurns his only true daughter, Cordelia, and falls into madness – no contradiction. On the other hand Macbeth follows the promptings of the wicked Lady Macbeth, and comes to grief – still no contradiction. But Hamlet? The Prince tramples on his sweetheart, the undeserving Ophelia, and it is she that goes mad while he strides forward to an avenging triumph! *Hamlet* contradicts the other tragedies! Or does it? After all, *Hamlet* still ends in a slugfest and a bloodbath, as they do. So the Prince did come to grief? *Hamlet* contradicts itself!

Similarly with Shakespeare's tempters. Cassius who starts Brutus towards murdering Caesar, Iago who ruins Othello and the Witches who overthrow Macbeth's virtue are all clearly evil. But who can call the much suffering Ghost of Hamlet's father evil, when he urges his son to avenge his murder? Does he make Hamlet fall, or rise to a noble self-sacrifice? Contradiction!

Now this contradiction inside *Hamlet,* and the special character of Hamlet amongst the Shakespearean tragedies, might be analyzed as follows: All these tragedies, including Hamlet, have a basic pattern of natural law, inherited from the medieval morality play, whereby the individual soul is confronted with a choice between good and evil; if it chooses love, it will create harmony and order in and all around itself, but if it gives way to the temptation to turn its back on love, then all hell breaks loose, both for the hero and for his society.

In *Hamlet* however, and in *Hamlet* alone, this natural pattern which we time-tag as medieval is heavily overlaid with what we might time-tag as the modern or Hollywood pattern, whereby all problems are the fault of society, so every hero is a rebel, every heroine should join him, and most villains are figures in authority – poor Bonnie Ophelia, what she should have done was help Prince Clyde kill her father! (Compare "Bonnie and Clyde," "Natural Born Killers," etc., etc.) Seen in this light, Hamlet is the four century-old trailblazer of Hollywood, one reason for the play's enduring appeal.

However, the medieval pattern is still there in Hamlet, which means contradiction. For in the modern pattern society is at fault, whereas in the old pattern, the central fault lies inside the individual. To make one and the same play simultaneously fit two such contradictory patterns required from Shakespeare a prodigious feat of theatrical counterpoint which the inside of the enclosed flyer means to disentangle for anyone who knows the play: in the three columns from left to right are the plot presented neutrally, then its medieval spin and its modern spin. Such an analysis does explain the many possible interpretations of the play, anywhere on the high tension grid between its contradictory poles.

But such tension is not humanly bearable, and must resolve one way or the other. This is what makes some distinguished critics even call Hamlet an unsatisfactory play. In any case the modern world obviously resolved the tension more and more in favor of the modern pattern, while Shakespeare himself reverted to the medieval pattern. In his very next play, *Measure for Measure*, he has the priest-like Duke of Vienna intervene to circuit-break the tragic process, and never again does Shakespeare seem to have been so nearly rocked off his medieval hinges.

Of course England's then apostatising from the Catholic Faith was enough to rock many a good man then and since off his medieval hinges. See the flyer's inner panel where precisely in *Hamlet* Shakespeare began bending the old theology in order to set the modern pattern. But in his own career it does seem to have been only a momentary departure, because hints scattered through the rest of his plays suggest that he was Catholic, only forced on the Elizabethan stage to keep his Catholicism under wraps. Which would explain many things:

Firstly, his popularity even with non-Christians but who respect the natural law which Our Lord came to defend and restore – Shakespeare's plays are constantly presenting nature as an order which one violates at one's peril. Secondly, the popularity of *Hamlet* in particular for rebels and all idealists dreaming of an escape from that order – many a romantic would rather enjoy his problem than have it solved, especially by resort to a God! Thirdly, Shakespeare's popularity with centuries of post-Catholic Christians or post-Christian liberals who can enjoy in his plays the natural order as defended by Christ, without having to submit to the Catholic Faith as commanded by Christ. Fourthly, however, since all such tasting fruits without feeding roots is doomed in the long run, then Shakespeare's present unpopularity is explained in the universities and schools where anti-Christian liberals reign supreme who reject all order of nature, let alone of supernature.

Yet Shakespeare can still be popular in the cinema because it is difficult to abolish that nature which, thanks to the Christendom that went before him, he understood so well! Hence the two recent films of Hamlet, and a Romeo and Juliet set amidst filling-stations in Vero Beach, Florida, in which the ancient verse can pop quite naturally out of the mouths of leather-jacket hoodlums!

Thus Shakespeare is true to life and his plays contain an enduring wisdom because his medieval heritage coming from Our Lord Jesus Christ gave him a clear grasp of human nature on the brink of modern confusion. Under severe pressure from the apostasy of England launching that corruption of the structure of society which makes many a rebel cut the figure of an avenging angel, Shakespeare in *Hamlet* teetered into that confusion, and gave us a glimpse of his nightmare future, our Hollywood present, in which the unnatural is become natural and the normal abnormal. But he himself drew back from the brink and went on to create a series of further plays on the medieval pattern, as reposing to a sane mind as they are disconcerting to minds of today which feel driven to "deconstruct" them.

For of course the world after Shakespeare went ahead with the confusion and undermining of the natural order. Anything tagged as medieval it has repudiated. The result is the emptiness, ugliness and death of theater, literature, music, art, as we have known them. For there is no way in which culture can replace religion. It cracks under the strain when press-ganged by liberals into doing so. Shakespeare, literature, etc., are an after-glow of the Faith, and they live by projecting its wisdom, but they die with its disappearance, because apostasy from Jesus Christ creates an environment so hostile to sane nature that less than ever can it survive without the help of Christ's grace, or supernature.

In conclusion, there is nothing – nothing – more organic to the problems of modern man than the solutions of Jesus Christ. Those problems are as complex as the Prince of Denmark, as deep as the questioning of God's natural order, as profound as rebellion against God. No mere bandaids will do for such a gangrene.

Nor can there be any other doctor than Jesus Christ, because He alone with the Father and the Holy Ghost is the one God that is being offended, and only the party offended, not the party offending, can lay down the terms for forgiving the offence. So only that Church which is His can have means efficacious to heal. So Our Lord Jesus Christ and His Catholic Church are not an optional extra.

Dear friends, pray for the priests who bring to you Our Lord Jesus Christ. Literature, culture, the world cannot survive if souls are not being saved through priests. We had one more priest from Winona ordained on June 21, as scheduled. It was a beautiful day, and how many souls went home spiritually refreshed by Mother Church's great ceremonies! This priest now leaves Winona to help look after your souls. Several seminarians stay in Winona for a few weeks to help provide you with Spiritual Exercises and a Doctrinal Session. If only Hamlet had done a Retreat!

Devotion to the Immaculate Heart of Mary

O N THE 21ˢᵀ and 22ⁿᵈ days of this month, the SSPX will be making an official pilgrimage to Fatima in Portugal, to honor the Sorrowful and Immaculate Heart of Mary, and to obtain through her intercession all possible graces for the Church, for the world, for the Society and for ourselves.

It would be difficult to exaggerate the importance today of the Devotion to the Blessed Virgin Mary's Immaculate Heart. Why devotions? Why the Blessed Virgin Mary? Why her Immaculate Heart?

New devotions have always arisen down the twenty centuries of Catholic Church history, but these devotions have never been entirely new, nor could they be, because neither God nor the Catholic religion can change. However, the world changes, the times they are always a-changing, and so men in a variety of different historical circumstances may need a variety of religious practices, or devotions, to help them to reach the same God. Within the Catholic Church it is God Himself, the Holy Ghost, who inspires these various devotions down the ages according to the differing needs of men (Jn. 16: 12, 13).

For instance, the one and only Catholic Mass by which Christ's bloody sacrifice on the Cross is made un-bloodily present again, cannot change in its essentials, but at the height of the Middle Ages God knew that the following centuries would need not to forget that Our Lord really is present beneath the appearances of bread and wine when consecrated, so He inspired and raised up in His Church the Devotion to the Blessed Sacrament. Thus Catholics could be ready 300 years later for the Protestant onslaught on the Real Presence.

Similarly when Protestantism had nevertheless taken firm root in half of Christendom, and risked also in the other half withering the Faith by its bitter-cold doctrines, then Our Lord made to a soul in the late 17th century the private revelation of the fire of His love for men burning within His breast, which gave rise of course, as He meant, to the great public Devotion to His Sacred Heart. Thus Catholics were spiritually forearmed, or forewarmed, against the icy blasts of rising scientism (idolatry of the material sciences), so that the growing cold of charity was then again seriously delayed.

Nevertheless the Christian nations continued to apostatize from Christ, especially by the French Revolution, whose liberalism poisoned the entire world. By this liberalism men were becoming too sick to take any strong medicine, and so for modern times, as St. Louis Grignon de Montfort had foretold in the early 18th century, Our Lord, to sugar the pill as it were, put forward His Mother, so Devotion to the Blessed Virgin Mary, in many forms, became more prominent than ever in the Catholic Church.

Thus in the middle of the 19th century, the Catholic Pope chose the Mother of God to drive a stake through the heart of liberalism by his definition in 1854 of the dogma of her Immaculate Conception – no, men are not all nice people born without sin and longing to follow the truth and do good the moment they know it – they are born in sin and borne to do evil by a mysterious curse brought down upon men by men, from which curse, alone amongst children of a human father, the Blessed Virgin Mary was protected by the privilege of her immaculate conception in the womb of St. Anne.

Objection: "Ah, but that extraordinary privilege cannot have been earned by the Blessed Virgin because she could not exist before she received it." True, but corresponding to the unearned privilege of her beginnings, the Catholic Pope in the middle of the 20th century defined the fully earned privilege of her bodily Assumption into Heaven at the end of her time upon earth. By her complete and unwavering fidelity to God and then to her divine Son, in every moment of her life, but especially at the foot of the Cross when fidelity to the will of God inflicted upon her motherly heart an overwhelming sorrow, she deserved, she fully deserved, at the end of her days to be taken by God not only with her soul but also with her body, into Heaven.

This is the mother whom God Himself has through His one Church put before modern mankind, a by now near terminally ill patient, as its only hope of healing. And how should she be this fount of healing other than through the heart by which a mother loves her sick child, bends over him, tends him, cares for him, and then turns to whoever can help to beg, beg, beg, for the means of a cure? As mothering is the essence of womanhood, so the motherly Heart is the essence of the Blessed Virgin.

By now we see all three elements of the Devotion to the Sorrowful and Immaculate Heart of Mary, and how suitable that devotion is to our times. It is like a summing up of all devotions to the Blessed Virgin, because it tells of the purity of her being (Immaculate), of her love in action (Heart), and of her love in suffering (Sorrowful). Just how important this Devotion now is,

Our Lord Himself tells. As the Second World War was beginning its slaughter, He said to a privileged soul, on July 2, 1940: "It is hearts that must be changed. This will be accomplished only by the Devotion to the Sorrowful and Immaculate Heart of My Mother being proclaimed, explained, preached, and recommended everywhere. Recourse to My Mother under this title which I wish for her universally, is the last help I shall give before the end of time."

In similar fashion we have been told by Our Lady that the present downfall of Church and world, which is endangering the salvation of all our souls, will only be turned around when Russia is consecrated by the Pope and bishops of all the world to her Sorrowful and Immaculate Heart. From then on how could Our Lord (who is omnipotent) allow any other means to save Church and world, without – perish the thought! – making His Mother into a liar? Therefore the devotion to the Immaculate Heart is, by the will of God, not a matter of choice for mankind, but an absolute necessity.

Enclosed is a copy of the prayer which all friends and members of the SSPX present in Fatima will be praying together, God willing, on August 22, the Feast of the Immaculate Heart, in this 80th anniversary year of her apparitions in Fatima. If you cannot be there that day, by all means join us in spirit by reciting the prayer at home.

Meanwhile thank you always for your support of the seminary, both material (which we always need) and moral. Particular thanks to several friends who sent letters of sympathy for the seminary's problems in May. But do not worry. We spent only a little time in weeping for fallen comrades. The war goes on.

Pray for vocations to the priesthood such as will understand and serve the Immaculate Heart of Mary, which unquestionably shares in the rejoicing of her Son: "I confess to thee, O Father, Lord of heaven and earth, because thou hast hidden things from the wise and prudent, and hast revealed them to little ones. Yea, Father, for so it hath seemed good in thy sight." (Lk. 10: 21)

The Death of Princess Di

LET ME TELL you a fairy tale.

Once upon a time a pretty little girl was born into a family which occupied a high rank in the kingdom. She was called Diana. Of course her father and mother should have behaved according to their rank, because that is what upper classes are for. Unfortunately when Diana was only six years old, her mother ran away from the home, which was a bad example, and a cruel blow to all the children in the family.

Nevertheless she grew up to be a beautiful young woman who loved going to parties. Now the Prince of the kingdom who was heir to the throne was quite a few years older than Diana, and he did not like parties, and he loved a woman called Camilla, but Camilla had married a different man. So when the Prince met Diana they fell in love and married. The wedding was like in a fairy tale. All the people in the kingdom were happy with their new Princess. She became their darling.

When she also became mother of two healthy boys, William and Henry, who could succeed to the throne after her husband, the people were even more happy. But things were not going well between the Prince and the Princess. Both of them loved their children, but they no longer loved one another. And so although as heir and heiress to the throne they should have given the best example to the kingdom, the Prince still loved Camilla and the Princess still loved parties of a kind suited maybe to unmarried young women, but certainly not to a future Queen. As a result, each of them became unfaithful to the other, and they began to live unhappily ever after.

Now if they had kept their unhappiness to themselves, they might have saved the home for their children. Or if they had let as few people as possible know about their unfaithfulness to their marriage vows, they might not have given bad example to the people. But the people of this kingdom were corrupt. They did not mind the bad example, perhaps because that made them feel more free to be unfaithful themselves.

So the Prince and Princess, instead of concealing their unhappiness, each made it known as widely as possible, to gain support amongst the people, because the Prince still wanted to become King, while the Princess wanted to be free. Of course death alone could stop them from being husband and wife, but nothing could any longer prevent them from separating, and breaking up the home of William and Henry.

At last the Prince was free to turn towards Camilla again (who had also abandoned the man she had married!), while Diana turned to one man after another. Were the people of the kingdom shocked, as they should have been? They did not seem to be. They seemed happy for the upper classes to be as low as they were. So, because the Prince lacked charm, they wondered whether they wanted him as King, but because Diana was charming and beautiful whenever she took it in her head to do what she liked to do, she was still the darling of their hearts, even if she had had to drop the title of "Royal Highness."

However, when her older son William, now a fully grown boy, learned of her idea of "marrying" her latest "partner," who was a complete foreigner with a strange religion, he was seriously upset. But who cared for the upset of William or Henry? Or who cared for the scandal being given to all good souls in the kingdom by the worldwide publicity given to their mother's adulteries? One cared, who is just.

Diana had chosen for partner this stranger with a powerful car. He in turn had chosen a driver who was confident he could choose to drink heavily and still drive fast enough to leave behind photographers whom he taunted to keep up with him, because the former Princess often chose to make use of them, only not this time. So how many elements were not chosen in the accident that then happened?

The "partner" and the driver were killed instantaneously, the Princess was wounded, unconscious. Had she had before impact, like the astronautess in "Challenger," a moment's consciousness to think of her two children? Within a few hours she was dead. The heirs to the throne had lost their mother, playing with a playboy in Paris.

Oh, how the people of the kingdom grieved! In the outpouring of sorrow for their fairy tale Princess to whom were given the honors of the kingdom, who dared mention God, or the Ten Commandments, or the scarlet A-word? Any bleat of protest would have been drowned in the worldwide floods of compassion! For who that had a heart could in that moment think of the betrayal of her children, her home, her motherhood? All the birds of the air fell a-sighing and a-sobbing, and all the people of the kingdom felt so much compassion that they felt good about themselves for at least a week. And so the fairy tale had a happy ending after all!

Dear friends and benefactors, we are all of us sinners, we will all of us go before God's judgment seat, we all of us need His mercy. We are sorry for the sudden and unprepared death of any human being, which includes Princess Diana, and we offer a prayer that God may somehow have been able to have mercy on her soul (she did come herself from a wrecked home). But there are certain principles we cannot forget.

Marriage is a divine and social institution. It is divine because it was instituted together with human nature by God to ensure the reproduction of that nature. Marriage is a primarily social institution because whereas men and women eat and drink to ensure their survival as individuals, they marry to ensure their survival as a species. True, to marriage as to nourishment, God has attached personal pleasures to make sure men will not give up marrying or eating, but whereas eating can only be personal, marrying is primarily social.

This is proved by the psychological wounds one can observe in the children of divorced parents. Especially when they are too young to rationalize their parents' selfishness, they suffer a deep sense of injustice because they instinctively know that they are not there for their parents' sake, nor even are the parents for the parents' sake, but, by the structure of marriage, both parents should be there for the children's sake (which does not mean spoiling them!). Justice lies in the children's practicing the same selflessness when they in turn will have children.

That marriage is primarily social is also shown by the duty and right of both Church and State to legislate, each for its own purposes, in matters of marriage. For instance, as the Church must do all she can to discourage mixed marriages, so the State must forbid homosexual "marriages." For both Church and State, it is a matter of self-preservation and survival.

It follows that when liberalism makes the individual sacrosanct, and makes society wholly subservient to the individual, then marriage (and Church and State) will be destroyed from within. Marriage will no longer be primarily social, its primary purpose will no longer be the children, as the Catholic Church always used to teach. The personal pleasures take over, as the New-church practices, and the children take second place.

Then of course adultery and divorce become unimportant, and the fairy Princess who sets the example of putting her sons behind the pursuit of other men becomes a Saint whom the media canonize, and whom millions of poor souls with empty hearts and empty lives would love to imitate. But the society that glorifies such princesses, however charming or beautiful, is in the process of disintegrating. From wrecked home to rock parties to wrecker of homes, was her smooth progression. To canonize her is to rock society's foundations, just as Rock expresses the suicidal instinct of the youth of a home-wrecking society.

Society must choose. It cannot both glorify the glamor and care for the children. It cannot both praise Princess Diana and repudiate Rock. Behavior like hers is where Rock music comes from. However, men may be deceived, but not God. At a given moment, with a cry of "Enough!," His justice will allow us to put together all the elements for our collective crash into the wall and swift extinction. "From dying unprepared for death, good Lord, deliver us!"

Good news from Fatima. The August 21, 22 pilgrimage went well, and the Consecration of Russia to the Immaculate Heart of Mary took place, as planned. We pray it obtains some graces for the Pope to perform the same Consecration, as Heaven desires.

The Sin of Homosexuality

THE CATHOLIC BISHOPS of the USA, more precisely their Committee on Marriage and Family, have just come out with a "Pastoral Message to Parents of Homosexual Children," which is a lamentable piece of work. Since this Pastoral Message is liable to make people, already confused, even more confused, let us restate some Catholic principles, because the question bears directly on Faith and Morals, and on people getting to heaven or falling into hell.

Homosexuality means the misuse between man and man or between woman and woman of those functions and parts of the human body which God designed for use exclusively between a man and a woman within a lawful marriage, for the primary purpose of the reproduction of the human race. The Law of God governing use of the reproductive functions can be broken in a variety of ways even between man and woman, but these sins, e.g., fornication or adultery, are at least natural to the extent that they observe the basic duality of man and woman. On the contrary sins of homosexuality violate even this basic natural structure of the reproductive function, rendering it necessarily and utterly sterile, void of its intrinsic purpose.

That is why homosexuality is sometimes called "the sin against nature."

In fact the sin is so unnatural that Mother Church ranks it alongside murder, defrauding the worker of his just wage, and oppression of the widow or orphan, as one of the four sins "crying to Heaven for vengeance." However, God did not wait for the founding of the Catholic Church to instill in men the horror of this sin, but He implanted in the human nature of all of us, unless or until we corrupt it, an instinct of violent repugnance for this particular sin, comparable to our instinctive repugnance for other misuses of our human frame, such as coprophagy.

That is why St. Paul in the famous passage on homosexuality in the first chapter of his Epistle to the Romans, verses 24 to 27, lambastes the Gentiles for practicing this sin even though they had no revealed religion, and He does so in terms chosen to reawaken that natural repugnance, e.g., verse 27: "And, in like manner, the men also, leaving the natural use of the women, have burned in their lusts one towards another, men with men working that which is filthy, and receiving in themselves the recompense which was due to their error."

Therefore to speak of homosexuality as an "alternate lifestyle" is as perverse as equating the violation of nature with its observance. It is as foully corrupt as to make no difference between recognizing God the author of nature, and defying Him.

Therefore what is "innate," or inborn, in human nature concerning homosexuality is a violent repugnance. Therefore to speak of homosexuality, or even just an inclination to it, as being "innate" in certain human beings, of course to excuse them, is to accuse God at least of contradiction, if not also of planting in men the cause of sin, which is implicit if not explicit blasphemy.

The very most that can be innate in a man of, for instance, homosexuality, is the raw material for his temperament which may be sensitive in one man, rough in another, but whether that sensitivity or roughness is molded into the compassion of a saint or the vice of a homosexual depends on a series of good or evil choices made by each individual. Homosexuality is a vice, or sinful habit, created by nothing other than a series of sinful acts, for each of which the individual was responsible. Homosexuality is a moral problem, which is why, fascinatingly, St. Paul in the same passage derives it from idolatry! (No space to quote, look it up!)

"Oh, but Our Lord had chawity, (unlike thumwun we know who wath tho nathty to Pwintheth Di!). Our Lord loved thinnerth, and faggotth, and tho thould we!!" So runs the objection!

Yes indeed Our Lord loved sinners, but not in their sin, on the contrary, despite their sin, which He hated. When Our Lord protected the unrighteous Mary Magdalene against the righteous Pharisees in a way which can bring tears to our eyes each time we read Luke, Chapter 7, He was protecting not her sin but her repentance. God will, as He has told us in the Gospel, go to almost any lengths to help the sinner who is trying to get out of his sin, but He abominates the sinner who wallows in it, and upon these modern cities that flaunt their perversity in annual homosexual parades, He is preparing such fire and brimstone as may make what fell upon Sodom and Gomorrah look like a fall of dew, because at least those cities never knew the Gospel (cf. Mt. 11: 20–24).

Woe then to the sinner who instead of casting away his sin, hugs it to his bosom, as do a mass of today's homosexuals, and as the Bishops' Pastoral virtually encourages them to do. God's patience is long, but if the sinner insists upon welding his sin to his soul, then one day God's patience runs out, and He hates sinners with sin, crying out to both, "Depart from me, ye accursed, into everlasting fire"(Mt. 25: 41). Therefore real charity, which wishes everlasting salvation to homosexuals, will, with all due prudence, not put a cushion under their sin, but paint it to them in its true colors to help them to get out of it.

But what does our American Bishops' Committee on Marriage and Family do? They dangerously downgrade the sin and dangerously upgrade the sinner, putting in effect a cushion beneath the sin.

As for the sin, they do still – to their credit – say that homosexual activity is intrinsically wrong. However, in at least two ways they diminish the wrongness. Firstly, they suggest homosexuality can be innate when they quote a Newchurch document from Rome to the effect that some homosexuals are "definitely such because of some kind of innate instinct," and when they say that "Generally, homosexual orientation is experienced as a given, not as something freely chosen," because "a common opinion of experts is that there are multiple factors – genetic, hormonal, psychological – that may give rise to homosexuality." Of course whatever is innate is not sinful.

Secondly, they make a true but in this respect dangerous distinction between the habit ("orientation") of homosexuality and the act ("activity"), saying there is nothing wrong with the orientation as long as it does not turn into activity. True, only the act and not the habit is a sin, but since when did habits (especially in this domain) not incline to acts? There may be even much virtue in resisting a bad habit, but am I helped to resist it by being told the habit is not bad? If the orientation is not so bad, why should the activity be so bad?

As for upgrading the sinner, watch how close the Committee comes to saying that God loves the sinner with his sin (which is blasphemy). I quote: "God loves every person as a unique individual. Sexual identity helps to define the unique persons we are. One component of our sexual identity is sexual orientation . . . Human beings see the appearance, but the Lord looks into the heart (I Sam. 16: 7)." How is this quotation to be interpreted other than as saying that God loves the homosexual in and with his orientation to homosexuality?

And if God loves the sinner with his sins how must men love him! From start to finish the Pastoral Message drips with honeyed words to prescribe how we must behave towards homosexuals. Let me reconstruct the general idea: (my own words in the quotation marks)

"With supportive love we must accept the homosexual persons challenged by the hurtful humor and offensive discrimination directed against their kind. We must reach out with honesty and commitment to help in the overcoming of their painful tensions. We must not be exclusive or judgmental but by significant communication as caring persons we must enable them to take a fresh and healing look at their dignity as human persons so they can learn to cope with their feelings. Sensitive to their authentic needs, and unconditionally supportive of their tender self-awareness, we must reach out and embrace them in intimate community" – oops! – it's dangerous to get in the honeyed groove!

And this stuff goes on for eight pages uninterruptedly! What other purpose or effect can such words have than to dismantle the individual's and society's instinctive defense mechanism against a sin stinking to high Heaven that wrecks both individual and society? And all this in the name of the Catholic Church??

Such a false love blurring sin and sinner has nothing to do with Catholicism! As St. Paul traced homosexuality back to idolatry, i.e., the breaking of the First Commandment, so the true remedy of the sin is for those practicing it to return to the true worship and love of the true God. But what chance do they have of being led back to it by churchmen who virtually promote such corruption as in this Pastoral Message? Almost none.

"Pray," said Padre Pio, who died in 1968, "there is nothing else left." But prayer, said the Cure of Ars, "is the powerlessness of the All-powerful, the all-powerfulness of the powerless."

And please be supportive and compassionate towards the sensitive feelings of the seminary's cashbox, presently hurt by a painful sense of rejection and emptiness, always in need of fulfillment! So do let yourselves be challenged to nurture it and fill it full with a healing flow of greenbacks, and it will not stop thanking you for your co-operation.

Dear readers, forgive me, the Bishops' Committee's language is getting to me! On the contrary, may the Lord God sustain every one of us in the real religion!

The Film
"The Sound of Music"

A S THE CHRISTMAS season comes round again, no doubt many Catholic households, especially but not only in the USA, will be preparing to watch, on public television or on videotape, The Sound of Music. This Hollywood film has repeatedly been the object of critical remarks in this letter. If readers have wondered why, let it now for the season be explained at length.

The problem with The Sound of Music is that it is not just the innocent entertainment that it seems to be, as will be shown. Nor is Hollywood alone to blame. For the 1965 film was the cinema version of the 1959 Broadway (New York) stage musical. Now Hollywood and Broadway, like all entertainers, are responsible for what they do to elevate or debase their public, but they cannot be primarily to praise or blame for the state in which that public comes to them.

Interestingly, in the years of grace immediately following World War II (it did teach some people some sense), the valiant Catholic magazine Integrity called in question the whole modern expectation of "entertainment," just as between the wars Fr. Vincent Mc-

Nabb, O.P., preacher in London, England, had called in question the whole of modern city-life because of the pressure it exerts on married couples to use artificial means of birth control. Obviously few souls paid much attention to Integrity or to Fr. McNabb, which is why we are now in the situation where few Catholics can see any problem with The Sound of Music. Let us then be aware that the problem runs deep, but let us here concentrate on its immediate manifestation in this one film.

Its story is based on a real life incident which happened in Catholic Austria just before World War II. The wife of an Austrian naval captain dies, leaving him with a number of children to look after. The captain appoints as governess for them a young unmarried woman who has just left the convent where she was trying her vocation. Fortune smiles as the captain and governess fall in love, but fortune frowns as the Nazis take over Austria in the Anschluss of 1938. To avoid serving the Third Reich, the captain manages to flee Austria with his new wife and children.

It would be interesting to read the original book by the real life governess, Maria von Trapp, to see just how far Hollywood departed from reality in the film starring Julie Andrews and Christopher Plummer. However, we need not know the original to see what Hollywood has done!

Firstly, Julie Andrews is nice (of course), but she is too high-spirited to be a nun (of course), for instance she dances over the Austrian mountain meadows, in springtime (of course), waving her arms around and singing (presumably to the grass) that "The hills are alive with the sound of music." The hills seem unmoved but they do look beautiful, as does Julie Andrews (of course. We know she would wear perfume and makeup to go jogging).

Fortunately the Mother Superior is also nice (of course, at least in 1965. Today she would be a child abuser), so she and the other nuns are very understanding and let Julie Andrews go, to try out being governess of a tyrannical widower's unruly children who have (of course) chased away several governesses before her. What shall she do? Have no fear! The Power of Positive Thinking (of course) – she sings a gutsy little number along the lines, "I have confidence in sunshine, I have confidence in rain . . . besides which you see, I have confidence in me." Bravo.

Sure enough, once inside the door she gives a dazzling demonstration of the superiority of liberty and equality over stuffy old Austrian ways! Immediately undermining – in front of the children – the Captain's tyrannical discipline over them, she proceeds to win their hearts (of course) by a combination of being their friend, taking their side, making them sing and have fun, all this without a trace of motherliness and all the time looking as cute as a kitten. She even looks cute when she prays, in fact who would not pray when it makes you look so specially cute?

Of course the stern Captain is soon won over by his domain being turned into a gigantic playpen, so he breaks out in that favorite Austrian number Edelweiss, whereupon they all burst into song because the family has been rebuilt on the liberty-equality model. By now Julie Andrews is looking goofy around the Captain (of course), so there is a ball, and they dance (of course), and dancing reveals more of her charms (of course), whereupon the Captain also looks goofy around her (of course).

But enter now the villains! Firstly a glamorous Baroness previously engaged to be married to the Captain, who schemes to get Julie Andrews out of the way, back to the Convent (but didn't you know, "The path of true love never did run smooth"?). Secondly, villain of villains, a

– a – a NAZI! (Original sin? – never heard of it! Isn't all sin Nazi sin?)

Pan back to the Convent for a heart-warming feminine dialogue: Mother: "You're unhappy." J.A.: "I'm confused." Mother: "Are you in love?" J.A.: "Oh, I don't know." Mother: "Go back to him." Him is of course delighted when she returns, so there is a duet of swooning, spooning and crooning by – guess what! – moonlight! "But will the children approve of our marrying?" Of course! Shiny white wedding dress (of course), wedding bells all over the place and a lovely ceremony (of course), to be spoiled only by the brutal reappearance of the nasty Nazi – the Captain must report for duty to the Third Reich!

The family try to sneak away. The nasty Nazi spots them, so now they all break out into singing Edelweiss. The nasty Nazi is foiled when the family escape to the convent (where else?), but drama rolls as the nasty Nazis close in on the convent. (But didn't you know, "Life is not just a bed of roses"?) The Captain is heroic (of course), but the dastardly villains are only foiled for good when their car is incapacitated by the nuns turned into mechanics (of course), and the last shots show the "family" climbing a mountain path to get out of the Third Reich, amidst hills which are once more – go on, don't tell me you couldn't guess! – "alive with the sound of music." How truly heart-warming!

Dear friends, please excuse this long excursion into the audio-visual scenery of an average modern Christmas, but no less may be necessary to rub noses in the falsity of this soul-rotting slush. Clean family edification? Nothing of the kind!

As for cleanness, many films may be worse than The Sound of Music, but stop and think – are youth, physical attractiveness and being in love the essence of marriage? Can you imagine this Julie Andrews staying with the Captain if "the romance went out of their marriage"? Would she not divorce him and grab his children from him to be her toys? Such romance is not actually pornographic but it is virtually so, in other words all the elements of pornography are there, just waiting to break out. One remembers the media sensation when a few years later Julie Andrews appeared topless in another film. That was no sensation, just a natural development for one canine female on a roll.

As for being a family film, by glorifying that romance which is essentially self-centered, The Sound of Music puts selfishness in the place of selflessness between husband and wife, and by putting friendliness and fun in the place of authority and rules, it invites disorder between parents and children. This is a new model family which in short order will be no family at all, its liberated members flying off in all different directions.

Finally as for edification, in The Sound of Music the Lord God is mere decoration. True, His Austrian mountains are beautiful (beautiful decoration), but His nuns are valued only for their sweetness towards the world and their understanding of its ways, while His ex-nun is wholly oriented towards the world.

Dear friends, any supposed Catholicism in The Sound of Music is a Hollywood fraud corresponding to the real life fraud of that "Catholicism" of the 1950's and 1960's, all appearance and no substance, which was just waiting to break out into Vatican II and the Newchurch. Right here is the mentality of sweet compassion for homosexuals and of bitter grief for Princess Di, of sympathy for priests quitting the SSPX for the Novus Ordo. Everything is man-centered and meant to feel good, the apostasy of our times.

But, somebody may object, The Sound of Music is only entertainment. Reply, is the world in a mess, or not? Now, has the world got to where it is by people listening to sermons in church? They do less and less of that. Then what do they drink into their hearts and souls and minds? Is it not their "entertainment," The Sound of Music in season and countless films more or less like it out of season? Then if the world around us is corrupt, it sure fits these films being corrupt, whereas if someone can see no problem with The Sound of Music (1965), how can he see a problem with Vatican II (1962–1965)? The simultaneity in time is no coincidence.

Dear friends, "entertainment" requires serious attention. Then what is to be proposed in place of The Sound of Music? For family time, amongst live human beings, better in general live games, talk or reading than mechanical TV or VCR, even good videotapes, let alone videotapes as false as The Sound of Music. Make your children (and your wife!) a Christmas present of your personal time, attention and guidance. That is more valuable to them than anything that comes in glitzy store-bought wrappings!

The seminary is nevertheless providing, as per the enclosed flyer, a wide variety of VCR tapes. Contradiction? Not quite. These tapes are instructional rather than entertaining, and well used they should make accessible a wealth of Catholic truth and beauty. However, note the new address at which to order either audio or videotapes. This is because, to get the material out, we have brought in professional help, only not resident in Winona. Note in particular the offer of a free 30-minute videotape. Anything (honest) to get real Catholicism back into circulation!

Family fathers should also consider this year's special Doctrinal Session at Winona from December 26 to 31, neither the Ignatian Exercises we normally give then, nor the Papal Encyclicals we normally give in the summer, but a new course, designed by Fr. James Doran to frame up for fathers the Catholic truths his eight years in SSPX parishes taught him they so need. Come! We are indeed offering alternatives to The Sound of Music.

May God bless you all, and give you light to discern these disguised hazards to our Faith.

"Perils from False Brethren"

W HEN A STORM blew up in the seminary here last May, and only a few paragraphs were devoted to it in the letter of June, some of you remained curious as to what it was all about. Since then a few more defections have taken place and the bleeding may not yet have stopped, so it is a reasonable guess that some more of you are asking questions like those that follow below.

The purpose of giving answers is to explain once more what the SSPX is doing, and how. "There must be also heresies," says St. Paul (I Cor. 11: 19), meaning that so long as men are men, there are bound to be errors and divisions springing up from within the Catholic Church. Wisdom's part is to make them serve to show the true spirit of the Church which they leave behind them:

Q: What happened in the Seminary last Spring?

A: A talented but proud young Argentinian priest who had been a Seminary professor at Winona for three and a half years, decided that the moment had come to break with the SSPX and form his own society, starting with one fellow professor and two seminarians who walked out with him.

Q: But did this priest walk out, or was he told to leave?

A: As soon as it became clear that he had for some time, from within the seminary, been secretly planning his own society, he was told to report in short order to the Superior General in Switzerland. When he refused, he was told within 24 hours to leave the seminary which he had been subverting from within by his intention – ingenuously disavowed – to take with him as many Society priests and seminarians as possible.

Q: What project did he have in mind for himself and his followers?

A: Let us call them Carlitists, from their Pied Piper's first name. In theory the Carlitists want something more intellectual and medieval than the SSPX has to offer. The Society has bravely resisted Vatican II, but they say it shares in such errors of the last few centuries as Jansenistic downgrading of nature, Jesuitical forcing of the will and individualistic devotions. So to renew "Catholic spiritual life," visionary young minds must group together in a vibrant new "Society of St. John" (Apostle of Charity!) to restore on a medieval and patristic model "theology, liturgy, piety, philosophy, political action, history, arts" (quote from their drafted "Proposal SSJ"). No less.

Q: That is quite a program! What does it mean in practice?

A: In practice it means that a group of seven former Society members are now back in the Novus Ordo, i.e., the Newchurch: four priests, two deacons and one seminarian. They are reported to be living with St. Peter's Fraternity in the Diocese of Scranton, PA, with Bishop Timlin's oral and as yet unofficial approval of their Church reform.

Q: But how can they go back to the Newchurch? Against everything they believed in when they were in the Society?

A: They are not the first to have lost their grip on the Truth. St. Peter's Fraternity began in 1988 when more than a dozen Society priests judged in Europe that Archbishop Lefebvre had gone too far by consecrating four bishops without Rome's permission. They returned to the Newchurch. Also at that time the Traditional Benedictine, Dom Gerard, led most of his monastery and countless followers back into the Newchurch. Like the Carlitists, he loved the Middle Ages and scorned the Counter-Reformation.

Q: What is wrong with loving the Catholic Middle Ages?

A: Nothing, but not to the point of scorning the Catholic Counter-Reformation which was the Church's self-defense when Protestantism broke up those Middle Ages. You do not dismantle defenses when the same enemy (neo-modernist Protestantism) is attacking stronger than ever!

Q: What did Archbishop Lefebvre think of Dom Gerard at that time?

A: Dom Gerard's defection from Tradition made him weep. He said that had Dom Gerard not betrayed, Rome would have been forced to do something right.

Q: What did the Archbishop think of St. Peter's Fraternity?

A: All those who had received the grace to belong to Tradition and then rejoined the Newchurch, he called traitors.

Q: Is that not rather a strong word?

Richard N. Williamson

A: The Archbishop was not playing games. He saw that the survival of the Catholic faith was at stake.

Q: *Do not the Carlitists say that it is normal for new societies to begin from within old societies?*

A: Yes, but not starting in subversion nor finishing in a personal dream. Father Vallet correctly and officially resigned from the Society of Jesus before founding several years later, again officially, his own little Congregation to preach the 5-day Exercises we know. Archbishop Lefebvre officially and correctly resigned from being Superior of the Holy Ghost Fathers two years before he founded the SSPX to defend the Church's real priesthood.

Q: *What are the Carlitists now doing?*

A: We are told that they have registered at Scranton University in order to acquire further qualifications. This fits their criticism of the Society that its priests have too many Mass circuits and too few university degrees.

Q: *And do Society priests have too many Mass circuits?*

A: As souls cry for help, so our priests can be stretched very thin to reach as many of them as possible, but here in the USA (and elsewhere), they are no longer stretched as thin as they once were. They can and do get vacations, and District Superiors keep an eye open for any dangerous fatigue over and above that not unhappy weariness which is normal for a priest who does his duty. At the seminary, the Carlitists objected to going on Seminary circuits. Martyrdom is romantic, but not the dry martyrdom of the Mass circuits!

Q: *Are the Carlitists looking after souls?*

A: By their ideals, they are elitists rather than pastors, which is another reason to call them Carlitists, but we hear that at least two of their (so far) four priests are offering Mass in or near centers where they operated as Society priests.

Q: Then is some cooperation not possible? Is it not the same Mass, the same "good fight"?

A: No way. They have quit the Society and gone over to the enemy, the Newchurch. They may pretend still to honor the Society, but to justify their quitting it, they are bound to attack it. The split must be clean, or there will be ongoing confusion. If they really wanted to work with the Society, all they had to do was not leave it! Actions speak louder than words.

Q: What about Society priests being undereducated?

A: It is true that relatively few have university degrees, but then did Our Lord Himself choose to make His Apostles out of Pharisees or out of fishermen? Our Lord needs from His young men faith, docility and common sense more than He needs frisbee-shaped certificates from Mickey Mouse university degree-courses!

Q: Did any of these strange ideas surface at the Seminary before last spring?

A: A little, and they were not encouraged. However, in general the Argentinian priest was trusted to be devoting his considerable talents to the service of the seminary. In fact he was all the time pursuing what he told one seminarian was, literally, a dream of his going back ten years, and which he is now trying to make real in Scranton. But all this was well concealed from most priests and seminarians for as long as he was teaching at the seminary.

Q: But did not this priest to a large extent have the Rector's support for his ideas while he was teaching at the Seminary?

A: Only insofar as it seemed that these ideas were serving, or would serve, the Society.

Q: *We are told that the Rector in Winona was bitter and furious when he discovered how he had been deceived. Is this true?*

A: Untrue. Anyone belonging to the SSPX since the early 1970's has known many such defections. They have always happened in the Catholic Church, and they always will, so long as Our Lord does not take away men's free will when He makes them His priests. He had a traitor amongst His own Apostles.

Q: *Then was the Rector indifferent to the whole affair?*

A: Not either. He was sorry for his comrades who quit, and for any more who may quit, but in war, bullets fly and shells land and comrades go down. There is half a minute for a handkerchief, then the war goes on.

Q: *How many seminarians were lost altogether in this affair?*

A: In and around this affair, over a dozen, of whom two may find their way back. The name of the game is "survival of the fittest."

Q: *And how is the Seminary now?*

A: Peaceful. Nine new seminarians entered this last September, two new priests should be ordained on Saturday, June 20, 1998, God willing. There is much to be thankful for, including the fact that this was the first group defection from the Society's North American Seminary since 1983.

Q: *How many priests were lost to the Society in this affair?*

A: So far (December 1), two from the Seminary and two from the US District. A few more names are being quoted as possible departures.

Q: *Does this mean another split within the Society in the USA?*

A: Carlitism looks like a minor split right now, but even if there was a major split tomorrow, what matters is still the purity of the Truth, not the numbers that stay with it. A collapse of numbers would oblige the Society to pull back and regroup, but that is all.

Q: *Does the Society need to do that right now?*

A: That is a day-to-day question for the District Superior to answer!

Q: *But can the Society afford to lose any priests at all?*

A: Quite honestly, if they have never understood, or have ceased to understand, what the Society is all about, yes, the Society can afford to lose them. This is because the Society cannot serve the Church by thinking one half, one quarter, or even one eighth like the Novus Ordo. For any and all mixtures of whisky and water to be possible, someone has to be producing neat whisky. For all degrees of Catholic compromise with the world not to collapse, somebody has to be generating pure Catholicism. Right now, as a worldwide organization, that somebody is principally – not exclusively – the SSPX.

Q: *But how can you be so sure that the Society is right, virtually against all the world?*

A: Because its Catholicism is clear, classical, and free of internal contradiction. On the contrary, take the most honorable of Newchurchmen, say, Cardinal Ratzinger – the more honorable he is, the more he contradicts his own liberal principles. How can Our Lord contradict Himself?

Q: *But did the Society lose so many priests when Archbishop Lefebvre was Superior General?*

A: It certainly did. Of the 400 priests he ordained in and for the Society, some 100 had defected before he died, evenly split between those who thought he was too hard and those who thought he was too soft! But as Scripture says the Lord commanded Joshua (Josh. 1: 7), the Archbishop deviated neither to right nor to left.

Q: *What do you mean?*

A: Not to the left: in 1975, in one of a series of shake-downs at the Society's central seminary in Ecône, Switzerland, a number of professors were quitting because the Society had just been "dissolved" by Rome. A seminarian went to the Archbishop to express his concern. The Archbishop's quiet reply: "Well, if all the professors leave, the seminarians will just have to teach themselves"! In other words, seminarians may come and professors may go, but a seminary's business is to teach a truth that cannot change.

Not to the right: in 1983, in the United States, when nine out of eleven Society priests in the seminary (then in CT) and the Northeastern District laid down to the Archbishop the terms on which they would allow that seminary and District to operate, he again quietly said, "Look, you go your way, we go ours, and if you are more successful than we are at saving souls, then may God be with you, but here we part company." In other words, seminary and/or District might collapse with only two priests out of eleven (and perhaps no properties!), but the Society's business was to continue a Church whose structure is not to be altered by men.

Q: *What you are saying is that the SSPX is not a question of numbers.*

A: Exactly. Numbers make democratism, but not Catholicism – "But yet the Son of Man, when He cometh, shall He find, think you, faith on earth?" (Lk. 18: 8). In the Old Testament, when Gideon gathered an army of 32,000 men to fight the Philistines, the Lord God told him they were too many. "Send home all those who for any reason do not want to fight." Still 10,000 men were ready to fight. "Still too many," said the Lord God. "Take them to a river to drink: separate the men who stoop right down from those who lift the water to their mouths with their hands." Only 300 did not stoop down. The Lord God ordered Gideon to send home the 9,700! And of course, because Gideon obeyed, the 300 were enough, with God's help, to rout the Philistines! Faith, and docility.

Q: *What about the New Testament?*

A: Same lesson. When Our Lord taught the Jews in the Synagogue at Capharnaum (Jn. 6) that they would need to eat His flesh and drink His blood to have life in them, then "many of His disciples went back and walked no more with Him," in other words they walked out on Him. Did Our Lord stop them, call them back and modify His teaching to make it more acceptable? No, He let the numbers go. And by next asking His twelve apostles if they also would leave Him, He almost seemed ready for the truth to be followed by nobody. But Simon Peter responded on their behalf, "Lord, to whom shall we go? Thou hast the words of eternal life," and with this faith and docility of a handful of men, Jesus Christ proceeded to build His world-saving Church.

Q: *But why is it so easy for priests to quit the Society?*

A: Because the split at the top of the Church between truth and authority since Vatican II means that untruths and many untruthful priests, formerly condemned by

Church authority, are now protected by it. Formerly an unfaithful priest had nowhere to go. Now he can go in a variety of directions without being condemned.

Q: But why are such priests not defrocked?

A: Because the Church authorities have in this crisis so lost their grip on the Catholic Faith that they punish the faithful priests instead of the unfaithful ones.

Q: How many more priests is the Society about to lose?

A: Only God knows, but that is not, for reasons given above, the important question. You should pray for the largest possible number to keep the Catholic Faith.

Q: But can they not keep the Faith by working with St. Peter's Fraternity or with the Institute of Christ the King or with the Indult Mass or with the Traditional Mass under Bishop Timlin of Scranton?

A: No. All these enterprises, and the new society if it is ever publicly approved within the Newchurch, are crippled in their preaching of the Truth by the fact that they cannot criticize the principles of Vatican II, deadly to Catholicism, on which the Newchurch is built: religious liberty, ecumenism, the independent dignity of the human person, etc. In order to tell the truth, such priests must offend the Newchurch. In order to be accepted (or stay) in the Newchurch, they must water down the Truth. Dilution is not Our Lord's way.

Q: When are there going to be no more cliques within the Society?

A: When Our Lord takes away His priests' free will! In other words, never. Pray not only for new vocations, but also for the faithfulness of old vocations.

Q: Is the Society being infiltrated?

A: It is quite possible. One reason why Our Lord included Judas Iscariot amongst His 12 Apostles was to teach His Church that this could always happen. Of course Our Lord was not deceived by Judas in the way that merely human superiors can always be deceived, but He wanted to teach His Church that it will work not on an absence of infiltration but on the presence of charity.

Q: Are there spies within the Society?

A: Maybe. Certainly superiors must keep their eyes open, and, for the common good, expel such enemies as soon as they are recognized. However, too much suspicion kills charity, the engine-oil of Catholic institutions, so an excess of spy-hunting would kill the Society.

Q: Was the Argentinian priest a plant from the Newchurch, Opus Dei, for instance?

A: That is like asking whether Paul VI was a Freemason. Maybe he was, possibly he had been one, in any case he did not need to be one because he certainly in large part thought like one. Whether or not the Argentinian priest always belonged to the Newchurch, in any case he finished up thinking like it, which is what matters.

Q: Why do American priests not yet hold key positions in the American District and Seminary?

A: Emphasize the "not yet." Because Americans have in their bloodstream the Revolution of 1776, whose liberal principles are essentially anti-Catholic, a fact readily recognized, even boasted of, by American non-Catholics, denied only by American "Catholics" who do not understand the Revolution. An example was the Bunker Hill referred to above, staged in the East in 1983 by nine Society priests out of eleven. For a long time afterwards none of the Catholics who stayed with the Society asked the question you just asked. Now it may arise again. But

Richard N. Williamson

truth must come before patriotism, whatever country we come from.

Q: Is that mini-Revolution of 1983 the reason why the Society seems comparatively light in the Northeastern USA?

A: No doubt. Mark you, the Society has to quite an extent rebuilt in the East, but it remains true that the revolutionary priests took with them out of the Society many properties and most of the people there at that time, inflicting numerical and material wounds still not entirely healed.

Q: But if priests are short in numbers, why do so many American priests get sent abroad? We need them at home!

A: On that reckoning, why should any non-American Society priests be, or ever have been, here? And where would the Society in the USA now be without those "foreigners"? The Catholic Church is above nations! Vocations come from wherever God calls them, and they go wherever He sends them. Be proud of your American priests abroad. Wherever they carry the true Faith, they are the true glory of the United States!

Q: Still, why does France, a small country compared with ours, have nearly 100 more priests than we do?

A: Because France has proportionally many more vocations and traditional Catholics than does the United States. It also has sent abroad numerically and proportionally many more Society priests than any other country. These are the glory of France.

Q: So what hope do we have for the Society in the United States?

A: Much, and in every way. Think firstly of the extraordinary rescue operation for souls that the Lord God has with it mounted in these almost impossible conditions for the last 25 years. It is wise to see in every true Mass celebrated (within a framework of the integral Catholic Faith) a triumph over the Devil. Then consider that with the Society you are guaranteed a roller coaster ride for nothing, all you have to do is hang on! Then again consider that in this crisis of neo-modernism Mother Church is carrying a heavy cross. Why should we not have to carry our part of it? Which is preferable, to belong to the Church and help carry her cross, or have no such cross to carry by not belonging to her?

Q: *No doubt it is better to belong to the Church.*

A: Then stay with the Society which continues to grow despite all setbacks. And remember Our Lord's words: "If any man will follow Me, let him deny himself, and take up his cross, and follow Me." (Mk. 8: 34) Dear readers, very many thanks for seeing the seminary through another calendar year. We live by your generosity for which we as rarely need to ask as we are always grateful. If you get out of Wall Street with profits before it crashes, remember who kept telling you that we are on the brink of the crack of doom!

But remember mainly the divine gifts brought to all of us by one shivering Child in one poverty-stricken manger. With no financing, no lobbying, no advertising, He transformed the world!

Fugitives to the Woods

SOME TIME AGO we learned at the seminary of the plight of 12 local children fleeing from their warm homes to brave the coldest months of a cruel Minnesota winter in cardboard and plywood shacks in the Winona woods. What happened to them? Were they for real?

They were for real, alright. The good news is what did happen to them. The bad news is why they were in the woods in the first place. Both good and bad news concern the family, so for the month of the Feast of the Holy Family, let us tell you about these 12 fugitives, seven boys and five girls, ranging from 11 to 16 years of age.

When they were discovered to be living in the woods on their own, with no desire to contact any adults at all, discreet inquiries at the local police station revealed that not one of the twelve children had had a "Missing child" notice posted about it! Did the parents not care? If only! The truth is that they must have cared, cared to keep the world in ignorance about the children, because if ever the wrong people came to find out why the children were missing, eleven fathers and one uncle could have found themselves in jail for several years each!

Twelve more or less long sequences of rape and incest, heterosexual or homosexual, committed against children, in the dear, sleepy, conservative, "decent," mid-Western 25,000-inhabitant town of Winona. These 12 cases came to light. Then think of all the cases that will not have come to light. Then imagine what is going on in the big cities!

As for the mothers, of course the children told them in each case what was going on, but these mothers either did not believe them, or, did not want to believe them. Now to wives in such circumstances, compassionate adults might cut some slack, but children have no such compassion. With their rigorous sense of justice, children rank such mothers as traitors alongside their fathers. That is why these twelve fled from all adults and took to the woods. Shakespeare's "Timon of Athens" did the same:

> Timon will to the woods where he shall find
> The inhuman beasts more kinder than mankind.

In the last century France had a horrible penal colony in French Guyana on the northern coast of South America. To it were shipped out all of France's worst criminals who had nobody there for company except one another. We are told that amongst themselves they had a high tolerance for all crimes except two: murder of father or mother, and the molesting of children. So strong was the family instinct even amongst hardened criminals. But not today amongst adults in the United States!

Is it any wonder then that so many children look like zombies? Are they not deadening their soul's nerve-ends against a nameless pain, because the adults are in denial? After all, what adults do not believe in liberty, democracy, money and pleasure? It stands to reason:

We worship liberty, as a goddess: "This is the land of the free. They are my children. They owe me everything. I can do as I like." We glorify democracy: "We, the people, are sovereign. There is nobody above me. Nobody – but nobody – tells me what or what not to do." We idolize money: "We give our children everything. What more do they want? They can't expect us to sacrifice our lifestyle, can they? We give them 'quality time'!" And of course the real religion of most people today is the three letter word (s_x): "I expect my wife to dress attractive around the house... Of course her girls imitate her... They develop physically, under my eyes... What do you expect a man to do?... And if there are no girls, why, boys are almost as cute at that age..."

As for the Catholic religion, it is powerless to restrain such horrors because it too has been made "cute" by the soft culture (e.g., "Sound of Music"), and it has been subordinated by Vatican II to American-style religious liberty: "I'm a good Catholic because now I go to Mass when I honestly feel like it, and not just when the rule book says so. Besides, we all know Fr. Joe is a _____ himself!"

Dear friends, eleven out of these twelve children came from "Catholic" homes. It is clear that as the Catholic Church became the Newchurch, so the horror of the Cross went out of the front door, and the horror of these sins returned through the back door. If men will not be nailed with Christ to the Cross, they will be nailed to sin by the Devil.

But people say, "Our American Way of Life is wonderful! Thanks to separation of Church and State, and our Supreme Court, God is banned from our schools, so now children are free to learn how to do it in biology classes in kindergarten! Isn't that wonderful? Besides, thanks to the First Amendment, we have no censorship! Pornography? It's a healthy outlet! The Internet? Women's underwear catalogues? What's your problem? We put it all in front of our children so that they learn to choose. Bishop, write about things nice! Write spiritual things to make us feel nice all over!"

What is it going to take to wake these people out of their Universal Dream? Out of their Dream "Catholicism"? Answer, severe suffering (and even then…). Fortunately, the God who rained down fire and brimstone upon Sodom and Gomorrah has not changed. He has been divinely patient with this 20th century, but He will not be mocked. At this beginning of 1998 we stand before great suffering. It will be a gift of God when it comes.

Meanwhile the story of the 12 children did have a happy ending. Attendance at the Old Mass when still available at some distance from Winona had made known an older couple around 60 years of age with a large farm and farmhouse left somewhat empty a few years ago when a car accident killed both their own teenage children. They were told of the 12 children. Might they take them in?

A dozen kids! Strangers. Out of the woods, possibly wild. No family or State support. Themselves at ages plus or minus 60! Yes, they would take them in. Now that is real religion! (James 1: 27)

And the children have been happy ever since. Of course it took a little time for the older couple to win their trust, which is a process still going on. Incest, etc., has scarred the children for life, but the scars are, as best they can be, healing. The one child from a Protestant home ran away because he could not take to life in the country. The littlest girl underwent two major operations because she had caught frostbite in the calf of a leg from the four months in the icy woods, where she had run away from two years of being attacked by her father. The frostbite turned gangrenous. Muscles were cut out of her back to put in the calf. Two months later the entire leg had to be amputated. Two weeks later, as she was hospitalized for the third time, she said to what might be called her real mother, who had had time to teach her to pray: "I shan't be coming home again. God has told me

I won't be suffering any more." She died a few days later, this last August, age 12.

But the ten remaining children are thriving, by time-honored, old-fashioned methods: affection, discipline, quantity time and attention, with a curse upon anything "politically correct." The boys are put to work on the farm while the girls – dare I tell you? – are put to work in the . . . in the . . . IN THE . . . KITCHEN! Even more horrible to relate . . . it works like a charm! For the littlest girl, there is an outstanding hospital bill of several thousand dollars, but what is money? Her little soul is surely now safe in heaven, and when she departed this life, the father who cared for her said it was just like losing his own children over again.

Dear readers, human nature, family structure and children's needs do not change, only our poor modern world changes for the worse all the time. Don Bosco promised a special blessing from God upon those who would look after abandoned children. Only, it takes wisdom as well as goodwill.

Two more candles in the darkness. Firstly, the Doctrinal Session here at the seminary after Christmas drew 63 men, our largest number ever, and everyone we know of was very happy with it. This must be because the concentrated course of doctrine was addressed directly to the needs of men and family fathers in today's dreadful situation. We have yet to hear from the wives, but we are sure they are, for the family's sake, happy to have let their men go for the week.

Secondly, a flyer from the Dominican girls' school in Idaho presents a compact disc of the girls' singing. Now nobody in their right mind pretends that schoolgirls (any more than schoolboys) are angels, but if the singing is angelic, imagine the landmarks of beauty and harmony being left in their souls for the rest of their lives! The Devil is not winning every battle!

Neither Sedevacantist nor Liberal

MERCIFULLY, NO MORE priests in the USA left the SSPX leftwards in the last two months to rejoin the Novus Ordo, but unexpectedly a priest of ours ordained a year and a half ago left us rightwards in December to join sedevacantists who quit the Society back in 1983. As the old song says, "If the left hand doesn't get you, then the right hand will"!

This young priest had seemed solid. Perhaps he was knocked off balance by having had to start his priesthood in the same house as a fervid Carlitist, who left the Society shortly before he himself did. In any case these left hand and right hand departures are an occasion to reason quietly, not in detail, which has been done before, but in general, on why the Society takes the position that it does, neither liberal nor sedevacantist.

The so-called "sedevacantists," named from their belief that the See ("sedes" in Latin) of Rome is vacant, are apparently the hardline opponents of softline liberals. The popes for the last 20, 30 or 40 years, they say, are too liberal to have been able to be real popes. Yet the general and deep down problem of liberals and sedevacantists is the same, even if neither would care to admit it: both forget just how far Our Lord can choose to allow the men of His Church to misbehave without it ceasing to be His Church.

This is because the Catholic Church, like its Founder, is truly human and truly divine. For when God became incarnate, or took flesh, then the Son of God, true God, became also true man, so that in Jesus Christ the divine and human natures are always both present and distinct but neither separate nor confused. Similarly in His one true Church, divine and human elements are always both present but especially must not be confused, because whereas the divine element is infallible both in Our Lord and in His Church, on the contrary the human element is sinless in Our Lord but fallible in His Church.

If then I blur the divine and human elements in the Church, the same confusion can go either of two ways. Either I will blur the human into the divine, and then, crediting mere humans with divine infallibility, I will hold the churchmen to be right whatever they say, and, if I blindly follow liberal popes, I will fall into liberalism. Or I will blur the divine into the human, in which case discrediting the stainless Church, bride of Christ, with the stains of fallible churchmen, I risk repudiating the bride and falling out of the Church, as did many Catholics when they became Protestants in Luther's time, and as have done a number of sedevacantists in our own time. On the contrary Catholics keep their balance by neither, like liberals, crediting the merely human with qualities divine, nor, like sedevacantists, discrediting the divine as merely human.

Of course when churchmen seriously misbehave, it can be difficult still to believe that the Church is divine. But let us remember Our Lord Himself. Which of us, had he been present at the original Way of the Cross, would have had no difficulty believing that this mocked, exhausted, bleeding man was God? So it is understandable if Catholics, watching the neo-modernists in Rome today make such a mockery of Catholic faith and morals, can hardly believe the popes are true popes. However, just as the disfigurement of the Man of Sorrows in His Passion did not prove He was not God, so all the present distortion of the Church does not necessarily prove the popes are not popes.

Does this mean that no amount of misbehavior in Rome could ever prove it? No. One day, maybe soon, the See of Rome could become vacant. There have been several false popes, or anti-popes, in Church history. Again, for our own times, or times not far off, Our Lady warned us at La Salette that Rome will become the Seat of the Antichrist. It is quite possible that with the death of John Paul II (which may not be far off) there will be a vacant See of Rome or an anti-Pope for a while. So sedevacantism may then become true, at which point it may no longer produce the bitter fruits associated with it in recent years. But "sufficient for the day is the evil thereof." Here and now the arguments for sedevacantism are rather less convincing than the arguments against it. How does our former colleague argue his case?

Of the 19 reasons he gives, why "in conscience" he had to leave the Society, ten concern the Church in general, nine concern the SSPX in particular. Of the ten concerning the Church, eight argue from the Church's infallibility (which no Catholic denies) to the invalidity of the Newchurch, of Vatican II and of JP2, because all these three are so fallible. (The remaining two arguments spell out that JP2 in particular cannot be Pope).

But Church history confirms just how much fallibility God can choose to allow inside His Church: the bulk of the Church in heresy (Arianism), a "Robber Council" (at Ephesus), and popes wavering on the brink of formal heresy (Liberius, Honorius) – Mother Church has seen it all! However even such grave defections of the human churchmen are not incompatible with the Church's divine indefectibility. Thus Our Lord Himself says of His Church at the end of the world that on the one hand it will still be there (Mt. 28: 20), on the other hand it will be so reduced in size as to be almost not there: "But yet the Son of Man, when he cometh, shall he find, think you, faith on earth?" (Lk. 18: 8)

This dark prophecy is essential to a correct understanding of the Church's divine gift of infallibility (or indefectibility in teaching). It means not that no bulk of the Church, no Council or no Pope will ever fall into error, but that (ordinary general infallibility) by a guarantee of God, the true and unchanging Deposit of the Faith will always be taught by the Church in a manner accessible to souls of good will down to the end of the world, while (derived particular infallibility) if the Pope as Pope ever imposes a definitive teaching of faith or morals upon the whole Church, God will specially protect him in that moment from teaching any error.

What has falsified and exaggerated infallibility in many Catholics' minds over the last 120 years has been the Church's strong discipline from the definition of papal infallibility in 1870 down to the 1960's and a series of relatively good popes (in doctrine and morals) from Pius IX to Pius XII inclusive. In a way, Catholics have it too good. That is why when John XXIII and Vatican II began seriously to err, easily most Catholics were caught off their guard. Whether they accepted error with their erring leaders and became liberal, or repudiated the erring leaders and left the Church or became sedevacantists, either way they lost their Catholic balance.

Archbishop Lefebvre on the contrary neither accepted the error nor repudiated the erring leaders, much to their annoyance. (They would have loved him to walk out of the Church, and tried in vain to declare him out of it in 1988). But the Archbishop's course was the wise course. He always used to say that to believe these popes are not popes means creating problems worse than the solution. If Church and Pope are no longer in Rome, where are they? If for the last 30 or 40 years there have been no validly elected popes, nor then validly appointed cardinals, where is another pope to come from? That is why sedevacantists have for the last 20 years been creating a little series of garage popes. Garage Masses, if need be! Garage popes, no thank you!

As for our former colleague's nine arguments against the Society, they mostly come down to the same "Either, or," to which the Society replies, "Both, and." Imagine a devoted son hovering by the bedside of his gravely ill and infectious mother. Our former colleague would tell him, "Make up your mind. Either you go right up to her because you love her, or you get right away, because she's infectious, but you can't just stand there, betwixt and between." To which the Society replies, "Our mind is made up. We must both stand close to that Church which is our Mother, and stand far enough off not to catch her disease and be unable to help her, so here we stand, in a contradictory situation, but not contradicting ourselves."

For indeed neither sedevacantists nor the Society are responsible for the contradictory situation of the Vicar of Truth being immersed in error, but the difference is that while the sedevacantists (and liberals) short circuit the contradiction, the Society endures it. Simplifications are always simpler, but they are not always true. They do, however, have their appeal to souls tired of complications, especially if the simplification carries an emotional charge as well.

In fact, the 19 arguments of our new sedevacantist may well be following his emotions, instead of his emotions following the arguments. In any case the end result is the same, once more, as with the liberals – disobedi-ence and enmity towards the Society. We pray for our former colleague.

Two minor consolations for his defection. If he left us in the opposite direction from the Carlitists, then the Society may be doing something right. As G. K. Chesterton once said "If I get attacked from all sides, then I can't be all wrong!." And secondly, this former colleague is the first American priest in nearly ten years to have defected from the Society to right or left, after doing all six years of his seminary in Winona and/or Ridgefield. We still have much to be thankful for.

Thank you in any case to all of you benefactors for your prayers and support for the seminary. As a wise reader recently wrote to us, such a seminary's very existence is in today's world an ongoing miracle.

The SSPX's Marriage Tribunal

A MONGST OTHER ACCUSATIONS recently leveled at the SSPX in the USA from former friends to left and to right is one that is delicate to handle in the public domain, and might have been better left in private. However, now that the issue has been raised, not by ourselves, it must not be thought that the Society has no answer. Also that answer throws much light on the nature of the Church and today's fight for the Faith. Let us then tackle the question head on: the question of marriage annulments.

The accusation leveled at the Society is that by undertaking to examine marriage cases, and by declaring the invalidity of even only a few of the marriages examined, the Society is taking upon itself an authority which can only belong to the mainstream or official Church. Thereby the Society is first going into schism, and secondly helping to dissolve the institution of holy matrimony.

The Society pleads not guilty on both counts!

Let us begin by remembering what the Church teaches concerning marriage and marriage annulments. Here is a classical definition of marriage: "Marriage is the union for common life between a man and a woman capable of that union, arising from a contract by which they give each other the exclusive and irrevocable right over one another's bodies for the procreation and rearing of children."

Between two baptized persons this union was raised by Our Lord to the status of a sacrament. If either or both parties are unbaptized, the union is still a sacred institution (Leo XIII), as designed by God for the continuation of the human race, all of whose members are meant for Heaven. Also by God the union, whether sacramental or not, is designed to be one and indissoluble. In other words one man may have only one wife, one woman only one husband, until death do them part. The main reason for this is that children are the primary purpose of the union, and children need a stable home with their own biological father and mother. Look around for the devastation caused by disregard here of God's law.

The union arises from the contract made between the man and woman when they exchange the right over one another's bodies for that act which generates children. If the contract was valid, the marriage is valid until the man or woman dies. If the contract was invalid, the marriage never exists nor existed. The first exercise of the marital rights does not validate, it merely consummates the marriage. Thus the validity of a marriage depends upon what actually happened when the contract was originally made. It is a question of establishing the facts and checking them against the rules that apply.

Now the rules for a valid marriage contract basically resemble the rules for any other kind of contract. For instance substantial fraud will invalidate a marriage, as when a girl marries a man because he tells her he is a prince and he turns out to be a slave. But just as with civil contracts, two parties can bitterly dispute over what was contracted between them, so that each country has a body of law to settle such disputes, and law courts and judges to apply that law, so with marriage contracts, spouses can be at war with one another or make war together upon their marriage, so that the Catholic Church has always had courts or the equivalent of courts to judge of the validity of marriage contracts.

For indeed firstly, the parties themselves cannot be judges in their own case, especially where such passions can be involved as in marriage cases. Secondly, the Church itself has a stake in marriages, as does the State, because upon marriages depends the future population of both. That is why both have a right and duty to legislate and adjudicate, in accordance with God's law, questions of marriage, because it is a primarily social and not just individual institution. That is also why the Church sets up a "Defensor vinculi," or defender of the marriage bond, in case both partners unjustly wish to tear it apart.

And a third reason why the Church must place at Catholics' disposal a means of resolving difficult marriage cases is that their non-resolution can be a real obstacle to the eternal salvation of the souls involved. May we, or must we, either separate, or live as brother and sister, or live as husband and wife? These can be agonizing questions, and they can call for an authoritative judgment. For just as God cannot require of men to believe in His Truth, on pain of eternal damnation, without making it accessible to them by an infallible teaching authority, so He cannot require of them to observe marriage laws making often severe demands upon their fallen human nature, without guaranteeing to them His Church's authoritative guidance as to the application of those laws. It stands to reason.

Hence the Catholic Church has always had priests or courts with authority to tell the law (ius-dicere, jurisdiction) on marriage contracts. And before Vatican II, amongst many contracts submitted for examination

Richard N. Williamson

by couples, usually in hopes of a judgment of invalidity, there always were a few marriage contracts which the Church authorities declared to have been, from the beginning, null and void. However, these "annulments" never dissolved a valid marriage, they merely declared one had never existed. The true Church cannot admit divorce.

But now what happened with the Second Vatican Council? Following the modern world's disordered glorification of the person, of the individual over society, the Council declared (e.g., *Gaudium et Spes* # 50) that children are no longer the one primary end of marriage, but its joint primary end together with the consorting of husband and wife, of which they are the fulfillment. Logically parents could now appeal to an Ecumenical Church Council for support to tear apart the marriage bond in their own interest, no longer subordinate to that of the children. Logically the Newchurch, soft on human passions and modern selfishness, began to declare more and more marriage contracts null. The situation became so scandalous in the United States that the Pope several years ago had to call the American Church to order for, in effect, creating Catholic divorce. Yet still we had the public scandal last year of Sheila Rauch Kennedy, Episcopalian wife of a supposed Catholic, appealing to the Catholic Church for help to defend her marriage, and being betrayed.

Of course many couples rejoiced in this "liberty" granted to them by the Newchurch. But what about Catholics who were serious about their faith? How could they look for a serious marriage judgment, in view of their eternal salvation, to authorities now capable of granting two "annulments" and a third marriage to a woman no older than 25 (case known in Detroit)? They heard the Pope himself calling these authorities to order!

Now if people deny that there is a crisis in the Catholic Church, then little that the SSPX does can make much sense. But if anybody grants that on the one hand the true Church owes to Catholics all the help they need to live up to its demanding laws, and that on the other hand the Newchurch is not providing that help, then it makes sense that the Society, amongst others, will step into that gap where it reasonably can, even if it has no territorial jurisdiction, and where it so steps in it may reasonably assume, in accordance with Canon Law, that the Church will, case by case, for the salvation of souls which is the supreme law, supply any missing authority or jurisdiction.

Upon that basis, as sins unfortunately continue, serious Catholics turn to Society priests for absolution from their sins, and these priests have jurisdiction supplied in emergency by the Church to grant absolution. Similarly, since marriage problems can also not wait until the end of the crisis in the Church to be resolved, Catholics may assume that if the Society sets about seriously examining marriage contracts in accordance with unchanging Catholic principles, then they may trust its declarations in the particular case to be receiving from the Church any jurisdiction lacking, and they may act before God in good conscience upon any such declarations.

Of course the Society may abuse such supplied jurisdiction, because to err is human. But that does not take away the Society's right to act in such cases, because the urgent need of souls may even make that right a duty, for reasons already given. This Church crisis was not of the Society's making, and it is not of the Society's ending. Pray, dear Catholics, not that the Society priests never assume emergency powers, but that for your sakes and theirs they make the right use of those powers. Prudently to assume these powers is not to cut oneself off from the Church, but to engage more completely in the Church's own work.

And do not think – second accusation – that the Society is opening wide the floodgates to "Traditional annulments." Here in the USA, since the Society undertook this ungrateful task, it has taken only some one hundred cases seriously enough to examine them, and of those one hundred it has declared in less than a dozen cases, I am told, that the contract of marriage was invalid from the beginning. That is, like before Vatican II, a trickle rather than a flood. However, in all one hundred cases the couples concerned can now trust that they know where they stand before God, and that is a great gift.

Enclosed is a flyer that attempts to shed light on the present "liberal" or "conservative" or "Traditional" or "sedevacantist" confusion amongst Catholics. It indicates that there is an objective basis to the subjective sway and swirl of opinions. It is that objective Truth that matters.

Meanwhile, let us profit by Lent to renounce, sacrifice and do our daily duty. Our fallen nature must be held in check, or we will "all perish", says Our Lord (Lk. 13: 3). May the thought of His Passion be with us in this season.

"Peter Schlemihl"

THIS LETTER DOES sometimes shock. I think it is necessary. Let me explain why with a story from German literature which I studied in school 40 years ago, but whose full meaning only came home to me several decades later: Peter Schlemihl by Adalbert Chamisso (1781–1838).

Peter Schlemihl is a bright young man who wants to get on in the world. So when a stranger in a grey frock-coat offers him all the gold he wants in exchange for his shadow, Peter accepts. After all, what use is his shadow? However, he then discovers that all the gold in the world cannot make up for the scorn he meets from everyone around him because he has no shadow. He is in despair when the man in the grey frockcoat sidles up to him again to offer him a second deal – for Peter to get his shadow back, all he need do is sign away his soul. The story ends with some compromise I have forgotten: Peter does not lose his soul, but there is still some price to pay for his original foolishness.

The story is charming, as I recall, and beautifully written. The stranger in the grey frockcoat is of course the Devil. Peter is Western man who has mutilated himself and placed his soul in peril for the sake of material prosperity and well-being. But what interests us first is the Devil's technique, as grasped by Chamisso. It is simple enough when one thinks about it, but it has enormous applications to the world around us.

The Devil traps Peter Schlemihl by stages. Firstly, gold in exchange for his shadow. Secondly, his shadow in exchange for his soul. Obviously the Devil could not care less about Peter's shadow except as a snare to catch Peter's soul. As it looks to Peter, having gotten into a serious mess by trading his shadow for gold, how strong the second temptation must be to get back his shadow and keep the gold by trading away his soul! The gold may have turned to dust, but he knows by now how valuable his shadow is. What does he know about the value of his soul?

Thus the devil has got Peter into the frying pan, and from the frying pan tempts him into the fire. Peter has fallen for the first temptation which is relatively minor, but the consequences are still grave enough to make him want to put them right by falling for an absolutely major temptation. He has got a minor but obvious thing wrong, his shadow. How tempting to put it right by getting a not obvious but major thing wrong, his soul.

Now Peter Schlemihl may be only a fairy tale, but fairy tales can tell a lot more truth than newspapers or television. Peter Schlemihl may help to explain why this letter has seemed to approve horrors like the Unabomber or films of Oliver Stone, while it certainly disapproves of sweet dreams of Catholicism and supposedly lovely films like The Sound of Music. Things are not what they appear.

Western man is like Peter Schlemihl. By the end of the Middle Ages he was getting a lot of little things wrong. So the Devil proposed a deal to Christians to put the little things right if only it would get the big things wrong. Christians split. Those who refused the deal stayed Catholic and kept the Faith. Those who accepted the deal became Protestants. They were rewarded by the Devil with prosperity and the repair of outward correctness, but they lost the Faith and lost their soul.

Thus the hallmark of the Protestant culture that emerged in England, Northern Germany where Chamisso wrote, and the United States, is prosperity and outward correctness, but inward wrongness. Outwardly everything looks fine and attractive, but inwardly there are deep and insoluble problems, insoluble because they are not recognized, because they are hidden from view by the attractive surface. To deal with these problems, Protestantism mutated into Liberalism, or the adoration of Liberty, which is in turn mutating into global tyranny, but while the surface is more brilliant than ever ("overcoming" of disease, hunger, distance), the deep down problems are in fact worse than ever (intellectual, moral and spiritual chaos – just think of modern art). For centuries now we have been buying from the Devil minor solutions in exchange for major problems, a prettier surface in exchange for uglier depths.

As for the Catholic countries that refused the Protestantism, alas, they then let themselves be infected by the liberalism until they were swept away by neo-modernism, which was the disaster of Vatican II. When at this point the Catholic churchmen themselves lost their grip on the solution, the puzzling of men's wills by the intangible loss of soul beneath an abundance of tangible gold and worldly goods became a worldwide problem.

This is my diagnosis of the Unabomber. You may say what you like about him as a criminal terrorist, etc., etc., and much of it is true. But the man, as is clear from his Manifesto (which is well worth reading), was at least trying to tackle, and publicise, serious and deep problems of man in a machine society. He has a Polish name. I wager his grandparents had the Catholic Faith, which he himself either never had, or has lost. But he still has a remotely Catholic sense of how technology brutalizes man. How Catholic on the contrary do all those technophiles deserve to be called who have – gladly – given up all such sense in order to wallow at ease in their computers? Give me the Unabomber's seriousness over their shallowness, any day of the week.

Similarly with Oliver Stone. I do not care for anything I know of the man, on the surface he is horrible, as are his films, but I can name five of them (including Nixon, JFK) which each from a different angle tackle one serious problem: what happened to the United States in the 60's? Outwardly, these films have nothing to do with the Faith, they are totally unsuitable for "family viewing," even for viewing by many adults (as I said at the time), but inwardly I again wager that the Catholic ancestry of Stone's French mother has much to do with his deep unease and preoccupation with the 1960's. Give me, again, any day of the week, the ogre who is serious about serious problems, over the sweetie-pies who willfully deceive themselves, or are deceived, for instance, that the American Way has nothing deep down wrong with it. The Constitution of 1787 is, for anybody who thinks it is a significant part of the solution, a significant part of the problem, and woe to any Catholic who thinks otherwise!

But even if we grant that, for instance, the horrible film Natural Born Killers has something serious to say about modern society beneath its ugly surface, was Oliver Stone bound to make the surface so ugly?

Unfortunately, one may say, yes, because if he made the surface nice, most of his audience would look no deeper. Their minds would happily click back into their normal Hollywood or "Sound of Music" mode. The world is sweet, all men are nice (except Nazis), life is a game, nobody goes to Hell. Serious Western artists have for the last 200 years been making their work uglier and uglier, partly to reflect Western reality, partly to shock Westerners into realizing what that reality is – the soul is more and more lost.

We are reminded of St. Augustine's famous prayer: "Lord, if you prepare to strike, we make all kinds of promises, but if you hang back, we do not keep them . . . If then you strike, we cry for mercy, but if you show mercy, by again sinning we force you to strike . . ." As God cannot win with His sinful people, so the man with any serious message cannot win with a modern audience. If he broadcasts on their wavelength, there is no way he can say what they need to hear. If he broadcasts on his own wavelength, they tune him out. Heads they win, tails he loses. Ours is a situation in which the Lord God soon tells Mr. and Mrs. Lot to walk away, and woe betide them if they look back.

Thus if the Seminary letter uses nice language to say nice things, readers feel really good about themselves and pay no attention. If it says nasty things but in a nice way, readers can escape from the nastiness by taking refuge in the niceness of the way, and still they are not disturbed as they should be. So that is why the letter must sometimes say nasty things in a nasty way, because even if a majority of readers were to turn away in disgust, still if a minority of readers were provoked into thinking seriously about real problems, it might be worth it. There is no hope for the "American Way," now being followed worldwide, from Catholics who believe in it. Its only hope is Catholics who will tackle its deep and serious problems, going back to Protestantism.

Peter Schlemihl may get back his shadow, but what use is it if he loses his soul? The modern world may get a lot of little things right, but what use is it if, almost in proportion, it gets the big things wrong? The Unabomber, Oliver Stone and apparent nastiness may get a lot of little things wrong, but how much does that matter compared with their trying to get some of the big things right?

Dear readers, pray the Rosary. Do not believe in Wall Street. Do not believe in Washington, D.C., nor in the Houses of Parliament in London. Do not believe in the dollar. Do not believe in pension funds. Do not believe in democracy, nor in the Constitution, nor in the British Monarchy. Do not believe in any of the works of modern man. He is a poor and forsaken creature, by his own choice. He has built on sand, and his sandcastles are on the brink of collapsing.

Believe in God, the Father Almighty, Creator of Heaven and earth, and in Jesus Christ, His only-begotten Son, who promised us that whosoever builds on His Gospel is building on rock. The winds and rain of the next few years are going to beat on that building, but it will not fall down. And if suffering comes our way, let us even be thankful, because it is the hallmark of real Catholicism, the surest sign that we are following in the footsteps of Jesus Christ on the way to Heaven.

NO. 175 | MAY 1, 1998

The Film *Titanic*

A FEW MONTHS ago there was released in the United States of America a film which has proved to be the biggest box office success of all time: *Titanic*. The film itself may be uninteresting, but its success must be a sign of the times. What times? Times that reverse the signposts of God to make them point in exactly the opposite direction!

The film's central interest is a fictitious love story set against the real life drama of the sinking of the famous ship *Titanic* on its maiden voyage in 1912 from Europe to New York. The story is well-known. Racing amidst icebergs in North Atlantic waters on the calm but dark spring night of April 14 to 15, this greatest and most luxurious of transatlantic liners yet to have been built, labeled "unsinkable," at 11:40 p.m. struck an iceberg, and at 2:20 a.m. sank.

What a lesson of life! One moment the *Titanic* was the pride of Western technology and the glory of the British Empire's shipyards, the next moment it was plunging in pitch darkness 2 miles to the ocean floor! One moment the first class passengers on board representing the flower of Anglo-Saxon high society and of Jewish finance were the lords of creation, the next moment they were like everybody else, helplessly awaiting their fate in mid-ocean with small chance of avoiding an icy cold death.

For of the 2207 souls on board when the *Titanic* set out across the sea, only 705 survived the sinking, to be picked up in their lifeboats at dawn. Lifejackets saved many hundreds more from death by drowning, but they could not long survive floating in the below freezing ocean.

And why had there not been enough lifeboats for all souls on board? Precisely because the floating palace was universally considered to be unsinkable. Its huge double-bottomed steel hull was divided into 16 compartments, each of which could be sealed off from the others by watertight bulkheads, so that even if several were flooded, still the liner could float. "God Himself could not sink this ship," was one deckhand's typical boast.

God did not need to sink it. It was men who designed the ship and built it; men who sent it through northern waters littered with icebergs because that route is, as for the airplanes, the shortest between Europe and New York; men who raced the *Titanic* amidst the icebergs to show what she could do; men who saw the fatal iceberg only in time to swing the bow to port enough for the glancing iceberg to open beneath the water line, like a tin-opener, a fatal front five of the 16 compartments. Had the liner crashed straight into the iceberg, it might not have sunk. Had only the front four compartments been punctured, it might still have floated. But as soon as the front five were flooded, the ship tilted far enough down in the bows for the water in the fifth compartment to slosh over the top of the bulkhead into the sixth, and so on, until the ship was bound to sink.

However, since no more than five compartments were originally breached by the iceberg, then the process of sinking took time. Hence an incomparable – real life

– drama, which has held the world's imagination captive ever since: 2207 souls trapped on the stricken liner, with only a minority having any serious hope of escape from a cruel death which they could watch approaching for two hours, as the great ship's bows tilted inexorably lower and lower in the water. Finally as the entire stern lifted out of the water, the unprecedented strain tore the ship in two. The front two thirds of the ship immediately sank, the stern third crashed back for a moment level on the water, only to flood rapidly, tilt forward until it was vertical, and slide in its turn beneath the waves. All that remained visible of the supposed pride and glory of Western industry was, besides assorted flotsam, a scatter of shivering lifeboats, and hundreds of bobbing life-jackets, crying out at first, but muted as cold and death closed in!

What a scene! What a signpost of God! What a reminder that "Man proposes and God disposes"! In 1912, after a century of "peace" and "progress," in the glow of the Edwardian age, men thought, especially Anglo-Saxons, that with their liberal principles they had the world under control. The Great War breaking out in 1914 would prove how wrong they were. Then surely the sinking of the *Titanic* was God's advance warning to the whole 20th century that modern man is not the master of his fate as he pretends. But does he want to learn this lesson?

All that the 1997 Hollywood film seems to want from the legendary sinking is a dramatic backdrop to highlight a romance of liberation. The film *Titanic* takes no interest in any of those grand lessons of life which are surely responsible for the disaster's having attained its legendary status. In the film, the ship's fate is merely of technical interest –who was to blame? Answer, the foolish owners and officers of the ship, who are part of a whole society set-up and establishment from which individuals, especially youngsters, must free themselves in order to lead their own lives and – be masters of their fate! Thus is the real lesson faded out and replaced by an unreal fantasy.

The film's hero, Jack, is a free soul, a young artist from backwoods Wisconsin with no strings and no affections, gambling his way at the last moment on board the *Titanic*'s lowest class accommodation, taking life and people as they come. The heroine Rose on the contrary is a high society girl feeling utterly trapped in her engagement to a domineering upper-class young plutocrat who is bringing her back across the ocean to marry her in her hometown of Philadelphia.

The hero and heroine meet on board when Rose in desperation is about to throw herself into the ocean. Jack cleverly and courageously saves her from doing so, for which he gets little recognition or recompense from her upper-class companions. However, by continually defying the undemocratic class distinctions imposed by them and by the ship's structure, he leads her to free herself progressively from the restrictions of her society, her family, her God, as she sheds, in order, her engagement, her mother and, mere hours before the ship hits the iceberg, her clothing, in scenes filmed with only enough restraint to avoid that "R" rating which might have been bad for the box office. Finally, as the ship is going down, she rescues him from a villainous imprisonment by her companions, while, once in the water, Jack rescues Rose upon a floating door with room only for one.

Jack has breath enough to preach to her one last time the gospel of self-fulfillment (old Tennyson's "To strive, to seek, to find and not to yield"), before he freezes dead and slips into the icy depths. But Rose will not forget this savior who has sacrificed himself for her. The film shows her having led the rest of her life in accordance with Jack's message of liberation. It has been a fulfilled life, and as she looks back in old age, she is given to declare solemnly that Jack saved her, "in every way that a person can be saved"!

Blasphemy! Conscious or unconscious on the part of the film's makers? God knows. Certainly Our Lord is nowhere in the film, except perhaps in the person of a Catholic priest shown ineffectively praying on deck in the ship's last moments while Jack is effectively striving to save Rose. Thus secular self-fulfillment is elevated to the status of a substitute religion. All the human heart's need for love, for sacrificial love, satisfied; its need for a knight to gallop to the rescue of a damsel in distress, and the knight raised to the rank of a religious savior, while all ten Commandments may be safely ignored – is this the key to the film's success?

Poor youth, flocking to see the film! In it is no inkling, not the least inkling, that the same human heart was made by the love of God for nothing less than to love God, mainly through the observance of those Commandments, defiance of which will fulfill not self but only sin and damnation. Who will give our youth the Catholic Faith, sole foundation of the true love of the true God, which is the sole fulfillment of every human heart?

Not liberalism, which is massively diluting and contaminating the Faith today by its systematic affirmation of man's independence from any truth or law to which he himself has not consented. Archbishop Lefebvre always used to say that one great antidote to liberalism is the circular letters written to the Catholic bishops of the world by the Popes from about 1800 to 1958. The Angelus Press has just published a Study Set of ten of these Papal Encyclicals, chosen by the Archbishop himself to teach anti-liberalism to his seminarians. The green flyer enclosed advertises both the set of Encyclicals and the Archbishop's teaching based upon them.

Richard N. Williamson

On the other side of the flyer the Angelus Press advertises the publication, no doubt for the first time in English, of a favorite book of Archbishop Lefebvre on the same subject, Fr. A. Roussel's *Liberalism and Catholicism*. Leaning much on the same Papal Encyclicals, Fr. Roussel teaches firstly the definition, origins and development of liberalism, and secondly the variety, subtlety and perversity of combinations of liberalism with Catholicism. The two absolutely do not mix, yet men mix them, Archbishop Lefebvre used to say, "in 36 different ways"! Nobody can pretend that this Encyclicals Study Set or Fr. Roussel's book make for easy reading. However, for anyone who has the Faith and ability to master such material, it is an incomparable fortification of their Catholic immune system against what Archbishop Lefebvre used to call the AIDS of neo-modernism, which is making the bows of the Church dip deeper and deeper under water. The pre-Conciliar Popes saw the liberal icebergs coming, they warned, they were not listened to . . .

For an easier introduction to these same Encyclicals, allow me to remind you of the existence of audio and video tapes of the Winona Doctrinal Sessions of the summers of 1996 and 1997. These have been now freshly and professionally packaged, and have not been designed to make money, in fact the Seminary tapes program is seriously in the red. But this doctrine must get out to Catholics, if all of us are not to go to the bottom of an ocean of eternal fire!

The ocean is icy all around us, and there may be only minutes to jump, but remember the baker on board the *Titanic* who paddled happily through the night, and was picked out of the water alive in the morning because in his last moments on board he consoled himself plentifully with a bottle of whisky! Drink down deep your Catholic Faith, and then you too will start heating up the ocean with your charity!

10 Years After the Consecrations

THE LAST DAY of this month will be the tenth anniversary of the famous Episcopal Consecrations performed by Archbishop Marcel Lefebvre and Bishop Antonio de Castro Mayer in Ecône, Switzerland, on June 30, 1988. How does that heroic event look ten years later? More heroic than ever! Let us recall its place in history.

Once upon a time, in the so-called Dark Ages, the Catholic Church reigned supreme as the undisputed mistress of civilization, and all Christendom was Catholic. Then at the end of the Middle Ages, the modern world began in earnest with the breakup of Christendom by Martin Luther. Half Europe turned Protestant, but the other half pulled its Catholic self together in the so-called Counter-Reformation, and the Church leapt across oceans to make many new Catholic peoples to replace those fallen away.

But of course the Devil would not leave the old or new Catholic nations in peace. Out of the juxtaposition of Catholic truth and Protestant error he developed a virulent new error, liberalism (What is truth? Who knows?

What does it matter?), with which he infected the politics in Catholic and Protestant nations alike, generating a series of Revolutions from the end of the 18th century which smashed Catholic altars and pulled down Catholic thrones. Mother Church reeled, but again she pulled her faith and her energy together, and made even of the liberal 19th century one of the greatest missionary centuries ever.

By now the Devil was resolved to break into the Church itself, but of course he could only do so by deceit. So he invented another error, as old as the hills but seeming new, a rerun of Protestantism and liberalism, whereby all the Catholic appearances would be maintained, but the substance would be changed or updated to get more in line with the modern world – hence the error's name of modernism. It caught several priests who wished to continue to appear Catholic while turning worldly, which is to sinful man an attractive combination!

However, just before modernism could strike Mother Church a mortal blow, the God-given Pope St. Pius X intervened in the early years of this century to denounce so clearly its perfidy and to smash it with such force that it was driven underground so as to even seem to many Catholics hardly to have existed. Basking then in the reprieve of 50 years (1907–1958) earned for Mother Church by the clear-sightedness and strength of the saintly Pope, the vast majority of Catholics had no idea of the storm being prepared for them.

Thus when Pope Pius XII died in 1958, too many churchmen were tired of resisting the modern world with its Protestantism, liberalism and modernism, so instead of electing another clear-sighted and strong Pope, the Cardinals chose John XXIII, a "Catholic" liberal who launched an Ecumenical Council to "update" the Church. At last the moment had come for the condemned modernists lurking in the shadows to step forward and grab power in the Church – John XXIII was on their side.

With his help they hijacked the Second Vatican Council from the beginning, and now the Church was in a desperate plight. When Protestants fell, the Catholic nations had stood. When politics in those nations fell, the Church had stood. When priests in the Church were all ready to fall, the Pope had stood. But now the Pope had virtually fallen – who was left to stand?

At the beginning of the Second Vatican Council in 1962, the good bishops were unorganized and the neo-modernists' onslaught took them completely by surprise. By the end of the Council, however, in 1965, some 450 truly Catholic bishops had grouped together to defend the Faith, and when they went home, they were resolved to continue working together to save the Church. Alas, they had reckoned without the structure of the Church, and Pope Paul VI.

By the structure of the Catholic Church, it is the Pope who commands, and Pope Paul VI was a liberal. Some Catholic bishops, he sacked. With some, he waited until they died. Others, he put under such pressure that they cracked, and resigned. He was resolved to break the back of their Catholic resistance, and by fair means or foul, he did just that. No doubt he was convinced he was acting for the good of the Church, but the Church was devastated just the same.

Then had Our Lord's promise failed, that the gates of hell would not prevail against His Church? No. Out of the 450 resistant bishops there was one who could not be sacked (he had already resigned), who would not crack under the pressure (despite Rome's best efforts), and who did not die until he had built a shelter to protect the Church's essential treasures for the duration of the storm – Archbishop Marcel Lefebvre.

What a man! Alone now, against Protestantism, against liberalism, against the Popes, against his fellow bishops, he was alone, alone, alone, except for a handful of scattered priests, and a handful of dear youngsters that he began to draw around him as seminarians. And with a few old priests and these youngsters he constructed that shelter, the Society of St. Pius X.

But under what pressure! In 1975 Rome pretends to "dissolve" the new-born Society. In 1976 it pretends to "suspend" the Archbishop from his priestly functions because his Society, which has refused to die, is just producing its first class of a dozen priests. The Archbishop and his youngsters continue ("Archbishop, do you realize what mistakes your young priests make?" "What do you expect me to do? The old priests won't stay with me!"). He hopes against hope that a few bishops will stand by him to help defend the Faith, but Providence so disposes that only in the early 1980's does Bishop de Castro Mayer from an obscure little Brazilian diocese at last step forward to associate himself with the stand taken by the Archbishop.

Meanwhile Rome is all the time resolutely transforming the Catholic Church into the Newchurch to be the religious spearhead of the New World Order. Pope John Paul II's Assisi event of October, 1986, placing Catholic truth on an equal footing alongside a dozen sectarian, heretical, Judaic and pagan errors, is a decisive alarm-signal for the Archbishop, by now 80 years old and feeling his end approaching. For the longest possible time he has negotiated with Rome and stayed within official structures to avoid even the appearance of breaking with the Roman Church, but soon he must choose. To ensure the continuance of ordinations for his priestly Society and of Confirmations for his now worldwide flock, either he must trust the Roman wolf to look after his Traditional sheep, or he must consecrate bishops of his own to look after them, at the risk of being condemned by Rome and even "excommunicated."

Hence the fateful decision of May 6, and the glorious action of June 30, 1988. But what a decision to have to take, and that he still had to take on his own! What calm! What clarity! What a man! And he died, as he had guessed, a few years later.

And of his heritage we have all received, and continue to receive, against the entire modern world, against bishops, cardinals and Popes, and against hell and high water, but with the Truth, with the Faith, and with God.

Your Grace, you can only be very high in Heaven. Thank you, thank you, thank you! Pray for us and intercede for us here below, that we may never abandon the Faith or Church which you defended, rather that with each passing ten years the anniversary of your glorious act may be more and more glorious!

Priestly ordinations take place here in Winona on Saturday morning, June 20 (celebrated by Bishop de Galaretta, not by Bishop Fellay as announced). There should be two new deacons and two new priests. That is not a large number, but it is worth a large number if they remain faithful. The crisis of modernism is about the Faith, not about numbers. All visitors welcome.

Remember also the Spiritual Exercises being given as usual at Winona in the summer, the men's retreat from July 6 to 11 still having places. And may you spend a pleasant summer, taking a vacation from worries but never a vacation from God!

Unreal Movies &
Real Catholicism

HAVING LAST MONTH looked at the long past leading up to the ten-year anniversary of the Episcopal Consecrations in Ecône of June, 1988, let us this month frame some storm-clouds of the future between some sunny skies of the present.

The sunshine to begin with is that the four bishops of the SSPX, consecrated mainly to give the sacraments of Confirmation and Holy Orders to the souls brought by the grace of God towards the Society, as you could read last month Archbishop Lefebvre himself telling them ten years ago, have quietly been doing just that.

For the last ten summers, including this one, I have been, at the US District Superiors' request, making a tour of Confirmations amongst mainly the Society's American churches and chapels and missions. This year I was in three out of four corners of the USA, Florida, California and Washington State, and in another ten or so States in between them.

Each year, I would have to say, it has been an encouraging experience. In easily most of these locations I have been more than once. This year I noticed many new faces, although in no chapel did numbers seem to have notably increased. This confirms a long-standing observation that the Society's action is rather a holding action than a glorious advance. However, a holding action in today's extra difficult circumstances is glorious enough. On this last Confirmations tour in the U.S.A., I may have confirmed some 400 adults and children. I often tap hard (as the rubrics do not forbid!) in order to warn confirmands how they will have to fight to live as Catholics, but in general the holding action does seem to be holding.

However, those extra difficult circumstances are not becoming any easier. Chaos in people's hearts and minds swirls all around us. Sister Lucy of Fatima called it "diabolical disorientation," and the Archbishop's dear little SSPX is going to need a miraculous protection if its faith is not also to perish in the universal storm, still rising. The old-fashioned barometer, reading lower and lower, is beginning to sway on the wall!

Let me take one case of this chaos, featured in many a Confirmation sermon this year, to try to help Catholics to grasp what a gigantic drama is playing out around them, because even most Catholics seem to think (or wish) themselves to be still living in the world of "The Sound of Music"! That world is gone, gone forever, as it deserved!

The case was apparently all over the media here in the USA several months ago. My knowledge of it is essentially confined to one long newspaper article sent to me by a friend, but the main outlines are clear. A 34 year-old schoolmistress from Washington State, married with four children between the ages of 4 and 13, entered into a relationship with a boy in her sixth grade class (age 11 or 12?), by whom she then had a baby girl. Tried and convicted for the offence against a minor, she was sentenced to jail for eight years, but the sentence was suspended because her "sweet and bubbly" personality must have seemed to everybody to be out of place in the "slammer." However, no sooner was she out than she made herself pregnant by the same boy for the second time, whereupon her judge threw her back into jail to serve the rest of her sentence!

The article prints an attractive color picture of her in court at the moment of her original sentencing: her pretty little chin perched on her folded hands, looking no older than a teenager herself, she looks wistfully across the courtroom, as though to say, "Why cannot these people understand true love?" For indeed, one of the quotations attributed to her by the article runs, "I have found true love at last." Can anyone doubt she has watched The Sound of Music 20 or 50 times? Not I.

"Oh, come on your Excellency! Get off movies, and leave that movie alone!" Dear friends, gladly, if only movies would get off Catholics and Catholics would leave that movie alone! But I have here under my hand a glossy "1998 Catholic Family and School Videos" catalogue, from a reputable conservative Catholic organization out of Colorado, which advertises one smiling, glamorous, sentimental, "uplifting" movie after another, page after page. Where is the blood? Where is the Cross? Where is the sacrifice?

Movies are unreal. Catholicism is for real. Catholic movies, unless they are strict documentaries, are virtually a contradiction in terms. Yet movies occupy the front, center, and back of most Catholics' hearts and minds, at least here in the USA! This is the drama of our poor schoolmistress who – you guessed – is one of seven children from a strongly conservative Catholic home! She was born in 1962. What did her home lack in those supposedly wonderful days, that she is now completely detached from reality? Catholics must ask themselves!

Listen to two more quotes of hers: "Some day we (she and the school boy!) will marry. We will all live happily together and my two families will be one, and everything will be just perfect!" (She means, she and her middle-aged husband and their four children and the schoolboy and their two children, will all live happily ever after, together? She is mad!) Again: "I couldn't be happier. I have a new life inside me. It's a sign, a sign that God wants us to be together, to be one!" She is using what remains of her Catholic Faith to justify her adultery and betrayal of a minor entrusted to her professional care! And she is watched and listened to with avid sympathy by media all over the country!!

Of course, she was herself betrayed: by all those (which means everybody) who encourage middle-aged women to look and behave like teenagers; by a co-educational school system which puts pretty women to teach adolescing boys; by her family values, anti-feminist father who himself rocked his family by a scandalous adultery; she was, one might say, betrayed by our whole crazy society (without that being an excuse!). Yet the problem is not just that she is completely detached from reality. The problem is that there are millions and millions, even of Catholics, living in the same unreal dream.

Question: can the Society withstand this tornado-force dream? Can Society Catholics, especially priests, withstand the mighty suction of Fiftiesism, that glossy version of Catholicism without the Cross, all the outer trappings of Tradition, but with none of the substance (cf. II Timothy 3: 5)? The glamorous modern world which seduced so many priests and bishops into Vatican II is more glamorous and modern than ever – what guarantees that the Society will not in turn go the way of all conciliar flesh?

Listen to a Society priest now working in the USA: "Here, either a priest fights like a hero, or he slips into

Fiftiesism without even realizing it. It's strange, but that's how it is. A priest must have unusual strength of character and rock-solid convictions to stand fast, or he will slide the way the whole modern environment encourages him to slide. So a polarisation is inevitable in all our parishes. That was not so yesterday, when a comfortable conservatism was still possible, but the days of those good conservative priests are gone. Today it's all or nothing. This or that priest may vigorously deny they are liberal, but if they are incapable of serious, steady, almost heroic action, they will give way in practice. You may even not be liberal, but if you do not do what you should do, you will still act like a liberal."

I have long asked myself whether the Society will last until the Chastisement. If it does, God will have given it a special protection. Time will tell if that is His will.

Meanwhile, another of the four bishops of ten years ago, Bishop Alfonso de Galarreta, performed the ordinations at Winona this year in bright sunshine. Lovely weather for the morning itself, and for the following day of the first Masses of the two new priests; a crowd of maybe 650 people; much Catholic happiness and many graces, as usual. God is good. He is still granting to the Society to bear good fruit. May He grant that we not become, following the Conciliar shell without substance, a Traditional shell without substance!

Let us also ask for good weather for the women's and men's retreats soon to take place here. The seminary grounds can be lovely at this time of year, when of a sunny evening all the green is bathed in a soft warm light, with no farm machine chattering, and with the occasional bird singing away the day. But man's cooperation is needed to mow God's creation, otherwise there are dandelions everywhere!

"Fiftiesism"

FOLLOWING ON THE mention of "Fiftiesism" in last month's letter, a reader reasonably asked what it is, and if there is anywhere he can read up on it. Since Fiftiesism is a serious threat to "Traditional" Catholics, and since little has to my knowledge been written about it as such, let us examine it here.

"Fiftiesism" is a name for the kind of Catholicism that was generally practiced in the 1950's, between World War II and Vatican II. To many Catholics who can look back that far, the 1950's seem like a golden age for the Church, because all kinds of Catholic systems were still up and running that crashed a few years later. On the other hand, precisely because so many Catholic systems crashed in the 1960's and 1970's, not all can have been well with the Church in those 1950's. There must have been "something rotten in the State of Denmark."

For instance the magnificent building now housing the seminary in Winona was put up by the Dominicans, sparing no expense, in the early 1950's, only to be abandoned by them in 1970, and sold for a song. And this Novitiate for their central United States Province was merely one Catholic institute amongst thousands all over the world that followed this path from riches to rags. Can the 1950's really have been such a golden age as they seem?

Fiftiesism is then the name for what was wrong alongside – or inside – all that was right in the practice of Catholicism in the 1950's. Church structures stood tall but termites were burrowing away within, so that with one strong push from Vatican II, the structures were all ready to fall over. Traditional Catholics today must take thought to avoid rebuilding a Church of the 1950's all ready to fall over again!

To illustrate what was good as well as bad in the Catholicism of the 1950's, let us think of English Catholicism in the 1520's, just before the Reformation in England of the 1530's and 1540's.

On the good side, England looked in the 1520's like a completely Catholic nation. It had been Catholic for nearly 1,000 years, with the result that for an Englishman then to be Catholic was the most normal and simple thing in the world. Young King Henry VIII was so Catholic that he was awarded by Rome the title of "Defender of the Faith" for his refutation of Luther's errors! As for the English people, a scholarly book was written a few years ago to prove how Catholic they still were, as though the Reformation was none of their fault.

Alas, on the bad side, what were the fruits of this 1520's Catholicism? By the end of the 1550's Catholics were being persecuted, and Queen Elizabeth I was skillfully and ruthlessly maneuvering England into national apostasy, wherein to remain Catholic was a glorious but highly dangerous avocation. Catholic priests were hunted down by her secret police, hanged, drawn and quartered as traitors, so that while an English priest in the 1560's had to have the same Catholic Faith and priesthood as a priest in the 1520's, nevertheless in the transformed circumstances he was called upon to be a quite new kind of priest. Hence the Jesuit Order, "old and new."

What had happened? The Catholicism of English Catholics in the 1520's had been tried by the Lord God and found wanting. As events of the 1530's and 1540's proved, their Catholicism, which we might call "Twentiesism," had been too much of a shellgame. The clergy had "lacked grace" (Thomas More). As for the people, they had resisted, for instance in the Pilgrimage of Grace, but not enough. So God punished English Twentiesism by letting it turn into the permanent shellgame of Anglicanism (known in the USA as Episcopalianism), founded on Elizabeth's Anglican Establishment.

Now imagine a Jesuit priest in England of the 1560's saying to the small congregations of his faithful remnant, "My dear people, all is changed, changed utterly, a terrible beauty is born. No more Twentiesism!," and you can see why a Traditional priest would say to Traditionalists in the 1990's, "No more Fiftiesism!"

In fairness to English Catholics of the 1520's, the problem of their shellgame had been building up over many generations before them, and it did not mean that every English Catholic was losing or would lose the Faith, because of course there was a glorious first harvest of martyrs under Henry VIII, and a second under Elizabeth I.

In fairness likewise to the Fiftiesism of our own time, the pre-Vatican II shellgame was the end-product of 150 years of Liberal Catholicism blending Church and world, attempting to combine the values of the Faith with those of the Revolution, and not every Catholic of the 1950's proved to be deep down in love with the world, because, as in Reformation England, a by the grace of God faithful remnant pulled through Vatican II to constitute the bedraggled but glorious remains of the Tridentine Church known to us as "Tradition," or the "Traditionalists"!

At the heart then of Fiftiesism in our own time is that while outwardly the Faith in the 1950's seemed to be lived, practiced and defended, and the Mass was the Mass of all time, nevertheless inwardly too many Catholics' hearts were going with the world. Thence it was simply a matter of time before all those strict priests celebrating the ancient liturgy with every detail in place, would throw away their birettas and loosen up with eucharistic picnics improvised from one moment to the next. Americans old enough remember how suddenly this change could take place, almost overnight. The inside was rotten. Many Catholics pretended to love God, but really they loved the world. God spat them out at Vatican II.

But why in the 1950's were so many Catholics inwardly loving the world? Because the modern world, industrialized and suburbanized, is too much with us, all-glamorous, all-powerful, all-seductive. For even if a man and his family are intent upon remaining Catholic, still man remains a three-layered creature, not only individual and familial but also social, and all three layers are connected. Hence society exerts an enormous anti-Catholic pressure upon Catholics when it has been, like ours, largely in the grip of Masonic Revolutions for the last 200 years.

To illustrate Fiftiesism here in the USA (since most readers of this letter are Americans, but of course Fiftiesism was worldwide, as was Vatican II), let us quote three anti-Catholic principles firmly believed in by many American Catholics of the 1950's (and 1990's?), one social, one familial, one individual, amongst many others.

False social principle: separation of Church and State. This deadly error means that Jesus Christ is no longer King over society, He is only King of the sacristy. Society can supposedly do as it likes, and Our Lord has nothing to say! On the contrary read in the Bible the history of the People of God from Abraham and Moses through David, Solomon and Ezra to see if God's religion tells peoples what as peoples they must do!

False familial principle: co-education. Boys are designed by God quite differently from girls because He has quite different parts for them to play in life. So the Catholic Church has always known and taught that from as early an age as possible, let us say no later than seven or eight, they should be taught differently and separately. Yet how many "Catholics" in the USA were accustomed to co-education in the 1950's and still see no problem with it in the 1990's? Not even in the most primitive tribes will you find co-education! They have too much sense!

False individual principle: the split between "religion" and real life. To how many "Catholics" in the 1950's was "religion" what one did on Sunday morning while in real life the world was being saved, for instance from Communism, by the American Constitution, free enterprise, etc. etc.? No doubt the Faith was believed in, every article of it, but how many "Catholics" let that Faith form their character and define their view of the world? How many "Traditionalists" to this day really put their trust in Our Lord Jesus Christ to solve problems of home, family, politics, education, economics, the arts, etc., etc.? How many on the contrary seek to "enjoy" the world as much as they can, to have all possible "fun," while keeping just short of mortal sin? That is pure Fiftiesism, and it will have the same disastrous results.

What is the solution to Fiftiesism, then and now? It is not complicated. The problem lies in pretending to put God first but not really doing so. The solution lies in obeying the First Commandment first, in loving the Lord God – Jesus Christ – with all our heart, with all our soul, with all our strength and with all our mind, and in putting no other gods or solutions before Him. Nor is it impossible to do so. The world, the flesh and the Devil may dominate our environment as never before in all history, but God remains God and we remain children of His Mother.

A powerful and practical means she obtained from her Son to help us put the First Commandment back in place is the Spiritual Exercises of St. Ignatius. These were given only twice at the seminary this year, but they brought forth a bouquet of testimonials from which we shall quote next month to encourage you to make use of one of the Society's three retreat houses in the USA. Go to the retreats where you hear they really knock down, drag out the retreatants! Those are where the action is!

And may Our Lord pull all of us back from the world, the flesh and the Devil, lest His Chastisement catch us still in Fiftiesism, ready for Hell!

NO. 179 | SEPTEMBER 1, 1998

John Paul II's "Personalism"

T HE MINDS OF most Catholic churchmen today are in a state of what Sister Lucy of Fatima called "diabolical disorientation." These churchmen are on the road to eternal perdition and they are taking millions of souls with them. How can that be? It is a mystery of iniquity. However, a little article which somebody sent to me recently throws – without meaning to! – much light thereon.

It is an article by a Fr. Richard Hogan, in a recent pro-life newsletter, on "The Theology of John-Paul II." It praises the Pope for providing the Catholic Church with a new way, acceptable to modern man, of presenting the Church's Faith and moral teaching. Little can Fr. Hogan realize that his article's clear presentation of the Pope's basic thinking makes clear not how this Pope helps to save babies, but how he helps to slaughter them! And yet no doubt the Pope, and Fr. Hogan, have the best of intentions! "Diabolical disorientation"!

In a nutshell, the Pope centers all on man. So, little human beings should be of supreme value. But, if the biological father and mother are also of supreme value, then why should they not get rid of the little fetus invading their supreme lives? The fight against abortion is no doubt a good cause, but no good cause is to be defended with bad arguments.

The problem with abortion is, first, last, and foremost, that it breaks the law of God. To try to fight abortion without bringing in God – to try to solve any of the modern world's real problems without bringing in God – is a fight lost in advance. Yet that is, basically, what Fr. Hogan praises the Pope for doing. No wonder this Pope, with – apparently – the best of intentions, is destroying the Church. Let us look at the article more in detail. It is not long.

The reason why the Pope's thinking is so valuable to modern Catholics, says Fr. Hogan, is because of his unique success in combining the modern philosophy he studied in Cracow with the Catholic theology he afterwards studied in Rome. By this combination modern minds with their new way of thinking can once more be reached with Catholic truth which was closed to them as long as it was cast, or expressed, in the age-old way of thinking. For whereas the old thinking was objective (based on the outward object, identically real or true for everybody) and deductive (concluding downwards from universal principles), on the contrary modern thinking is subjective (based on inward realizations, valid maybe only for the individual having them) and inductive (concluding upwards from a series of individual experiences, like democracy, says Fr. Hogan).

The gulf between these two ways of thinking is so deep that for as long as Catholic truth was only cast in the old way, it was inaccessible to modern minds thinking only in the new way. What Karol Wojtyla did as far back as 1958 with his philosophy of "personalism," as Fr. Hogan calls it, was to bridge this gulf between object and subject by putting the human person in the center, for in the human person objective and subjective meet and are no longer opposed to one another.

How? On the one hand, by being created as an object in the image and likeness of God, the human person reflects the ultimate, objective, universal Reality from whom all else is deduced. On the other hand by being created as a subject individual and inward to himself, the human person has subjectively valid experiences from which he mounts inductively upwards, e.g., to God.

Fr. Hogan concludes by rejoicing that Karol Wojtyla's re-thinking of Catholic Revelation transforms all Catholic theology! The fusing of objective and subjective in the human person gives us brand new notions of creation, the human body, the human family, the human person, the person of Christ; of the Church, the sacraments, grace, sin, death, Judgment, Heaven, and Hell! Fr. Hogan apparently loves these new notions, and ends by begging readers to study the Pope's "personalism."

However, has the good Father Hogan stopped to think? The Pope's version of Hell is indeed new. The Pope promoted to cardinal the Swiss "theologian" Hans Urs von Balthasar who said that Hell is empty. A charming thought. But if nobody goes to Hell, why should any abortionist stop aborting? Because of "the dignity of the human person"? Don't make me laugh! As a Scottish convert to Catholicism once noteworthily said, "A Kerk (=church) without a Hell isn't werth (=worth) a damn!" Exactly. The Newchurch, emptying out hell, is not "werth a damn"!

Where then, in Fr. Hogan's version, did Karol Wojtyla go wrong? (No doubt Fr. Hogan has rather simplified the issues, but his simplification is essentially just.)

Firstly, Fr. Hogan bases the achievement of Karol Wojtyla's "personalism" on its overcoming of the split between object and subject, between objective thinking and subjective thinking. But this split is false. For while objective reality and subjective man are indeed different, they do not exclude one another, as Fr. Hogan suggests.

For indeed what is objective, the vast real framework of the universe, includes what is subjective, human beings and their inner realizations. That is why ancient thinking took full account of everything subjective within the framework of objective reality. Only modern thinking gives such importance to the subject as to shut out objective reality. Thus ancient thinking fires on all four engines, modern thinking only on two. There is no need to respect modern thought or modern ways of thinking! Hopping on one leg may be amusing, but as a means of movement it cannot compare with walking on two legs!

Therefore, secondly, not only is there no need to recast the Catholic Faith from an objective into a subjective way of thinking, but also there is a positive need not to do so! It is the sheerest common sense that the truths of the Catholic Faith have nothing whatsoever to do with my inward realizations, or my sacred subjectivity! I may or may not have a beautiful inward realization, a NIF (nice internal feeling), of the Immaculate Conception, but all the NIFs in the world have nothing to do with whether a particular Jewish maiden was, or was not, miraculously protected by God from the stain of original sin at that moment in history when she was conceived in the womb of St. Anne! Alas, common sense is not modern man's strong suit!

But democracy is. Notice how Fr. Hogan slipped it into the modern way of thinking. Listen to modern catechism teachers: "Children, what do you all, democratically, feel, about the Immaculate Conception, inside yourselves? Jane, you feel it's true? Then it's true for you! John, you don't? Then it's false for you! But let's take a vote, in order to all induce together!" Ridiculous!

Hence, thirdly, as for Pope John Paul's "personalism" as presented by Fr. Hogan, it is true that the human being is created in the image and likeness of God, and so reflects to a tiny extent the objective truth and goodness of God. And it is true that this human subject can have all kinds of thoughts or feelings, upwards or downwards, especially since God gives him free will. But whether these subjective thoughts are true or not, valid or not, depends not upon whether they are subjectively held (they cannot not be if they are thoughts or feelings), but upon whether they match objective reality.

In other words, the real value of the human person lies not in his merely being.a human person, regardless of whether he is full of truth or falsehood, which is what this Pope basically thinks. The real value of the human person lies in the use he makes of his free will to subjectively recognize and love the ultimate objective reality, i.e., God.

If the human person refuses to align his human subjectivity upon the objective Divinity, that is not just a regrettable failure leaving his "human dignity" untouched as he goes to Heaven whether he wants to or not. It is a damnable sin and offence against the goodness of God, cause of eternal damnation in the objective fires of Hell. Who do modern "theologians" think they are to be extinguishing those fires? Benefactors of mankind? On the contrary!

This Pope is the leader of a dream. His Newchurch is a dream. Into that dream he is helping to pull thousands upon thousands of priests like Fr. Hogan, and millions upon millions of unsuspecting Catholics. Unsuspecting? God knows. In any case they – and all of us – are due for a harsh awakening with tomorrow's reality check. How soon does it arrive? God knows. But that is one check that will not bounce! So we must pray for this poor Pope that he may wake up to reality before it is too late for him to save his soul. And we must pray for Fr. Richard Hogan that he put his fight against abortion on solid foundations, namely the existence of God, His Fifth Commandment, and the existence of Hell for grave disobedience to any of God's Ten Commandments.

The Pope and Fr. Hogan may reply that God, Commandments and Hell are objective notions which no longer have any grip on subjective modern man. The answer is that a strong conviction will still put them over to many men, and if those many reduce themselves to a handful, like in Noah's time, then the rest must be left to the Flood. As Dr. Samuel Johnson said, "The prospect of imminent execution wonderfully concentrates the mind"!

In any case it is useless to fight sin with man-centered arguments, because sin is man-centeredness. The sinner has won before the fight starts! That is why the Newchurch is so weak. To reach out to modern man on modern man's terms means that, heads he wins, tails God loses. Fr. Hogan, think again!

On the 10th of October, Deo volente, I shall be in Ecône for the blessing of the handsome new stone church at the mother-seminary of the SSPX in Switzerland. Pray for the occasion, and for the dear Society, which is still reaching out to modern man on God's terms. It will have the success that God grants.

Co-education

C O-EDUCATION, EDUCATING BOYS and girls together, has always been condemned by the Catholic Church. For instance, Pope Pius XI on 1929
called it a "pernicious error, which, to the immense harm
of youth" is "spreading far and wide among Christian
peoples." Why then can many "Catholics" today not see
what is wrong with it? Because it naturally follows from
four great false principles of the modern world, universally held to be true.

The first and most radical of these false principles is
religious liberty. If the State cannot decide which religion is true, then religious ideas are not that important,
so we don't need no education (unless it's material), we
don't need no thought-control, "truth" is just opinions,
strawberry fields for ever, and school time has no reason
to be anything other than one long party for boys and
girls together.

Now when this way of thinking is laid out so crudely,
no self-respecting Catholic can think he is affected by
it. However, just how seriously do our "Catholics" take
education that is not material or technological? Judge
by their pocket books, or wallets, not by their words.
Which in fact comes first? That expensive car, or that

expensive Catholic tuition for the child? Things spiritual like old-fashioned Catholic education get lip service, but things material get the real service. So, the drive of boys towards girls and of girls towards boys being an unalterable given of human nature, then to deny its easy gratifications to one's youngsters requires a higher motivation, otherwise the lower drive will take over. Co-education betrays a lack of such motivation, a lack of belief in the seriousness of life. Had I anything really serious that I wished to teach these boys or girls, then the first thing I would do, if I could, would be to separate them. The army and navy are no longer serious, so now they are mixed. American football is still serious, so who ever heard of mixed American football training camps?

Second great modern principle: relations between the sexes are not a social matter with which, for instance, schools should concern themselves, they are purely a private matter for the individuals concerned. Therefore education has no business to be getting in between the sexes, and liberty requires that they be free to mix with no interference from school.

It is an enormous error of our age that relations between the sexes are a purely individual affair. True, by the pleasures attached, insofar as the individuals alone concerned can enjoy them, those relations resemble eating and drinking, but as to the purpose governing these pleasures, those relations are wholly different. Whereas eating and drinking are ordered to the survival of the individual, those relations with their whole range of material and spiritual pleasures are ordered to the survival of the species, or mankind. Therefore they are a matter of society's survival, and of its legitimate concern. The society that refuses to interfere in the individuals' use or misuse of those relations and what goes with them is a society like our own, committing suicide.

Again, the problem lies rather in the disappearance of higher belief and motivation than in the constant re-appearance of lower drives. Just as the jagged rocks on the sea floor of a tidal harbor are no problem at high tide when the ships float freely above them, but at low tide, without their having moved an inch, they paralyze shipping, so if men are spiritually motivated they can sail above their lower instincts, but if that motivation ebbs away, they fall foul of those instincts which have not changed. Modern co-education betrays modern society's lack of spiritual or intellectual motivation, or faith.

Third great modern error behind co-education: the denial of original sin. "Boys and girls are just friends." "The more they are mixed together, the less they notice one another." "Separation is artificial." "Mixing is necessary to teach and test virtue." "Amongst Catholics everything should be fine." And, of course, "MY children are angels."

Well, as the saying goes, if you believe that, you can believe anything. Yet it is astonishing how many "Catholic" parents do believe it! They have all learned about original sin in their catechism, but of course the catechism is only a book and their children are of course the exception! I can remember how, when the mother of a teenage girl wanting to hang around seminarians tried to reassure the suspicious Seminary Rector that her daughter was "not like that," he snorted. "Oh," she pouted at him, "I do wish you wouldn't be like that!" He snorted again.

In what world do these parents live? Answer, in a foolish world which all around them affirms the innate goodness of man. ("Ah, but America is different" – I suppose you are talking about Bill Clinton?) What grasp then does the Catholic catechism have upon the minds and hearts of such "Catholic" parents? Poor things. Not much. But then, as everybody knows, religion is only for

Sundays mornings. Alas! Catholics immersed in a Protestant culture, as in English-speaking countries, must exert themselves constantly not to become Protestants who merely go to Mass on Sundays, even if it is the true Mass!

Original sin is for real! Since when has throwing young men and women together been anything other than like tossing lit matches on a heap of dry straw? Since modern times, when mankind is so advanced? Oh yeah? Ask the US Navy, since it began a few years ago sending scads of young sailoresses to sea together with the young sailors – the aircraft carriers return to port turned into love boats, and half the ratings have to be dismissed for pregnancy!

"Oh, bishop, I do wish you wouldn't be like that!" Pleeeeeeease! Where has the common sense gone? Since when, if you wish to keep two magnets apart, do you put them close by one another? In truth, co-educators do not want the young magnets to stay apart, they are quite happy to see them clinching. After all, "Mixing is necessary to learn to interact normally," and "They will mix all their lives so they might as well start now," and "To condemn casual mixing is just being hyper-reactive", and after all, "Catholics must not be too different from the world around them." Oh no? Alas, the denial of original sin is so embedded in the proud modern world that not all the mockery in China will prise it out again. "The facts can go to blazes! Our dream is so much nicer! We are now God!"

However, almost as catastrophic as the denial of original sin is the fourth hidden principle of co-educators, namely that between the two sexes – let the crudity of the expression awaken to the shocking stupidity of the error – there are only minor differences of plumbing! In our enlightened age, so runs the argument, girls are no longer inferior to boys but are interchangeable with them, so it is against equality to educate them separately or train them for different functions, especially when the rising divorce rate may require either to perform what used to be regarded as the other's functions.

But if the divorce rate is so rising, is not one of the main reasons precisely this scorn for the God-given distinction and complementarity of the two sexes? Children especially need a manly man to be their father and a womanly woman to be their mother, but of course the modern world thinks it knows better. There are volumes to be written on this subject, so often addressed in these letters, but space is running out. Here is how Pius XI summed up the error in his 1929 Encyclical on the Christian Education of Youth, quoted above:

> Co-education . . . is founded . . . upon a deplorable confusion of ideas that mistakes a leveling mixity and equality for the lawful association of the sexes. The Creator has ordained and disposed perfect union of the sexes only in marriage, and, with varying degrees of contact, in the family and in society. Besides, there is in nature itself, which fashions the two sexes' quite different organisms, temperaments and abilities, nothing to suggest that there can be or that there ought to be mixity, and much less equality, in the training of the two sexes. These, in keeping with the wonderful designs of the Creator, are destined to complement each other in the family and in society, precisely because of their differences, which therefore ought to be maintained and encouraged during the years of formation, with the necessary distinction and corresponding separation, according to age and circumstances. These principles, with due regard to time and place, must, in accordance with Christian prudence, be applied to all schools, particularly in the most delicate and decisive period of formation, that namely of adolescence . . .

Richard N. Williamson

Of course, Traditional Catholic schools today, especially when they are starting out, must make do and mend, and they may not have the means to establish immediately all separation desirable of the sexes. But let Catholics at least not approve in principle of any mixity they may be obliged to put up with for the time being in practice. Nor let them say that Pius XI was speaking for 1929 but not for 1999 (what makes the difference? – Vatican II??), or that he was speaking for Europe but not for America (did the Freemasons change human nature?).

In sum, education of youth is much too serious to allow for fooling around with mixity. Co-education is not just a matter of individuals' free choice, it is an issue for society and its schools. Co-education is a massive occasion of sin, given the weakness of human nature due to original sin. And co-education massively disrespects God's design in the natural distinction and complementarity of the sexes.

Why We Do Not
Cooperate with Rome

WHY MUST SO-CALLED Traditional Catholics take their stand against today's Rome? Why, when traditionalists with their "strong faith" have "so much to offer the Church," do they insist on "cutting themselves off"? Why can they not, like conservative Catholics, make the best of both worlds by using Rome's 1984 Indult allowing (within strict limits) the Tridentine Mass?

The answer to these questions emerges yet again, clearly, from an address of Pope John Paul II to a leading group of conservative Catholics who were down in Rome last weekend because they believe in cooperating with Rome.

The occasion was the gathering in the Eternal City from Friday Oct. 23 to Monday Oct. 26 of members of the Fraternity of St. Peter to celebrate the tenth anniversary of their Congregation, founded in 1988 by priests leaving the SSPX in protest against Archbishop Lefebvre's consecrating four bishops that summer without Rome's permission. It will be remembered that the Archbishop said at that time that the Catholic Church's leaders had shown themselves by, for instance, the Assisi event of October 1986, to be incapable of defending the true Faith, so Tradition had to be given interim bishops of its own. On the contrary, said the handful of his priests who broke away to form St. Peter's Fraternity, the Church's present leaders are good Catholics under whom the Traditional Faith can perfectly well be continued. So these conservative priests put themselves back under the direct control of Rome through the *Ecclesia Dei* Commission, named after the document of July 1988 in which Rome condemned the consecration of the four "Traditional" bishops.

To avoid the accusation of making unfair omissions, the following text of the Pope's address to members of St. Peter's Fraternity in Rome on October 26, 1998, is given in full. His words are in italics, commentary is in normal print.

"I bid you cordially welcome, dear pilgrims wishing to be in Rome for the 10th anniversary of the Motu Proprio *Ecclesia Dei*, to strengthen and renew your faith In Christ and your fidelity to the Church. Dear friends, your being in the presence of 'the successor of Peter who more than anyone else has to watch over the unity of the Church' (Vatican I, *Pastor Aeternus*) is particularly significant."

From the outset, the Pope emphasizes unity, and himself as the center of Catholic unity. For 17 years, the only answer of Popes Paul VI and John Paul II to Archbishop Lefebvre's accusations based on truth was this argument of unity . . .

"To safeguard the treasure entrusted to the Church by Jesus while remaining steadfastly turned towards the future, the Church must be constantly reflecting on her link with Tradition coming to us from the Lord through the Apostles, such as it has been established down the centuries."

The Pope does now evoke the Deposit of faith (as a "treasure") and Tradition, but neither as being absolute truth, rather he hints they are caught up in time ("towards the future", "down the centuries"). Does truth move with the times?

"According to the spirit of conversion in the Apostolic Letter 'Tertio Millennio Adveniente' (# 14, 32, 34, 50), I encourage all Catholics to take steps towards unity and to renew their attachment to the Church so that all legitimate differences and varying sensibilities worthy of respect may not be separated from each other, but may be an incentive to proclaim the Gospel together; thus, under the impulse of the Spirit uniting the various charisms, all will be able to glorify the Lord, and salvation will be proclaimed to all nations."

Conservatives must admit that JP2 is here treating their attachment to the Tridentine Mass, etc., as no more than a legitimate "sensibility" varying from the – one must suppose – equally legitimate, actually much more legitimate, sensibility of modernists to the Mass of Paul VI. Traditionalists on the contrary say that the Paul VI Mass is a betrayal of the Catholic Faith, undermining the Real Presence, the Present Sacrifice, the Sacrificing Priesthood. Do conservatives agree with JP2 in reducing these dogmas to a matter of "sensibility"?

"I wish all members of the Church to remain heirs of the faith received from the Apostles, worthily and faithfully celebrated in the holy mysteries, with fervour and beauty, so that they may receive ever more grace (cf. Trent s. VII, Decree on Sacraments) and live in a relation of close intimacy with the Holy Trinity."

The sentiments are impeccable, but can JP2 not see that the humanism intrinsic to the man-centered Mass of Paul VI necessarily militates against "worthy and faithful celebration"? No, in truth, he cannot see it (partly, no doubt, because his own priesthood began and grew up with the Tridentine Mass, which is no longer the case for young priests now).

"While confirming that the liturgical reform desired by Vatican II and carried out by Paul VI was justified, the Church does also give a sign of comprehension for people 'attached to certain previous liturgical and disciplinary forms' (Motu Proprio *Ecclesia Dei*' #5). This is the standpoint from which the Motu Proprio '*Ecclesia Dei*' is to be understood and applied; I wish it all to be lived in the spirit of Vatican II, in full harmony with Tradition, aiming at unity in charity and fidelity to the Truth."

This is the central paragraph of JP2's address to the conservative priests of St. Peter's. Notice the firm affirmation that the Paul VI liturgical reform was good, the corresponding reduction to mere "attachment to previous forms" of any protests against that reform, and the serene conclusion that Tradition is nothing that can be out of harmony with "the spirit of Vatican II." Do conservatives accept this understanding of "Tradition" as being perfectly compatible with the "spirit of Vatican II"? So Tradition and Truth do change with the times?

But now comes the practical clincher. Back in 1988, the new St. Peter's Fraternity obtained from Rome the Tridentine Mass and approval by Rome, but they did not obtain the bishop of their own that they had asked for. Since then, they have had to depend on diocesan or Novus Ordo bishops who thus retain essential control of the whole St. Peter's operation. Alas for St. Peter's, reports come from all over the world of how those bishops block their operation. St. Peter's Fraternity is liable to appeal in vain over their heads to the Pope. The Pope habitually refers them back to the same bishops! Now judge whether or not the blocking by those bishops is the will of the Pope:

"Led by 'the activity of the Holy Ghost, whereby the whole flock of Christ is preserved and progresses in unity of Faith' (Vatican II, *'Lumen Gentium'* # 25), the Successor of Peter and the bishops successors of the Apostles, teach the Christian mystery; in a quite particular way the bishops, gathered together in ecumenical Councils with Peter and beneath Peter, confirm and strengthen the doctrine of the Church, which is the faithful heir of Tradition existing now for nearly 20 centuries as a living and progressing reality, giving new impulse to the whole Church community. The three last ecumenical Councils, Trent, Vatican I and Vatican II, have been particularly concerned to throw light on the mystery of the Faith, and have undertaken reforms necessary for the good of the Church while ensuring continuity with apostolic Tradition, already gathered together by Saint Hyppolitus."

Note in passing the dangerous definition of "Tradition" as "a living and progressing reality, giving new impulse to the whole Church community." Also the incredible ranking of the anti-dogmatic Vatican II alongside the super-dogmatic Trent and Vatican I. But this paragraph has served mainly to prepare the "coup de grace," or finishing blow:

"So it is the task of the bishops, first and foremost, in communion with the successor of Peter, to lead the flock with firmness and charity, so that the Catholic Faith may be everywhere safeguarded (cf. Paul VI, Apostolic Exhortation 'Quinque Iam Anni'; New Code of Canon Law, can. 386) and worthily celebrated. For indeed, as Saint Ignatius of Antioch stated, 'Where the bishop is, there too the Church is' (Letter to the Smyrnians, VIII, 2). I extend also a fraternal invitation to the bishops to show understanding and renewed pastoral concern for Catholics attached to the old rite of Mass, and, on the threshold of the third millennium, to help all Catholics to experience the celebration of the holy mysteries with a devotion truly nourishing their spiritual life and bringing them peace."

In other words, St. Peter's Fraternity need only obey the diocesan bishops in order to be sure of their Faith being safeguarded and of their liturgy being worthily celebrated! Is that their experience? As for the "understanding and renewed pastoral concern" to be shown to Catholics with a St. Peter's Fraternity "sensibility," well, of course, what that means was explained above – the Pope wants it "all to be lived in the spirit of Vatican II." He concludes:

"Entrusting you to the intercession of the Virgin Mary, perfect model for the following of Christ, and Mother of the Church, dear brothers and sisters, I grant you the Apostolic blessing, and to all those dear to you."

According to the "Wanderer" report of the *Ecclesia Dei* weekend, Cardinal Ratzinger assured the conservative Catholics that their problem is the diocesan bishops. In other words, like Pope John Paul II he is convinced that the replacement of the old liturgy is fine, that at most that replacement is being misapplied.

No, Your Holiness. No, Your Eminence. Nice conservatives may let themselves be persuaded that Vatican II and the Novus Ordo Mass are good texts, just being badly applied, but nasty "Traditionalists" know that they are bad texts. Not just the new practice, but the new principles are wrong. And the greatest service "Traditionalists" can render to both of you, and to conservatives, is to take this stand "against" you until you too see it. Then you will thank us for having "cut ourselves off."

So the SSPX goes its way. The solemn blessing of the new church of Ecône Seminary in Switzerland on October 10 was a great success. Lovely weather, many people, a beautiful Pontifical High Mass celebrated by the Superior General, Bishop Bernard Fellay. It recalled the rededication of the Temple in Jerusalem amidst the Macchabean Wars (I Macch. 4) . . .

Pray to and for the Holy Souls in the month of November, and please do not forget the seminary in your generosity.

One Year to the Millennium: Quo Vadimus? – Where are We Headed?

WITH ONLY 12 months to go before we enter into the third millennium, it is reasonable to wonder where we are going. Since the beginning of JP2's pontificate in 1978, he has not ceased to present the year 2000 A.D. as being about to usher in a great new age for Church and world. He may be right, but certainly not in the way he thinks.

Q: Why may he be right?

A: Because by this end of the 20th century, Western liberalism has broken down, as it was bound to do, because of the disintegration built into its principles. Whatever new integration follows will have to be so different that anyone will call it a new age.

Q: Where do you see the breakdown?

A: At ground level, a friend wrote two years ago from New York City, "The people in the streets are misled and show their hatred and arrogance. One of them said to my wife, 'It is nothing personal, but we'll have a battle in the streets. There'll be bloodshed'. New York City seems to be a powder-keg waiting for someone to light the fuse." Another friend from the Eastern United States has noticed for years that the anger is coiled up inside people like a snake ready to strike. They have for years been taught, and have accepted, to live for material goods which leave their nevertheless spiritual souls deeply unsatisfied, and now they look like losing even their material goods.

Q: *How is that possible? The New York stock market dipped in the summer but soared again in the autumn!*

A: As much as an engine depends upon oil circulating, an economy depends on money circulating. But modern money has two serious problems. Firstly, it consists merely in paper or book-entries or electronic blips which can only serve for money as long as people have confidence in them. With backing by gold deliberately discredited, that confidence could easily evaporate. And secondly, modern money is brought into existence as debt with interest on it, which can only be paid back by ever increasing debt, which must come to a halt when people or nations are "maxed out" in debt. That point is being reached. This autumn the US Federal Reserve saved public confidence by drastic interest rate cuts putting more funny money into circulation, but this has merely delayed the day of reckoning which, the longer it is delayed, the worse it will be. Insiders know that the system is on the brink of seizing up, like an engine without oil.

Q: *But cannot the politicians rescue the economic system?*

A: It is the immorality of the politicians and of the peoples voting for them so as to get a free lunch, which produced this doomed economic system in the first place. There is no such thing as a free lunch. Only dishonesty can pretend there is. But the American people today so rejoice in dishonesty that they re-elected as President and now refuse to impeach, a man whom they all know to be a liar, an adulterer and a perjurer, and many hold that those are not the worst of his crimes. What do the people care, so long as he seems to be delivering the material goods? And if the people get disgusted with their own politicians, who do they turn to? Here in Minnesota, they just elected a former professional wrestler as governor! Maybe he will do better than the professional politicians!

Q: But what does this breakdown of economics and politics have to do with religion?

A: Everything. As politics govern economics, so religion governs politics. The turning away from God generates the dishonesty (no Ten Commandments) and the materialism (what else is there to live for?). That is why the same media that trashed Presidents Nixon and Reagan for comparatively minor misdemeanors now shield and protect a President for major crimes, an incredible contradiction until one recalls that the former two put brakes (or half-brakes) on the destruction of Christendom, while the latter has his foot hard down on the accelerator. It is the City of God, in however broken-down a form, against the City of Man. Only this religious perspective can explain many contradictions, for instance why, similarly, the feminists loved the "molested" Anita Hill whose lies denounced a conservative, whereas they abandoned the molested Paula Jones whose truth-telling denounces this President. For liberals, the end justifies the means. All contradictions are justified in the war on God.

Q: *Where does this breakdown of sanity and morals end?*

A: If God does not intervene, then like in the cities of Sodom and Gomorrah, good men will finally not be able to live in peace even within their own homes, but bad men will be breaking down their doors, etc. (Gen. 19: 4–10). And just as the ancient Roman Empire succeeded in pinning on Christians the blame for its own misdeeds and misfortunes, so the liberals and their media are now beginning to blame the "religious right" for the consequences of their own criminal folly, and the corrupt people will rejoice in having such a scapegoat.

Q: *Please, can we have some good news?*

A: Actually, the good news is that the news is so bad!

Q: *What on earth do you mean?*

A: If wallowing in mud worked for modern man and made him happy, that would suggest he is a pig. If it does not work but makes him unhappy, that suggests that man is not meant to live like a pig. Thank goodness the modern world does not work!

Q: *I suppose you will say that Vatican II was modern man "pigging out" inside the Catholic Church?*

A: That is right. This autumn one of the major American media (PBS) broadcast a nearly two-hour program on the Second Vatican Council. Cardinals, bishops, priests and large numbers of laymen and laywomen were interviewed, one after another, mostly of course to tell how wonderful the Council was. They were pathetic. Practically none of them mentioned or seemed to think of God! They have lost their Faith and lost their way.

Q: But did not something like Vatican II have to hap-pen inside the Catholic Church in mid-20th century? Had not the Church become for instance too clericalist and legalist, too centered on priests and too bound up with laws?

A: That is a good question. There was a real problem which called for a real solution. It was given a false solu-tion by Vatican II.

Q: How?

A: By the 1950's, the substance of Catholicism had been for a long time draining out behind the appear-ances of the Church. The true solution would have been to put back the substance – easier said than done! The solution of Vatican II – easily said and done – was to pull down whatever appearances were standing, and that process is still going on. However, to be fair to Vatican II, the problem of Catholic appearances without Catholic substance had been building up over a long time, so that something like it had to happen. It is no use pretending that Vatican II was just an unhappy accident which we can get over by rebuilding the Catholicism of the 1950's.

Q: How far back does the problem go?

A: Plus or minus, 700 years. The Middle Ages (500 – 1500 A.D.) had their moments of darkness which the Church's enemies seize on to be able to dismiss those ages as "Dark Ages," but that was nevertheless the time when the Church most filled the world with the light of Christ. As the Middle Ages declined, so the rebellion of Protestantism broke out and the Catholic Church began her magnificent rearguard action with the Counter-Ref-ormation, but Vatican II was like the breakdown of the Counter-Reformation. That is why JP2 is quite right that the Church must move into a new age, but he is quite wrong in thinking that the new Catholic age will be built on the principles of Vatican II, which are intrinsically godless.

Q: How can you say that the Counter-Reformation has broken down? How can the Catholic Church break down?

A: Of course the Catholic Church is in her essence unchanging and imperishable, but at various times in history, the living Church adopts various modes. The Counter-Reformation mode presupposed, and relied upon, a heritage of faith and morals left over from the Middle Ages, a heritage steadily eroded down the following centuries and now virtually exhausted. To this extent the believers in Vatican II are right: Church and world are now so out of joint that the Church must enter a new age. Only, it will never be the New Age of the modernists' globalist and godless dreams, to be entered into and baptized by the Catholic Church changing essentially and beyond all recognition. "Heaven and earth shall pass away, but my words shall not pass away," says Our Lord (Lk. 21: 33).

Q: So the followers of Vatican II are wrong in wanting to change the Church's essence, whereas the followers of Catholic Tradition would be wrong if they did not want her to change even her mode?

A: Correct. All grave heresies derive their power from some truth, for instance the oneness of Christ's person is the force behind the great heresy that he has only one nature. The truth that serious change had to come in the sclerosed Church of the later 20th century is the force behind Vatican II and behind the terrible errors of, for instance, Cardinal Ratzinger and JP2.

Q: How dare you speak of terrible errors of the reigning Pope and of his Prefect for the Congregation of the Doctrine of the Faith?

A: By reading what they write! As for Cardinal Ratzinger, the English translation just appeared in the US of Milestones, his memories of the first 50 years of his life. He shows himself there to be a highly intelligent, "pious" and "nice" man, but at the same time he shows that modern errors have such a grip on his thinking that he has no idea what Catholicism is about! The heart may be "sweet," but the head is rotten. Piously one may hope God will judge him on his heart, but meanwhile with his head he is quite unable to defend the Faith, which is his official function!

Q: *And what, pray, is your evidence of the Pope's "terrible errors"?*

A: Also just appeared recently in English translation (Angelus Press) is the third volume of Prof. Johannes Dörmann on John Paul II's Theological Way to Assisi. It analyzes the Pope's 1981 Encyclical *Dives in Misericordia*, on God the Father. Did you know that the prodigal son's conversion consists in his realization, thanks to his father's welcoming him back, that he has been a good fellow, full of human dignity, all along? Sin? Forget it! Repentance? Forget it! All men are good and will go to Heaven, whether they know it or not, whether they want to or not! Conversion is just the becoming aware of one's inalienable human dignity. In German has also recently appeared Prof. Dörmann's fourth volume in the same series, on the Pope's Encyclical of 1987 on the Holy Ghost, *Dominum et Vivificantem*. It is equally hair-raising (there is no other word). Not only does the Holy Ghost not proceed from the Son (Photian heresy), but also the Son proceeds in a way from the Holy Ghost. What for? No doubt, so that the religion of the Son (Catholicism) will be merely one amongst a variety of lawful religions all proceeding, in a way, from the Holy Ghost! That is what Vatican II virtually taught (Decree on ecumenism), and what this Pope actually put into practice, notably at Assisi.

Q: Is Prof. Dörmann arguing that this Pope is in his encyclicals transforming the three persons of the Holy Trinity?

A: Yes, and the best proof that Prof. Dörmann is correct is the actions of JP2, e.g., the series of interreligious meetings which merely started with the Assisi event of October, 1986.

Q: Does this Pope know what he is doing?

A: Some people think he must do, because he is an educated man and thoroughly knew true Catholic doctrine before Vatican II. However, other people say that he was not educated but miseducated before Vatican II, having plunged, like Cardinal Ratzinger, into modern philosophy which bent both their minds clean out of shape and falsified all their subsequent studies of doctrine. Before all these neo-modernists flew into the cloud, they could see, and when they flew into the cloud their guardian angels must have been flashing red lights and sounding alarms in their cockpits, but, once they were inside the cloud, they became blind and were flying blind from then on.

Q: Are you saying then that this Pope is not to blame for now flying blind?

A: No, because not only must his guardian angel have warned him before he flew into neo-modernism, but also now God must, logically, be offering all kinds of graces to His one and only Vicar to fly His Church out of the cloud, and that Vicar must be spurning those graces in order to be so obstinately flying onwards in the same cloud as he is doing.

Q: But can nobody tell the Pope what he is doing?

Richard N. Williamson

A: Archbishop Lefebvre tried to tell both Pope Paul VI and Pope John Paul II that they were going seriously wrong, but neither would listen. After all, of all the Cardinals and thousands of other Bishops, half tell JP2 that he is horribly conservative, the other half tell him he is wonderfully conservative. How could he take seriously the lone voice, or with Bishop de Castro Mayer, lone voices, telling him that in his principles he is not conservative at all? Pope John Paul II and Cardinal Ratzinger must more or less politely laugh any time anyone suggests they are not Catholic – "But we are the heads of the Church!" Our best information is that JP2 completely ignores the Traditional movement. It has for him no significance at all. He is wholly occupied with preparing, so to speak, the Assisi Millennium.

Q: But won't the series of earthquakes virtually devastating Assisi in 1997 have told John Paul II anything?

A: The "loving God" of JP2 is not any God who would use natural disasters to warn or punish men.

Q: Then how can the Lord God get through to him?

A: Either by an overwhelming grace which Catholics could obtain by their prayers if there were enough of them to mourn for the stricken Church and to hunger and thirst for righteousness. Or, if too many Catholics will prefer their inalienable dignity and guaranteed salvation to mourning and hungering and thirsting, then by a major Chastisement, of which Our Lady is meant to have warned us many times in this century, and which makes a great deal of sense, even if the Church has so far abstained from approving all these warnings.

Q: But why does a major Chastisement make so much sense?

A: Precisely because the mass of Catholic churchmen are so sunk into neo-modernism that, short of a miraculous turnaround on their part, nothing less can save the Church. Also, in today's state of mankind, nothing could bring so many souls to their knees as a major Chastisement.

Q: *Still, why did the Lord God allow His churchmen to get into such a mess in the first place?*

A: Because He so respects our human dignity, in the real sense, that He insists upon allowing us to make free use or misuse of our free will, and that includes His own churchmen. He will never allow them to go so far as to destroy His Church, but He can certainly make use of them to purge His Church, which is what is now happening.

Q: *So in the end, the Immaculate Heart of Mary will triumph, as she promised at Fatima in 1917?*

A: Yes, but not sentimentally. Rather, following on a major Chastisement, as said, insofar as it is hard to see what else could clear the way, and followed by the arrival of the Antichrist.

Q: *Now having said what this new age of Church will not be like, can you say what it will be like?*

A: Some prophecies say it will be the greatest triumph of the Catholic Church in all her history, proportional to the greatest distress ever in which we see her today. If we can reasonably imagine a large part of mankind perishing in the Chastisement, we can also imagine how deeply the survivors will have relearned the fear of God, almost forgotten today even amongst the best of men. From that salutary fear will spring up in men's hearts a true love of God which will soar above the false dilemma, dead Tradition or live heresy. Everything these survivors do will naturally be both faithful to Tradition and full of life, in modes we will then instantly recognize to be Catholic but on a scale we can hardly now imagine.

Q: But if this new age of the Church will be so glorious, how will the Antichrist arrive?

A: At La Salette in 1846 Our Lady said that 25 years of plentiful harvests would make men forget the ravages of sin. At that point it will take very little time to rebuild all the distracting gadgets of today's materialism because they will not need to be reinvented but only remembered.

Q: Have you a timetable for these events?

A: No way. The Lord God is enormously patient, but when He strikes, it could be swift. At a sheer guess, the reign of the Antichrist might be in about 60 years' time, but that date is only to provoke thought. The real date is God's secret.

Q: And where does the SSPX fit into this cosmic drama?

A: As the Counter-Reformation systems of the Catholic Church are, in a manner of speaking, shutting down in the crisis merely precipitated by Vatican II, so Catholics are enveloped in darkness and cold. The SSPX is like an emergency power system designed to provide minimal light and warmth for Catholic souls until the main power is turned on again. Or, the SSPX is like the pilot light in a stove. It can do no cooking to speak of, but its function is to stay lit to enable cooking to be done when the gas is turned on again. Or, the SSPX is like the guardian of a sacred deposit entrusted to it for safe keeping: the Catholic Mass and priesthood threatened all around with destruction for a mysterious period of time. Or, as the only worldwide Catholic organization of priests keeping the integral Catholic faith, the SSPX may prove to be the backbone of the hyphen joining the pre-Chastisement to the post-Chastisement Church. Or, the SSPX is like the ugly fat man anchoring the end of a tug-of-war line – nobody tugging on his side loves him but they all need him. Or . . .

Q: Enough images! Does the SSPX claim there is no salvation outside the SSPX?

A: No, because God has allowed it to stay too small in numbers to reach directly more than relatively few souls. Rather, He wishes it to give witness to Catholic Tradition, by which it indirectly serves an enormous number of souls. So what the SSPX does claim is that there is no salvation outside of that Tradition to which it presently gives witness.

Q: But aren't many SSPX priests (and bishops) somewhat young?

A: As modest as the SSPX must be concerning the persons who compose it and their talents, so uncompromising must it be concerning the Truth which they serve. As Our Lord said (Jn. 7: 16), the Society's doctrine is not the Society's doctrine. It is the Father's doctrine.

Q: But we keep hearing that the SSPX is infiltrated, that this or that prominent member is a Freemason.

A: Such rumors need not to be heeded until there is serious evidence of an infiltration, as opposed to groundless suspicion, which is forbidden by Catholic charity. The presence of Judas Iscariot among the Apostles teaches us there may always be infiltrators. The problem is not so much to identify them, which God alone can unfailingly do. The problem is rather to have an organization healthy enough to carry them so that they will not do too much harm before being discovered.

Richard N. Williamson

Q: And what can layfolk do to help the Church in this her hour of need?

A: Duty of state, duty of state, duty of state. There is no substitute for duty of state. If every man would do his duty, said Pope St. Pius X, the world would not be in its present trouble. Catholics are liable to look for things glamorous or difficult to do, but glamor is deceptive and there is difficulty enough in keeping God's Commandments in daily life today. Daily duty is humble and humbling, always there, and in plentiful supply. Done with a supernatural intention and in the state of grace, it unfailingly merits in proportion to the love of God with which it is done. Here is how the Church will be rebuilt, one person or one day at a time, and, of course, by quiet, steady, unceasing prayer.

Q: Nevertheless, did Archbishop Lefebvre have any particular recommendations for the rebuilding of the Church?

A: When his successor as SSPX Superior General, Fr. Franz Schmidberger, asked him a year or two before he died how the SSPX could reach souls today, the Archbishop replied, by schools and by the Spiritual Exercises. Notice how both these apostolates are hard work, reliable means of long-term sanctification, reaching into the soul. The Archbishop did not mention sensational actions, or publicity campaigns.

Q: And how much should we concern ourselves with the future or with the Millennium?

A: Up to a certain point and not beyond. For instance a family father must provide for his family as best as he can foresee, but nobody can foresee all that is going to happen in the next few years. For whatever we cannot foresee, God requires of us to trust Him, and not to worry. It insults a father when his children do not have confidence in him. On the contrary, when children show the right kind of trust in their father, he has the utmost difficulty in letting them down. Our Heavenly Father is omnipotent. No difficulty can make Him disappoint souls that trust in Him. As far as the future is concerned, the end of the Ambrosian Hymn is the last word: "Have mercy upon us, O Lord, have mercy upon us. May Thy mercy, O Lord, be upon us, according as we have placed our hope in Thee. In Thee, O Lord, have I placed my hope, let me never be put to confusion."

Dear Friends and Benefactors, the seminary has successfully completed another calendar year, with your support. We have at present 36 seminarians including six who entered the seminary this last September, and two who should be ordained priests this coming June 26. We are always grateful for your support. To express that gratitude is the purpose of this letter, even if it does not always say so.

INDEX

A

abortion, 96, 119, 126, 152, 183, 308
abortionists, 126, 152, 183, 309
absolute supremacy, 23
absolute Truth, 65, 75, 321
absolution, 277
Action Française, 46, 47
activism, 8
adolescents, mixed school classes of, 82, *see also* education system; teenagers
adultery, 15, 234, 236, 237, 299
Africa, 43, 45
Age of Apostasy, 171, 172, 178, 185
Age of Christendom, 172
Age of Mary's Triumph, 171, 172
Age of the Antichrist, 172
Agnoli, Carlo, 113
Alfred E. Murrah Building bombing, 195
altar girls, 152, 171
Americanism, 120, 161, 162, 163–168
Americanization, 64
American priests, 259
Amerio, Romano, 113, 169, 185
The Angelus, 112, 166, 290
Anglicanism, 162, 303
Anglo-Saxons, 287
anonymous Christians, 112
anti-Americanism, 96, 197
Antichrist, 51, 133, 151, 158, 172, 269, 335, 336
anti-culture, 4, 5
"Antidote to Oklahoma," 53
anti-liberalism, 48, 123, 197, 289
anti-modernism, 147
anti-religion, 47
anti-Semitism, 96
anti-Vietnam War parades, 108
apostasy, 67, 101, 138, 139, 172, 197, 225–226, 247, 302
Apostolic authority, of Pope, 44
Argentina, Argentine
          priests, 253, 259
Arian crisis, 109, 110
Asia, 158–161

Assisi
    earthquakes in, 334
    International Prayer Meeting, 25, 294, 320, 333, 334
        and John Paul II, 24–28
atheists, 10
authority
    Apostolic authority, of Pope, 44

B

Barabbas, 126
Bea, Cardinal, 101
Beatles, 187
Belgium, 68
Benigni, Msgr., 149
betrayals, 299
Billot, Cardinal, 46
Bishops' Committee on Marriage and Family, United States, 237, 240
blasphemy, 10
    films, *see* films
Branagh, Kenneth, 221
Brezhnev, Leonid, 105
Bride of Christ, 115, 268
Bruskewitz, Bishop Fabian, 126, 127
    and SSPX, 122–128
Buchanan, Patrick
    campaign of, 116–122
Buddhism, 159

C

Cairo, 27
Calmel, Fr., 182
Calvat, Mélanie, 150
Canon Law, 277, *see also* Church Law
    New Code
        Cannon 386, 323
Canons, *see* Church Law
Carlitism, Carlitists, 252, 253, 255, 267, 272
Carmelites, 68
Carmels, 39
catechisms, 315
Catholic Church, 48, 51, *see also* Rome; Vatican I; Vatican II
    absolute superiority, 164
    democratism in, 43–47
    divine indefectibility, 270
    FAQ on the future of, 169–185
    God's plan for, 171
    infallibility

divine gift of, 270
layfolk's role in, 338
level of, 170–171
and State, split between, 52, 165–166
Catholic doctrine refusal, as insulting God, 11
Catholic dogma, *see* dogma
Catholic girls, 6, *see also* women
Catholic Liberals, 145, *see also* liberalism, liberals
Catholic Magisterium, 76
Catholic Middle Ages, 251
Catholic schools, 1, 4, 6, 103, *see also* education system
Catholic Tradition, *see* Tradition, Traditionalism
Chambers, Whittaker, 66
Chamisso, Adalbert, *Peter Schlemihl,* 279–284
chaos, 55, 58, 60, 297
charismatic globalism, 64
charity, 23, 137–143
of St. Pius X, 144–150
Charriere, Bishop, 84
chastisements, 334, 335
Chesterton, G.K., 272
children, *see also* education system; families
disciplining, 190, 193
engaging with good activities, 190–191
indisciplined exception, 192
Christendom, 141, 209, 291
Christian civilization, 66, 155
Christian marriage, 102–103, *see also* families; Holy Family; marriages
Church Law, 93, *see also* Canon Law
Ciceri, Fr., 145
civic liberty, 22
civilization, *see also* Christian civilization
Western civilization, 4
civil war, 51
Civitavecchia Madonna, 48
clergy, 155
clothing
teenagers' choice, 2
Cobain, Kurt, 194
co-education system, 305, 313–318, *see also* Catholic schools; education system
collegiality doctrine, 114
commodification, 3
Communism, 105
computer games, 2
concentration camp, 199–204
Conclave, 175
The Conduct of Pius X in the Fight Against Modernism, 144
Congar, Fr. Yves, 111

Consecration of Russia to Mary's Immaculate Heart, 1988, 11, 92
        decade after, 291–296
conservatism, conservatives, 85, 300
conservative Catholics
        avoidance of, 8–13
contraception, *see also* abortion
corporal punishment, for school children, 80
corrupt politics, 183
Cortés, Donoso, 79
Counter-Reformation, 251, 291, 330–331, 336
Crosby, Bing, 167
        Catholicism, dangers of, 157, 167
Crowley, Fr. Mateo, 34
Curé of Ars, 242

D

Dalledonne, Professor, 101, 102
Dante Alighieri, 102
dark judgment, on future, 170
darkness, 173
Davies, Michael, 179, 180
de Castro Mayer, Bishop Antonio, 98, 291, 294, 334
Declaration of Human Rights, 63–64
Deep Blue chess computer, 215–221
"Defensor vinculi," 275
de Galarreta, Bishop Alfonso, 300
de Joma, Fr. Benoit, 111
De Lai, Cardinal, 146
de Mallerais, Bishop Bernard Tissier, 88
democracy, 53, 117, 310
democratism
        in the Catholic Church, 43–47
Descartes, 4
determinism, 217
Devastated Vineyard, 152
The Devastated Vineyard, 151, 155
diabolical disorientation, 297, 307
Diana, Princess, death of, 232–237, 247
Dietrich von Hildebrand Institute, 73, 77
dignity, 19, 125, 130, 311, 335
disobedience, 173
Diuturnum Illud, 51, 54
Dives in Misericordia, 332
divided mind, 165
divine order, 44
divorce, 184, 235, 236, 276, 317, *see also* families
dogma, 75, 170
Dominican Sisters, 70, 199

of Fanjeaux, 68
of Idaho, 38, 42, 65
school for girls, 266
Dominum et Vivificantem, 332
Doran, Fr. James, 248
Dostoevsky, Fyodor, 133, 136
doublethink, 52, 53
Dörmann, Fr. Johannes, 24, 25, 27, 28, 99, 100, 332, 333

E

Ecclesia Dei Commission, 320, 322
Wanderer report of, 324
Ecône, Switzerland, 35, 67, 85, 88, 99
new church of 1998, 324
economic system, and politicians, 327
ecumenical prayer meeting at Assisi, *see* Assisi Prayer Meeting 1986
ecumenism, 62, 92, 111, 112, 140, 141, 153, 159, 160, *see also* religious liberty
education system, 32
co-education, 313–318
corporal punishment for school children, 80
denial of difference between boys and girls, 82
modern education, woes to, 210–214
egalitarian democratism, 46
Eisenhower, Dwight D., 105
Eliot, T.S., 66
"Wasteland," 194
Elizabeth I, Queen, 302, 303
encouraging words, New Year 1995, 29–32
Encyclical on the Christian Education of Youth (1929), 317
England, 67, 161–162
English Catholicism, 302
English literature, 202
entertainment, modern expectation of, 243, 248
Epinay, Fr. Pierre, 88
Episcopalianism, 303
Epstein, Brian, 187
equality, 44, *see also* liberalism
Euclidean geometry, 203
Europe
forebodings and reassurance from, 66–72
euthanasia, 126
evolutionary theory, 170
excommunication of SSPX bishops, 1988, 126
external liberty, 14
extremism, extremists, 142
of Archbishop Lefebvre, 156

F

false ecumenism, *see also* Assisi Prayer Meeting 1986; ecumenism
false familial principle, 305
false individual principle, 305
false religions, 124–125
   tolerance of, 62
families, 38, 40
   children, *see* children
   Rosary prayers, 214
fascism, 47
fast food, 2
Faust, Edwin, 166, 167
Fellay, Bishop Bernard, 88, 94, 114, 115, 325
females, *see* women
femininity, 39
feminism, 40, 64, 76
Ferrari, Cardinal, 145, 146, 147, 148, 149
Fiftiesism, 177, 299, 301–306
films, 104, 106, 243–249, 280, 285–291, 297
   protest films, 41–42
First Amendment of the US Constitution, 167, 264
First Vatican Council, *see* Vatican I
fix-it mentality, 197
Ford, Henry, 203
forebodings and reassurance, from Europe, 66–72
fornication, 237
Founding Fathers, 167
France, 6, 43, 68, 111, 260
fraternisation, 105
freedom, 13, *see also* liberty
Freemasonry, Freemasons, 64, 66, 107, 113, 126, 337
free will, 14, 15, 16, 17, 133, 311
French Guyana, 263
French Revolution, 228
FSSP, *see* St. Peter's Fraternity (FSSP)
fugitives to the Winona woods, 262–267

G

Gaume, Msgr., 29, 32
gays, *see also* homosexuals, homosexuality
General Patton, 204
Gerard, Dom, 181, 251
Germany, 111
   influence on Vatican II, 112
Gibson, Mel, 221
globalism, 181
glorification, 20, 21

of the person, 276

God

    knowledge of, 141

    man as, 138

    neglect of, 192–198

    plan for Catholic Church, 171

    wake-up calls, 195

    wrath of God, 162

God is God, 140

Gottardo, Msgr, 145

Great Apostasy, 183

H

Hamlet, 221–227

Heaven, 44, 138, 142, 159, 185

hedonism, 145

Henry VIII, King, 302, 303

Hiss, Alger, 104, 105

Hogan, Fr. Richard, 307, 308, 310, 311, 312

Holy Family, 31, 102, *see also* families

Holy Matrimony, 273, *see also* marriages

homosexuals, homosexuality, 184, 247

    marriages, 235

    sin of, 237–242

hormonal treatments, 70

Hospital Orders of Sisters, 39

human dignity, *see* dignity

humanism, 321

humanities studies, 202

human society, 44

Hutus, 45

I

Idaho, 38, 42, 65, 266

Ignatian Spiritual Retreats, 134, *see also* Spiritual Exercises of St. Ignatius

Immaculate Conception, 310

Immaculate Heart of Mary, 335, *see also* Consecration of Russia to Mary's

Immaculate Heart, 1988

    devotion to, 227–231

Immortale Dei, 53–54

Incarnation, 10

incest, 265

individual, glorification of, 81

individualism, 184

Indult Masses, 178, 179, 258

    1984, 319

industrial technology, 130

impact of, 130–132
infallibility, 109
Institute of Christ the King in Gricigliano, Italy, 258
Integrity (magazine), 243
internal liberty, 14, *see also* natural liberty
Interreligious World Prayer Meeting, Assisi, *see* Assisi Prayer Meeting 1986
Iota Unum, 113, 169
Italy, 97

J

Jackson, Michael, 204
Japan, 158, 159
Jesus Christ, 10, 30, 140
Jews, 207
JFK (film), 106
Joe, Fr., 264
John Paul II, Pope, 62, 63, 99, 111, 114, 170, 175, 294, 319, 321, 324, 326, 331, 333
     and Assisi Prayer Metting 1986, 24–28
     Ecclesia Dei, see Ecclesia Dei Commission
     ecumenism, 153
     evidence of terrible errors, 332–333
     as a head, 92
     on Hell, 309
     personalism, 307–312
     weaknesses of, 154
Johnson, Lyndon, 105
Johnson, Samuel, 312
John XXIII, Pope, 98, 110, 113, 270, 292
Jones, Paula, 328
Joseph of Arimathea's tomb, 205
Judeo-masonry, Judeo-masons, 138, 141, 172, 181
Julius Caesar, 222

K

Kasparov, Gary, 215
Kennedy, John F., 105
Kennedy, Sheila Rauch, 276

L

La Salette, 269, 336
     150th Anniversary of, 150–157
Latin, 201
Lee Kwan Yew, 159
Lefebvre, Archbishop Marcel, 25, 114, 132, 151, 160, 179, 214, 252, 256, 270, 290, 293, 296, 334

anti-Revolution, 84
consecration by, 87, 319
           of Russia to the Immaculate Heart of Mary, 88
Declaration of Nov. 21, 1974, 85
on Dom Gerard, 251
excommunication of June '88, 93
and Fr. Synder, 36
ordination by in 1976, 86
recommendations for rebuilding of the Church, 338
on St. Peter's Fraternity, 251
solution to pluralism, 77
Lefebvre, Joseph, 88
Leftism, 132
Leonine Encyclicals, 103
Leo XIII, Pope, 51, 53, 102, 145, 168, 274
lesbians, *see also* homosexuals, homosexuality
Le Sel de la Terre, 110
Letterman, David, 22
Liberal Catholicism, 145, 303
Liberalism and Catholicism (Roussel), 290
liberalism, liberals, 32, 47, 50, 67, 94, 95, 107, 125, 162, 173, 228, 268, 281, 292, 326
           education, errors of, 79–83
Liberius, Pope, 91, 110
Libertas, 53
liberty, *see also* liberalism, liberals
           civic liberty, 22
           definition of, 13
           moral and natural, 13–23
Lincoln, Abraham, 50, 63, 107
Longinqua Oceani, 168
Lorans, Fr. Alain, 98
Lovey, Fr. Philippe, 99
Luther, Martin, 91, 268, 291

M

machines, 213, *see also* industrial technology; television
Madonna of Syracuse, Sicily
           blood on, 48
           weeping, 49
male milk, 70
man as God, 138
Maoism, 105
Marcille, Fr. Philippe, 109, 110
Marie-Christiane, Mother, 68
Marie-Dominique, Fr., 88
Marie, Fr. Pierre, 110, 111
marriages, 235, *see also* children; families

Marriage Tribunal, 273–278
Martin, Malachi, 151, 152, 153, 154, 155, 156, 170, 175
martyrs, 185
materialism, materialists, 71, 160, 189, 215
McNabb, Fr. Vincent, 243–244
Measure for Measure (play), 224
media, *see also* television
Merton, Fr. Thomas, 35
Middle Ages, 280
middle-class liberalism, 40
Milan Seminary, 147
millennium
        approaching towards, 326–339
        future of, 338–339
Mindszenty Report, 194
miracles, 48
modern education, woes to, 210–214
modernism, modernists, 43, 146
moral chaos, 57, 58, 60, 61, 65
moral liberty, 13–23
Mother Church, 39, 79, 80, 162, 292
music, teenager's choice, 2
Mutara III, Tutsi King, 45
Mystical Body of Christ, 38, 39

N

Nagasaki, 159
National Rosary March, 8
Natural Born Killers, 38–42, 50, 106, 223, 282
naturalism, 8
natural liberty, 13–23, *see also* liberalism, liberals
natural order, 45
Nazi death camps, 199–204
Nebraskans, 123
neglect of God, 192–198
neo-modernism, neo-modernists, 95, 102, 173, 178, 179, 261, 281, 333, *see also* modernism, modernists
neo-Nazism, 96
Newchurch, 62, 63, 64, 93, 100, 112, 236, 240, 247, 251, 258, 259, 264, 276, 277, 294, 309, 311
Newfaith, 100
New Mass, *see* Novus Ordo Mass (NOM)
Newthink, 102
New World Order, 52, 62, 64, 105, 153, 155, 160, 175, 180, 201, 202, 210, 294
New York City, 61
New York stock market, 327
Ngo-dinh-Thuc, Archbishop, 95

Nick (a teenager's story), 1–7
NIF (nice internal feeling), 310
1984 (novel), 52
Nixon (film), 104
Nixon, Richard, 117
       career of, 104–109
non-Catholics, 140
non-Christian religions, 112
North America, 155
Notes from the Underground, 133
Novus Ordo Mass (NOM), 22, 84, 176, 178, 220, 247, 267, 322, 324

O

Oklahoma bombing, 50, 51, 195
Olivier, Sir Lawrence, 222
Onoda, Fr. Thomas, 158
Opus Dei, 259
original sin, 23, 79, 80, 100, 166, 315, 316
Orwell, George, 52
Our Lady, message from, 48–54

P

paganism, 201
papacy
       dissolution of, 176
Papal Encyclicals, 134
papal infallibility, 173
parents, 1, 4, 83, 156, 190, 202, *see also* children; families
       responsibilities of, 80
       role in disciplining their children, 190
Pascendi, 145
Pasqualacci, Professor[AQ: Please verify spelling.], 99
Pasqualucci, Professor[AQ: Please verify spelling.], 100
patriotism, 21, 64
Paul VI Mass, 321
Paul VI, Pope, 85, 98, 110, 111, 123, 259, 293, 322
PBS (American media), 329
peer pressure, 81
Pentecost, 207
"Perils from False Brethren," 249–262
personalism, 307–312
Peter, 208
"Peter Schlemihl," 279–284
Pfluger, Fr. Niklaus, 112
Philippines, 159
physical liberty, 14
Pie, Cardinal, 31, 32

Pilate, Pontius, 126
Pink Floyd, 129, 193
      "The Wall album," 186–192
Pio, Padre, 149, 242
Pitt, Msgr., 34
Pius X, Pope, 46, 144, 162
Pius XI, Pope, 313, 317
Pius XII, Pope, 46, 112
pluralism, 73–78, 164
Pluralist Magisterium, 76
political religion, 63
politics, 96
Pontifical Biblical Commission, 98
Pope, *see also specific popes*
           Apostolic authority of, 44
           infallibility of, 91
Pope John Paul II's Theological Journey to the Prayer Meeting of Religions in Assisi (Dörmann), 24
pornography, 247, 264
prayers, 39
pre-Council Catholicism, 177
Protestantism, 50, 90, 95, 100, 118, 178, 183, 228, 251, 268, 281, 283, 291, 292, 330
protest films, 41–42
psychological liberty, 14
public school system, 32
Puritans' Progress, 203

R

Rahner, Fr. Karl, 112, 113
Rangel, Bishop Licinio, 98
Rao, John C., 73, 74, 75, 76, 77, 163, 164, 166, 168
Ratzinger, Cardinal Joseph, 48, 99, 255, 324, 331, 332, 333, 334
Rausis, Gratien, 88
Reformation, 162
Reformation England, 92, 303
religion of society, 32
religious liberty, 21, 32, 58, 92, 96, 119, 124, 125, 163–168, 195, 313
           principle of, 60–65
religious right, 118
Rerum Novarum, 54
The Rescue, 145, 147
Resurrection
           historical fact, 205–209
retreats, 134, 306, *see also* Ignatian Spiritual Retreats
revisionism, 96
Revolution, *see* Vatican II
Ritter, Fr. Bruce, 55, 57, 58

rock music, 129

Rome, 86, 94, 126, *see also* Catholic Church
     New Code of Canon Law, *see* Canon Law, New Code

Rosary, 214

Roussel, Fr. A., *Liberalism and Catholicism,* 290

Russia, 105, *see also* Consecration of Russia to Mary's Immaculate Heart, 1988

Rwanda, 43, 44, 45, 46

S

St. Anne, 229

St. Athanasius, 91, 94

St. Augustine, 71, 190, 283

St. Dominic Barberi, 71

St. Don Bosco, 266

St. Hyppolitus, 323

St. Ignatius, 129, 323

St. Ignatius' Spiritual Exercises, *see* Spiritual Exercises of St. Ignatius

St. Joan of Arc, 94, 172, 185

St. John Bosco, 83

St. Louis Grignon de Montfort, 228

St. Madeleine-Sophie Barat, 40, 42

St. Margaret Mary, 172

St. Mary's, Kansas, 134

St. Paul, 71, 174, 238, 239, 241, 249

St. Peter, 205, 322

St. Peter's Fraternity (FSSP), 178, 251, 258, 319, 320, 322, 324

St. Pius X, Pope, 292, 338
     charity of, 144–150
     Motu Proprio, 44

St. Thérèse, 129

St. Thomas Aquinas, 101, 207

St. Vincent de Paul, 77

salvation, 10, 27, 83, 112

sanctifying grace, 100, 191

San Sebastian de Garabandal, Spain, 66

Satanism, 155

Satanist rituals, 170

Schmidberger, Fr. Franz, 100, 101, 338

school system, *see also* education system; public school system
     for girls, 39–40

scientism, 145

Scotton, Msgr Andrea, 145, 146, 147

Scotton, Msgr. Gottarao, 146, 147

Second Vatican Council, *see* Vatican II

secular humanism, 170

sedevacantism, sedevacantists, 173, 175, 267–272

seduction, 29

See (Sedes) of Rome, 269
self-glorification of man, 19
self-value, 22
seminarians
        duties of, 9
        and Rosary March, 9
Seminary of Milan, 146
sentimentalism, 64
sexual identity, 241, *see also* homosexuals, homosexuality
Shakespeare, William
        Hamlet, 221–227
        Julius Caesar, 222
Shintoism, 159
Simoulin, Fr. Michel, 89, 99
sin
        of homosexuality, 237–242
        original sin, 23, 79, 80, 100, 166, 315, 316
        sincere sin, 55–59
        sincere sinners, 60
sincere sin, 55–59
sincere sinners, 60
Singapore, 159
Siri, Cardinal, 153, 191
Si Si, No No Congress, 97–104
Sister Lucy of Fatima, 297, 307
Sisters of Charity in Nazareth, Kentucky, 35
Snyder, Fr. Urban, death of, 33–37
social equality, *see* equality
society, importance of, 184
Society of Jesus, 252
Society of Saint Pius X (SSPX), 61, 70, 181, 294, 336–337
        25th anniversary, 84–89
        and Bruskewitz, Bishop Fabian, 122–128
        and charity, 137–143
        Doctrinal Session, 266
        Dominican building (Winona), *see* Winona seminary
        and Dominican Sisters in Idaho, 38
        in Ecône, *see* Ecône, Switzerland
        FAQ on, 90–96
                on the future, 169–185
        flyer from the Dominican girls' school in Idaho, 266
        infiltration in, 258, 337
        loss of priests, 254–258, 267
        Marriage Tribunal, 273–278
        Mass circuits of priests of, 252
        noncooperation with Rome, 319–326
        North American Seminary, 254
        number games, 256
        obedience to Rome, 123

pilgrimage
  to Fatima, Portugal, 227
political agenda, 96
priests
  education of, 253
  youngsters, 337
retreats, *see also* Ignatian Spiritual Retreats; Spiritual Exercises of St. Ignatius
Revolution of 1983, 260
and Rome
  disobedience, 91, 173, 174
  possibility of dialogue between, 180
Rosary March, 8
and salvation, 337
school, palace revolt 1977, 86
schools, 79
spies within, 259
stand on John Paul II, 91
true Church, 90, 91
and unity of Traditional priests, 181
in the USA
  split in, 255
Winona, *see* Winona seminary
Socrates, 204
The Sound of Music (film), 243–249, 280, 297
South Korea, 158
Spadafora, Msgr., 97, 98
Spain, 66
Spellman, Cardinal, 58
Spiritual Exercises of St. Ignatius, 306
spiritual virility, 31
Sri Lanka, 160
sterile contraception, 75
Stone, Oliver, 41, 104, 106, 129, 280, 282, 283
suburbanism, 41
suicide, among youngsters, 188
Sunday Celebration in the Absence of a Priest, 171
Super-Church, 27, 28, 112
supernatural Doctrine of Jesus Christ, 114
supernatural Faith, 4, 23, 139
supernature, 79, 226
Switzerland, 67

T

teenagers, 1–7, *see* adolescents, mixed school classes of
television, 3
Ten Commandments, 1
'Tertio Millennio Adveniente,' 321

Theological Way to Assisi, 332
Thomism, 102
Timlin, Bishop, 258
Titanic (film), 285–291
tradecumenism, 9
Traditional annulments, 278
Traditional Carmel, 39
        in Quiévrain, 68
Traditional Mass, 258, *see also* Tridentine Mass
Tradition, Traditionalism, 6, 39, 63, 86, 90, 303, 305, 324
Tridentine Mass, 84, 85, 121, 179, 319, 322
troglodytism, 136
truth, consequences of prioritizing unity over, 64
Tutsis, 45
Twentiesism, 303

U

Unabomber Manifesto, 128–136, 193, 280, 281, 283
The Union, 147, 148
United Nations, 105
United States, 69, 111, 161–162, 276, 301
        Bishops' Committee on Marriage and Family, 237, 240
        Federal Reserve, 327
        Fiftiesism in, 304
        influence on Vatican II, 112
        Nixon Buchan, 119
        pluralism in, 164
        religious liberalism, 58, 163–168
unreal movies, and real Catholicism, 296–300

V

Vallet, Fr., 252
Vatican I, 109, 320
Vatican II, 4, 11, 21, 26, 52, 58, 61, 81, 87, 97, 120, 123, 160, 177, 247, 258, 270, 293, 299, 303, 322, 324, 329, 330, 336
        characterizing as "pastoral" Council, 98, 115
        Freemasonry, *see* Freemasonry, Freemasons
        German influence on, 112
        influences of, 109–115
        Protestant influence on, 101
        US influence on, 112
Verbum, 195
Vietnam War, 105, 106, 108
virility, 39
virtual reality, 211
von Balthasar, Fr. Hans Urs, 309

W

"The Wall album," 186–192
Wall Street, 69
  bubble, 70
warning, from God, *see also* wrath of God
Washington, George, 50, 167
Watergate scandal, 105
Way of the Cross, 268
weeping statues, 48–54
Western civilization, 4
Wilde, Oscar, 173
Wilson, Woodrow, 107
Windswept House, 151, 154
Winona seminary, 7, 65, 77, 121, 137, 192, 209, 226, 249, 301
  Doctrinal Sessions, 168, 290
  National Rosary March, 8
  in priestly ordinations, 295
  Rector in, 254
Winona wood, fugitives to, 262–267
Wojtyla, Cardinal Karol, 25, 99, 100, 153, 308, 309
women, *see also* femininity; feminism
  female administrators, 152
  female Eucharistic ministers, 152
  schooling, 39–40
  self-sacrifice, 39
women-priests, 126
world crisis, and Church crisis, 169
World War II, 34, 230
wrath of God, 162

Y

youth, youngsters, 19, 22, 33, 211
  suicide among, 188

CPSIA information can be obtained
at www.ICGtesting.com
Printed in the USA
LVHW051105180621
690535LV00007B/122